# The Longman Practical Stylist

# The Longman Practical Stylist

## SHERIDAN BAKER

PEARSON
Longman

New York  San Francisco  Boston
London  Toronto  Sydney  Tokyo  Singapore  Madrid
Mexico City  Munich  Paris  Cape Town  Hong Kong  Montreal

Publisher: Joseph Opiela
Managing Editor: Valerie L. Zaborski
Project Coordination and Text Designer: Electronic Publishing Services Inc., NYC
Senior Cover Design Manager: Nancy Danahy
Cover Designer: Laura Shaw
Art Studio: Electronic Publishing Services Inc., NYC
Senior Manufacturing Buyer: Dennis J. Para
Electronic Page Makeup: Electronic Publishing Services Inc., NYC
Printer and Binder: Courier Corporation
Cover Printer: Courier Corporation

ISBN 0-321-33349-7

2345678910—CRS—08 07

# Contents

# ✒ Preface

*The Longman Practical Stylist* lays out, step by step, the simple poetics of persuasion, the processes of argument, the essence of our attitudes, our thinking, our conversation, our writing. Responding to suggestions from the thousands of students and teachers who use in it colleges and high schools, I have again provided the simple basics while eliminating some of the accretions of time, bringing other things up to date, especially in the burgeoning electronic world, renewing examples and suggestions for exercises, and expanding the treatment of usage.

The book remains essential, while providing a more helpful course through the process of persuasive writing—finding oneself and one's subject, making a thesis, the inner organizer, and managing the outer structure. In easy steps, we begin with the whole essay. Many books on writing begin with small trials, then lead the student timorously up to the ominous essay looming ahead. But students find early confidence in the opposite approach: "Why yes, even I can do it!" Once they see how easily one turns any familiar subject from Ping-Pong to nuclear energy into a thesis and then see the simple essentials of structure, they can proceed effectively to discover the successively smaller and more powerful elements—paragraphs, sentences, and words, where the real glory of writing is.

I continue to emphasize argument because argument indeed subsumes the other expository modes—description, narration, and exposition— and teaches easily the firmest organization of one's ideas. I discuss briefly the possibilities in prewriting, which teachers may amplify and adjust to suit their own practices and classes. I include examples of students' writing and revision, which, again, teachers may easily illustrate further from the copious and immediate examples in their own classrooms. Rather than "Exercises," I make "Suggestions for Exercise" to encourage teachers to bring in their own, and to work more directly with their classes in discovering subjects and theses, in paragraphing, in writing various kinds of sentences and punctuating them, in using words and spelling them, in handling various figures of speech. I encourage students to play with language, to write unusual and complicated sentences for fun, to juggle with words, and especially to achieve clarity by learning to recognize and eliminate the endemic wordiness that everywhere befogs our prose.

A chapter on the research paper draws everything together in a complete student's paper, "Can Animals Talk?" As it helps the student discover the library's and the computer's resources, and how to cite and present them, it also provides a helpful introduction to these resources for classes not requiring a research paper. A handbook of punctuation, spelling, capitalization, and usage, beginning with a chapter on "The Trouble with Grammar," completes the book. Inside the front cover is a "do's" list against which students may check their work; inside the back cover, a set of symbols for marking the "don'ts."

The teacher will find plenty of room here for any convenient approach, and ample opportunity for that almost necessary bonus of academic gratification, disagreeing with the book, out of which much of our best teaching comes. A great deal will certainly be familiar. Nothing here is really new. I am simply describing the natural linguistic facts discovered again and again by the heirs of Aristotle, in which lineage I inescapably belong. For I have found that the one practical need in all writing is to mediate gracefully between opposite possibilities—between simplicity and complexity, clarity and shade, economy and plenitude, the particular and the general.

I again wish to acknowledge my great and unending debt to the teachers who, from the responses of more than three million students, have given me their encouragement and suggestions. I am grateful to the following reviewers for their helpful comments and suggestions: William Adair, San Joaquin Delta College; Louis Avery, Houston Community College; Linda Carter, Morgan State University; Vincent Cassaregola, Saint Louis University, MO; Robert Dees, Orange Coast College; Kathleen Duguay, North Adams State College; Sarah Harrison, Tyler Junior College; Michael Hogan, University of New Mexico; Ann Johnson, Community College of Denver; George Kennedy, Washington State University; Mary Levitt, North Adams State College; Christopher MacGowan, College of William and Mary; D'Ann Madwell, North Lake College; Mark Miller, North Adams State College; Richard Mulkey, Converse College; Amy Pawl, Washington University, MO; Gary Peterson, College of the Redwoods; Jim Riser, University of North Alabama; Arthur Wagner, Macomb Community College; Russ Ward, Aims Community College; John White, California State University, Fullerton; Eugene Whitney, Portland Community College; Sue Williams, Olivet Nazarene University; Robert Wiltenburg, Washington University. I continue to be no less grateful to the individual students and private citizens who have written me from as far away as Kenya, Australia, and Japan, and as near home as Ann Arbor.

*Sheridan Baker*

# The Longman
# Practical Stylist

# 1

# The Point of It All

## WRITE FOR YOUR SHARE

Writing is one of the most important things we do. It helps us catch our ideas, realize our thoughts, and stand out as fluent persuasive people both on paper and on our feet in front of the meeting or the boss. Reading and writing have already enlarged your education and your speech. Even television, in its news and advertising, and in most of its shows, pours into our thoughts the words and habits that literacy—and written scripts—has built into our speech and thinking.

This language we share is Standard English—sometimes called edited Standard American English, as if it were some labored necessity for the business we would rather not do. But actually we "edit" almost everything we say, as several psychologists and linguists have noted.* We instinctively select one word or another, one way of saying, when we talk to friends or our friends' parents, to dignitaries or children, to the boss or the new file clerk. Whatever our backgrounds in different parts of the country or city, in different ethnic and linguistic surroundings, we come together in this common language of ours as our minds spontaneously edit the choices. We automatically edit all our fragmentary thoughts, intuitively filling in the grammar, expanding, rephrasing, just as if we were writing and rewriting: ". . . er . . . I mean . . . but really . . . ."

So writing is an extension of the way we naturally handle language. Writing simply straightens out and clarifies our intuitive editing and, in turn, makes the editing itself more fluent. Writing is a process of discovery.

---

*Lev Vygotsky, *Thought and Language* (Cambridge, MA.: MIT Press, 1962), with "Comments" by Jean Piaget; James Moffett, "Writing, Inner Speech, and Meditation," *College English 44* (1982): 231–246.

Writing perfects thought and speech. Indeed, during the millions of years from our first emotive screams and gurgles of pleasure to the bright dawn of literacy, writing—thinking well-dressed for its purpose—seems to be where speech has been going all the time.

Your composition course prepares you for the challenges not only of college but also of discovering yourself in your group, your community, or in the business of life ahead, whether it be in the executive suite or the courtroom, the hospital or the consulate, the legislature or the press room. You must write in almost every course. You must write not only to recognize yourself but also to apply for admission to postgraduate studies. You must write proposals for grants and programs. You must write on your computer. You must write to persuade people of your worth—demonstrated in your literacy—and of the worth of your ideas. You must write to develop and advance them—and yourself. You must write for your share of life. Thinking and persuasion are your business, and the business of your course in composition. All communication is largely persuasion. Even your most factual survey as an engineer or an educator must persuade its audience to approval by its perception and clarity and organization—in short, by its writing.

## ATTITUDE

Writing well is a matter of conviction. You learn in school by exercises, of course, and exercises are best when taken as such, as body builders, as flexions and extensions for the real contests ahead. But when you are convinced that what you write has meaning, that it has meaning for you—and not in a lukewarm, hypothetical way, but truly—then your writing will stretch its wings. For writing is simply a graceful and articulate extension of the best that is in you. Writing well is not easy. As it extends the natural way we express ourselves, it nevertheless takes unending practice. Each essay is a polished exercise for the next to come; each new trial, as T. S. Eliot says, a new "raid on the inarticulate."*

In writing, you clarify your own thoughts and strengthen your conviction. Indeed, you probably grasp your thoughts for the first time. Writing is a way of thinking. Writing actually creates thought and generates your ability to think: you discover thoughts you hardly knew you had and come to know what you know. You learn as you write. In the end, after you have rewritten and rearranged for your best rhetorical effectiveness, your words

---

*"East Coker."

will carry your readers with you to see as you see, to believe as you believe, to understand your subject as you now understand it.

## Don't Take Yourself Too Seriously

After all the heat of scribbling and stating and restating what you think you think, cool off for a minute. Take your subject seriously—if it is a serious subject—but take yourself with a grain of salt. Your attitude is the very center of your prose. If you take yourself too importantly, your tone will go hollow, your sentences will go moldy, your page will go fuzzy with *of*'s and *which*'s and nouns clustered in passive constructions. In your academic career, the worst dangers lie immediately ahead. Freshmen usually learn to write tolerably well, but from the sophomore to the senior year the academic mildew frequently sets in, and by graduate school you can cut it with a cheese knife.

You must constantly guard against acquiring the heavy, sober-sided attitude that makes for wordiness along with obscurity, dullness, and anonymity. Do not lose your personality and your voice in the monotone of official prose. You should work like a scholar and a scientist, but you should write like a writer, one who cares about the economy and beauty of language and has some individual personality. Your attitude, then, should form somewhere between a confidence in your own convictions and a humorous distrust of your own rhetoric, which can so easily carry you away. You should bear yourself as a member of humankind, knowing that we are all sinners, all redundant, and all too fond of big words. Here is an example from—I blush to admit—the pen of a professor:

> The general problem is perhaps correctly stated as inadequacy of nursing personnel to meet demands for nursing care and services. Inadequacy, it should be noted, is both a quantitative and qualitative term and thus it can be assumed that the problem as stated could indicate insufficient numbers of nursing personnel to meet existing demands for their services; deficiencies in the competencies of those who engage in the various fields of nursing; or both.

Too few good nurses, and a badly swollen author—that is the problem. *Nursing personnel* may mean nurses, but it also may mean "the nursing of employees," so that the author seems to say, for a wildly illogical moment, that someone is not properly pampering or suckling people. Notice the misfiring *it* (fourth line), which seems to refer to *term* but actually refers to nothing, and the ponderous jingle of *deficiencies in the competencies* would do for a musical comedy. The author has taken the wrong model, is taking herself too seriously, and is taking her readers almost nowhere—*or both*, as she might say—leaving us scratching our heads.

## Consider Your Readers

If you are to take your subject with all the seriousness it deserves and yourself with as much skeptical humor as you can bear, how are you to take your readers? Who are they, anyway? You might start with your classmates as your audience. This is a good beginning. But the problem remains with all those other classes; with those papers in history or social science; with the reports, the applications for jobs and grants, the letters to the editor. At some point, you must become a writer facing the invisible public.

To some extent, your audiences will vary. You imagine yourself addressing slightly different personalities when you write about snorkeling and when you write about nuclear reactors. If you write about baseball, you assume an audience aware of the pitch with the bases loaded, with two outs, and with the count at three and two. But if you write about baseball to a British friend or for a British newspaper, you assume a different audience. Your language would vary as you reach out to their needs for understanding: "The pitcher is under great pressure to throw the ball within the required rectangle of space over the home base so that the batter cannot hit it effectively and allow one or more of the runners already on bases to advance to home base and score." If you knew something about cricket, you could explain baseball even more effectively for your British readers. Whatever you write, you must sense your audience's capacity, its susceptibilities and prejudices.

Be wary of biases built into our language over the ages. English lacks a singular pronoun to include both sexes, having settled for the masculine by default. Look out for references to an officer, a judge, or a student as only a *he*, or to a nurse, a baby-sitter, or a spouse as only a *she*, confusing some readers and angering others. An accidental *welshing* or *Dutch treat* may offend those whose ancestry reaches to Wales and Holland as you innocently color your language. My *color* there, in my sentence about bias, might get under someone's skin or bring a laugh at my expense. At a formal reception on a very hot day, the governor's lovely and tactful wife said to Yogi Berra, dressed a bit too casually in white short-sleeved shirt and white pants, "You look wonderfully cool, Mr. Berra," and the Yogi replied, "Well, you don't look so hot yourself." So watch your language, and don't lose your audience.

But even as you adjust your language to differing audiences, you are working within a comfortable range. You are *writing*, which immediately eliminates some ways of speech. The written word presupposes a literate norm that frees you from worry about your personal vocabulary. Your only adjustment is generally toward a kind of verbal worldliness, a grammatical tightening and a rhetorical heightening to make your thoughts clear, emphatic, and attractive.

Consider your audience a mixed group of intelligent and reasonable people. You want them to think of you as well informed and well educated. You wish to explain what you know and what you believe. You wish to persuade them pleasantly that what you know is important and what you believe is right. Try to imagine what they might ask you, what they might object to, what they might know already, what they might find interesting. Be simple and clear, amusing and profound, using plenty of illustration to show what you mean. *But do not talk down to them.* That is the great danger in adjusting to your audience. Bowing to your readers' supposed level, you insult them by assuming their inferiority. Thinking yourself humble, you are actually haughty. The best solution is simply to assume that your readers are as intelligent as you. Even if they are not, they will be flattered by the assumption. Your written language, in short, will be respectful toward your subject, considerate toward your readers, and somehow amiable toward human failings.

## THE WRITTEN VOICE

### Make Your Writing Talk

That the silent page should seem to speak with the writer's voice is remarkable. With all gestures gone, no eyes to twinkle, no notation at all for the rise and fall of utterance, and only a handful of punctuation marks, the level line of type can yet convey the writer's voice, the tone of a personality.

To achieve this tone, to find your own voice and style, simply try to write in the language of intelligent conversation, cleared of all the stumbles and weavings of talk. Indeed, our speech, like thought, is amazingly circular. We can hardly think in a straight line if we try. We think by questions and answers, repetitions and failures; our speech, full of *you know*'s and *I mean*'s, follows the erratic ways of the mind, circling around and around as we stitch the simplest of logical sequences. Your writing will carry the stitches, not those editorial loopings and pauses and rethreadings. It will, on its own, carry some attractive color and rhythm from your personal background, but it should be literate. It should be broad enough of vocabulary and rich enough of sentence to show that you have read a book. It should not be altogether unworthy to place you in the company of those who have written well in your native tongue. But it should nevertheless retain the tone of intelligent and agreeable conversation. It should be alive with a human personality—yours—which is probably the most persuasive rhetorical force on Earth. Good writing should have a voice, and the voice should be unmistakably your own.

Suppose your spoken voice sounded something like this in one of your classes:

> Well, I think what Davis says about Freud is, I don't know, prejudiced, or biased. He, or maybe Freud, well they think sex is the only thing. I guess the Oedipus and Electra bit is true all right. But what about friendship, I mean, what about the kind of friends, your friendship with another girl, or another boy, that has nothing to do with whether you want to marry your mother or kill your father and all that. It's finding someone like yourself, or maybe just a little different, someone to share your feelings with and laugh at the same things, like that. That hasn't anything to do with sex.

Your written voice, after several revisions, might then emerge from this with something of the same tone but with everything straightened out, filled in, and polished up:

> Davis's Freudian psychology omits at least one essential human experience: friendship. Davis seems to connect all human relationships to the sexual drives that begin with the infant's sensual relationship with its mother. But the famous Oedipus complex has nothing to do with the friendship between people of the same sex in which the individual psyche discovers that it is not alone, that another one shares the same fears and pleasures. Friendship is a bond somewhat different from the basic sexual drives.

You might wish to polish that still more. You might indeed have said it another way, one more truly your own. The point, however, is to write in a tidy, economical way that wipes up the lapses of talk and fills in the gaps of thought, and yet keeps the tone and movement of good conversation in your own voice.

## Establish a Firm Viewpoint

"In my opinion," the beginner will write repeatedly, seeming to say "It is only *my* opinion, after all, so it can't be worth much." The writer has failed to realize that the whole essay represents an opinion—of what the truth of the matter is. Don't make your essay a personal letter to Diary or to Mother or to Teacher, a confidential report of what happened to you last night as you agonized upon a certain question. "*To me*, Robert Frost is a great poet"—this is really writing about yourself. You are only confessing private convictions. To find the public reasons often requires no more than a trick of grammar: a shift from "*To me*, Robert Frost is . . ." to "Robert Frost is . . . ," from "*I thought* the book was good" to "The book is good," from you and your room last night to your subject and what it is. *Generalize* your opinions and emotions. Change "I cried" to "The scene is very moving." The grammatical shift represents a whole change of viewpoint, a shift from self to subject. You become the informed adult, showing the reader around firmly, politely, and persuasively.

Once you have effaced yourself from your assertions, once you have erased *to me* and *in my opinion* and all such signs of amateur terror, you may later let yourself back into the essay for emphasis or graciousness: "Mr. Watson errs, I think, precisely at this point." You can thus ease your most tentative or violent assertions and show that you are polite and sensible, reasonably sure of your position but aware of the possibility of error. Again: the reasonable adult.

You go easy on the *I*—in short, to keep your reader focused on your subject. But you can use the *I* as much as you like, to *illustrate* your point, once established, using a personal experience among several other pieces of evidence or even all by itself. Of course, your instructors will sometimes ask for a wholly autobiographical theme. Indeed, some courses focus altogether on the *I* of personal experience, and your autobiographical résumés in applying for medical and law school and for grants and jobs will of course require the *I*. But for the usual essay, I repeat, use the personal anecdote and the *I* to illustrate a point or to interject a tactful remark.

Effacing the *I*, and then letting it back in on occasion fixes your point of view. But what about the other pronouns, *we, you, one*? *One* objectifies the personal *I*, properly generalizing the private into the public. But it can seem too formal and get too thick:

FAULTY: *One* finds *one's* opinion changing as *one* grows older.
REVISED: Opinions change with age.
REVISED: *Our* opinions change as *we* grow older.

That *we* is sometimes a useful generalizer, a convenient haven between the isolating *I* and the impersonal *one*. *We* can seem pompous, but not if it honestly handles those experiences we know we share, or can share. Suppose we wrote:

As I watched program after program, I got bored and began to wonder what values, if any, they represented.

We can easily transpose this to:

As *we* watch program after program, we are progressively bored, and *we* begin to wonder what values, if any, they represent.

(Notice that shifting to the present tense is also part of the generalizing process.) Thus, *we* can generalize without going all the way to *one* or to the fully objective:

Program after program, TV bores its audiences and leaves its sense of values questionable.

*We* also quite naturally refers to earlier parts of your demonstration, through which you have led your reader: *as we have already seen*. But you will have noticed from the preceding examples that *we* tends slightly toward wordiness. Used sparingly, then, *we* can ease your formality and draw your reader in. Overused, it can seem too presumptuous or chummy. Try it out. See how it feels, and use it where it seems comfortable and right.

*You* raises similar problems. The first is the one we have been discussing: how to generalize that *I* effectively into something else, either *one* or *we* or full objectivity. The indefinite *you*, like the indefinite *they*, is usually too vague, and too adolescent.

FAULTY: You have your own opinion.
FAULTY: They have their own opinion
REVISED: Everyone has an opinion.
REVISED: We all have our own opinions.

*You*, like *we*, can also seem patronizing, attributing to you things not like you at all:

FAULTY: Like most people, you probably learned to hate grammar because your teacher also hated it.

REVISED: Many people dislike grammar because their teachers also disliked it.

I have consistently addressed this book to *you*, the reader. But this is a special case, the relationship of tutor to student projected onto the page. None of my own essays, I think, contains any *you* at all. Our stance in an essay is a little more formal, a little more public. We are better holding our pronouns to *one* or *we*, an occasional I, or none at all, as we find a comfortable stance between our subject and audience and find our written voice.

## THE POINT: ARGUMENTATION

The point is persuasion. Your written voice, your personal style, remember, is a part of your persuasiveness. But having a point to make is the real center of persuasion, the likely goal of most of your writing and speaking in college and in contemporary life. Hence, the center of your composition course is indeed argumentation. Even explaining the Battle of Lexington or the Oedipus complex invites an argumentative thrust as you persuade your readers of the most significant causes and crucial events. Argumentation thus ranges through the coolest explanation, or exposition, up to the burning issues you support. Argument, as we will see as we move along, absorbs for its ends every kind of writing you can think of. Narration, dialogue, anecdotes, exposition, description, newspaper headlines, statistical tables, and chemical formulas may all illustrate the point you are making in that written personality of yours that gives it life.

### Plan to Rewrite

Again, writing is a process of discovery. "How can I know what I think till I see what I say?" a little girl once said,* putting the secret of writing in a nutshell. Seeing is discovery. Seeing is understanding. Seeing is knowing. Seeing is believing. Writing puts it all together. The inner impulse of thought is unrealized until *seen*, and once seen, once discovered, or uncovered, it prompts more *saying* to get that thought fully realized and more visions and revisions to get down before your and your reader's eyes what

---

*Graham Wallas, *The Art of Thought* (New York: Harcourt, 1926), p. 106; W. H. Auden in Rudolf Arnheim, W. H. Auden, Karl Shapiro, and Donald A. Stauffer, *Poets at Work: Essays* (New York: Harcourt, 1948), pp. 173-4.

your mind has come to know and what your voice has found to say. Revision is seeing again and discovering once more. You are realizing, making real, for yourself and everyone, the misty point barely glimpsed at your first impulse to say something, to put yourself and your argumentative point in the world beyond you. So as you write your weekly assignments and find your voice, you will also be learning to groom your thoughts, to present them clearly and fully, to make sure you have said what you thought you said.

This is the process of composition, of putting your thoughts together, beginning with jotted questions and tentative ideas, all to be mulled over, selected, rejected, expanded as you discover your ideas and write them into full expression. Ultimately, good writing comes only from rewriting. Even your happy thoughts will need resetting as you join them to the frequently happier ones that a second look seems to call up. I like to start by jotting with pencil on paper and then writing out more fully in pencil. Others can handle it from the first on the PC. Either way, even an apparently letter-perfect paper will improve almost of itself if you simply run it through again. You will find, almost unbidden, sharper words, better phrases, new figures of speech, and new illustrations and ideas to replace the weedy patches not noticed before. Indeed, this process of rewriting is what strengthens that instinctive editing you do as you speak extemporaneously or write impromptu essays and exams when revision is out of the question. Rewriting improves your fluency, making each rewrite less demanding.

So allow time for revision. After you have settled on something to write about, have written out your ideas for a while, have found an argumentative point, and feel ready to write the whole thing out, plan for at least three drafts—and try to manage four. Thinking of things to say is the hardest part at first. Even a short assignment of 500 words seems to stretch ahead like a Sahara. You have asserted your central idea in a sentence, and that leaves 490 words to go. But if you step off boldly, one foot after the other, you will make progress, find an oasis or two, and perhaps end at a run in green pastures. With longer papers, you will want some kind of outline to keep you from straying and probably some jotted notes even for short ones, but the principle is the same: step ahead and keep moving until you've arrived. That is the first draft.

The second draft is a penciled correction of the first print out. Here you refine and polish, checking your dubious spellings in the dictionary, sharpening your punctuation, clarifying your meaning, pruning away the deadwood, adding a thought here, extending an illustration there—running in a whole new paragraph. You will also be tuning your sentences, carefully adjusting your tone until it is clearly that of an intelligent, reasonable person at ease with your knowledge and your audience. Your third draft, a runthrough and smoothing of your penciled revision, will generate further improvements.

Your PC revises in a wink—so easily, in fact, that successive local revisions may stall your flow of ideas. As with any first draft, revise here and there as you go, as we do spontaneously in speech and in any writing, but push on to the end. Your PC can help you with quick checks for spelling and typos, and you can even have it list out your favorite bad habits. But, for best results, you should print out every draft and revise it in pencil for better control over words and the whole. Then make your corrections on the PC with its facility in revising wording and punctuation, in recasting sentences and paragraphing, and in shifting whole paragraphs and sections.

Here is an assignment that has gone the full course. To get the class underway, the instructor asked for a paragraph on some pet gripe, something close to home, written to persuade others.

### FIRST DRAFT WITH PENCILED CORRECTIONS

German is probably the hardest language to learn. It is rigid

routine learning with nothing creative asked for. College chokes off

creativity with too many requirements. In a college education,

students should be allowed to ~~make~~ *choose* their own course. ~~Too many~~ *All the*

requirements, ~~are discouraging to~~ *they must take discourage* people's creativity, and they

cannot learn anything ~~which is~~ *they are* not motivated ~~for him~~ to learn.

~~With~~ *R*equirements, *restrict* their freedom to choose ~~what he is interested in~~ *and their eagerness to learn.*

*They are only discouraged* ~~is taken away~~ by having to study dull subjects like German, ~~which~~ *in which*

*they can see no relevance to their interests.* ~~he is not interested in.~~

Though this student starts with a gripe about German, he discovers, as he writes, a wider interest in freedom of choice. He recognizes this when he reads the printout by cutting his first two sentences as he also tightens up his phrasing. Below you see what he handed in after a second run (and some further changes) with the instructor's marks on it. Then you see the final product handed in again as this assignment on the process of revision required, with the whole idea of creativity dropped to strengthen the point about freedom and make it more coherent.

## THE PAPER, WITH INSTRUCTOR'S MARKINGS

*can you get rid of the passive?*

*redundant?*

*relevant?*

*true?*

*activate?*

College chokes off creativity with too many requirements. In a college education, students <u>should be allowed</u> to choose their own curricula and select their own courses. <u>All the requirements they must take</u> stifle their creativity. Moreover, <u>they cannot</u> learn anything they are not motivated to learn. Requirements restrict their freedom to choose and their eagerness to explore the subjects they are interested in. <u>They are only discouraged</u> by having to study dull subjects like German, in which they can see no relevance.

## REVISED PAPER

Students should choose their own education, their own curricula, their own courses. Their education is really theirs alone. Every college requirement threatens to stifle the very enthusiasms upon which true education depends. Students learn best when motivated by their own interests, but, in the midst of a dozen complicated requirements, they can hardly find time for the courses they long to take. Requirements therefore not only restrict their freedom to choose but destroy their eagerness to explore. Dull subjects like German, in which they can see no relevance anyway, take all their time and discourage them completely.

# AIMING FOR A STYLE OF YOUR OWN

By writing frequently, you will create a style of your own—and with it, a good bit of your future. But what is style? At its best, it is much like style in a car, a gown, a Greek temple—the ordinary materials of this world so poised and perfected as to stand out from the landscape and compel a second look, something that hangs in the reader's mind like a vision. It is a writer's own voice, with the hems and haws chipped out, speaking the common language uncommonly well. It comes from a craftsman or craftswoman who has discovered the gnarls and potentials in the material, one who has learned to enjoy phrasing and syntax and the very punctuation that keeps them straight. It is the labor of love, and like love it can bring pleasure and satisfaction.

But style is not for the gifted only. Quite the contrary. Indeed, as I have been suggesting, everyone already has a style and a personality and can develop both. The stylistic side of writing is, in fact, the only side that can be analyzed and learned. The stylistic approach is the practical approach: you learn some things to do and not to do, as you would learn strokes in tennis. Your ultimate game is up to you, but you can at least begin in good form. Naturally, it takes practice. You have to keep at it. Like the doctor and the lawyer and the golfer and the tennis player, you just keep practicing—even to write a nearly perfect letter. But if you like the game, you can probably learn to play it well. You will at least be able to write a respectable sentence and to express your thoughts clearly, without puffing and flailing.

In the essay, as in business, trying to get started and getting off on the wrong foot account for most of our lost motion. So we will next consider how to find a thesis, an argumentative point, which will virtually organize your essay for you. Then we will study the relatively simple structure of the essay and the structure of the paragraph—the architecture of spatial styling. Then we will experiment with various styles of sentences, playing with length and complexity to help you find the right mix to convey your personal rhythm. Finally we will get down to words themselves. Here again you will experiment to find those personal ranges of vocabulary, those blends of the breezy and the formal, that will empower your personal style. Here, in the word, is where writing tells; here, as in ancient times, you will be in touch with the mystery. But again, there are things to do and things not to do, and these can be learned.

# 2 Making a Beginning: From Subject to Thesis

## GETTING SET

Get set! Writing an essay isn't exactly a 50-yard dash, but you do need to get ready and get set before you can go to it. Writing requires a time and place, an habitual environment to coax and support those inspired moments that seem to flow spontaneously into language. Your best scheme is to plan two or three sittings for each assignment. Your place should be fixed. It should be comfortable and convenient. Your times should be regular, varied in length from short to long, and set to fit your schedule and your personal rhythm as morning person or night owl, sprinter or long-distance runner. Arrange your first period for a time as soon as possible after assignments, perhaps only a half-hour for scribbling and thinking on your PC or paper. Your next two sessions should be longer, the last with expandable time to get the job done.

## WHAT SHALL I WRITE?

First you need a subject, and then you need a thesis. Yes, but *what shall I write?* Here you are, an assignment before you and the screen as blank as your mind, especially if your instructor has left the subject up to you. Look for something that interests you, something you know about, some hobby—something that shook you up, left you perplexed, started you thinking.

Writing will help you discover that something. Don't stare at the void. Set yourself the task of writing for ten minutes no matter what. Start moving and keep going, even beginning with *Oh no! What shall I write? Write on anything, the assignment said. OK, but what what what what what? Fishing? Baby-sitting? Skipping rope? Crime? Nuclear power? Oh no. Crime? Rape? How about the time I ripped off a candy bar and got caught? The shock of recognition. Everyone's done it at some time or other. Everyone's guilty. Everyone's tempted. Something for nothing. The universal temptation of crime.* . . . Keep going until your watch tells you to stop. That's a good start. A subject is rising from that candy bar. Take a break and let your thoughts sink in and accumulate.

Probe your own experiences and feelings for answers as to why people behave as they do, especially in times of crisis. Prestige? The admiration of peers? Fear of not going with the gang? Why is fishing (let us say) so appealing to you? Why more so than water skiing or swimming or sailing or tennis or painting? Why don't some people like it? What might they object to? Now have another bout, perhaps just jotting the questions down, perhaps discovering some answers as you go. You have found your subject—and indeed have already moved a good way toward a thesis. The more your subject matters to you, the more you can make it matter to your readers. It might be skiing. It might be dress. It might be roommates, terrorism, a political protest, a personal discovery of racial tensions, an experience as a nurse's aide. But do not tackle a big philosophical abstraction like Freedom or a big subject like the Supreme Court. They are too vast, and your time and space and knowledge all too small. You would probably manage no more than a collection of platitudes. Start rather with something specific like running, and let the ideas of freedom and justice and responsibility arise from there. An abstract idea is a poor beginning. As you move ahead through your course in writing, you will work more directly with ideas, with problems posed by literature, with questions in the great civilizing debate about what we are doing in this strange world and universe. But again, look for something within your concern. The best subjects lie nearest at hand and nearest the heart.

You can personalize almost any subject and cut it down to size, getting a manageable angle on it. On an assigned subject, particularly in courses like political science or anthropology or sociology, look for something that connects you with it. Suppose your instructor assigns a paper on Social Security. Think of a grandparent, a parent, a neighbor, a friend—or perhaps yourself as a student—receiving or not receiving benefits and how reductions would or would not affect your life. You will have a vivid illustration as well as one corner of the huge problem to illuminate. Nuclear energy? Perhaps you have seen on television the appalling space suits and mechanical arms required to handle and get rid of the radioactive stuff. Perhaps you remember an article or a sentence that started you thinking. With subjects to find, keep an eye and an ear open as you read the newspaper or *Time*, or watch TV, or talk with your friends. Scan the Internet and the World Wide Web. A small group, in class or out, can storm up a subject and help compose it. If you watch for them, your classes and textbooks will inevitably turn up subjects for your composition course that you can bring into your personal range. Pollution? All of us have seen a local swamp or dump or have choked on fumes in traffic jams. You need to find a personal interest in your subject to have something to say and to interest others.

## FROM SUBJECT TO THESIS

Suppose, for the present, we start simply with "Drugs." Certainly, most of us have been tempted, or had to resist or to go along, have experimented or gotten hooked, or have known someone who has—especially if we include cigarettes and alcohol. "Drugs" is a subject easily personalized. Taking a subject like this will also show how to generalize from your own experience and how to cut your subject down to manageable size. Your first impulse will probably be to write in the first person, but your experience may remain merely personal and may not point your subject into a thesis. As I have said, a personal anecdote makes a lively *illustration*, but first you need to generate your thesis and establish it for your reader. You need to move out of that bright, self-centered spotlight of consciousness in which we live before we really grow up, in which the child assumes that all his or her experiences are unique. If you shift from *me* to *the beginner* or *the young adult*, however, you will be stepping into maturity by acknowledging that others have gone through exactly the same thing, that your experiences have illustrated once again the general dynamics of the individual and the group. So instead of writing "I was afraid to refuse," you write:

> **The *beginner* is afraid to refuse and soon discovers the tremendous pressure of the group.**

By generalizing your private feelings, you change your subject into a thesis—your argumentative proposition. You simply assume you are normal and fairly representative, and you then generalize with confidence, transposing your particular experiences, your particular thoughts, and your reactions, into statements about the general ways of the world. Put your proposition, your thesis, into one sentence. This will get you focused. Now you are ready to begin.

## WHERE ESSAYS FAIL

You can usually blame a bad essay on a bad beginning. If your essay falls apart, it probably has no primary idea, no thesis, to hold it together. "What's the big idea?" we used to ask. The phrase will serve as a reminder that you must find the "big idea" behind your several smaller thoughts and musings and drafts before you can start to shape your final essay. In the beginning was the *logos*, says the Bible—the idea, the plan, caught in a flash as if in a single word. Find your *logos*, and you are ready to round out your essay and set it spinning.

Suppose you had decided to write about a high-speed ride—another case of group dynamics. If you have not focused your big idea in a thesis, you might begin something like this:

> **All people think they are good drivers. There are more accidents caused by young drivers than any other group. Driver education is a good beginning, but further practice is very necessary. People who object to driver education do not realize that modern society, with its suburban pattern of growth, is built around the automobile. The car becomes a way of life and a status symbol. When teenagers go too fast, they are probably only copying their own parents.**

A little reconsideration, aimed at a good thesis sentence, could turn this into a reasonably good opening paragraph, with your thesis, your big idea, asserted at the end to focus your reader's attention:

> **Modern society is built on the automobile. Children play with tiny cars; teenagers long to take out the car alone. Soon they are testing their skills at higher and higher speeds, especially with a group of friends along. One final test at extreme speeds usually suffices. It is usually a sobering experience, if survived, and can open one's eyes to the deadly dynamics of the group.**

Thus your thesis is your essay's life and spirit. If it is sufficiently firm, it may tell you immediately how to organize your supporting material. But if you do not find a thesis, your essay will be a tour through the miscellaneous, replete with scaffolds and catwalks—"We have just seen this; now let us turn to this"—an essay with no vital idea. A purely expository essay, one simply on "Cats," for instance, will have to rely on outer scaffolding alone (some orderly progression from Persia to Siam), because it really has no idea at all. It is all subject, all cats, instead of being based on an idea *about* cats with a thesis *about* cats.

## THE ARGUMENTATIVE EDGE

### Find Your Thesis

The *about*-ness puts an argumentative edge on the subject. When you have something to say *about* cats, you have found your underlying idea. You have something to defend, something to fight about: not just "Cats" but "The cat is really our best friend." Now the hackles on all dog people are rising, and you have an argument on your hands. You have something to prove. You have a thesis.

"What's the big idea, Mac?" Let the impudence in that time-honored demand remind you that the most dynamic thesis is a kind of affront to somebody. No one will be very much interested in listening to you deplete the thesis. "The dog is our best friend." Everyone knows that already. Even the dog lovers will be uninterested, convinced they know better than you. But the cat. . . .

So it is with any unpopular idea. The more unpopular the viewpoint and the stronger the push against convention, the stronger the thesis and the more energetic the essay. Compare the energy in "Democracy is good" with that in "Communism is good," for instance. The first is filled with platitudes, the second with plutonium. By the same token, if you can find the real energy in "Democracy is good," if you can get down through the sand to where the roots and water are, you will have a real essay because the opposition against which you generate your energy is the heaviest in the world: boredom. Probably the most energetic thesis of all, the greatest inner organizer, is some tired old truth that you dig to spurt with new life, making the old ground green again.

To find a thesis and to put it into one sentence is to narrow and define your subject to workable size. Under "Cats" you must deal with all felinity from the jungle up, carefully partitioning the eons and areas, the tigers and tabbies. But proclaim the cat the friend of humanity, and you have pared away whole categories and chapters and need only think up the arguments sufficient to overwhelm the opposition. So put an argumentative edge on your subject—and you will have found your thesis.

Neutral exposition, to be sure, has its uses. You may want to tell someone how to build a doghouse, how to can asparagus, how to follow the outlines of relativity, or even how to write an essay. Performing a few exercises in simple exposition will no doubt sharpen your insight into the problems of finding orderly sequences, of considering how best to lead your readers through the hoops of writing clearly and accurately. It will also illustrate how much finer and surer an argument is.

You will see that picking an argument immediately simplifies the problems so troublesome in straight exposition: the defining, the partitioning, the narrowing of the subject. Not that you must constantly be pugnacious or aggressive. I have overstated my point to make it stick. Actually, you can put an argumentative edge on the flattest of expository subjects. "How to build a doghouse" might become "Building a doghouse is a thorough introduction to the building trades, including architecture and civil engineering." "Canning asparagus" might become "An asparagus patch is a course in economics." "Relativity" might become "Relativity is not so inscrutable as many suppose." Literary subjects take an argumentative edge almost by nature. You simply assert what the essential point of a poem or play seems to be: "*Hamlet* is essentially about a world that has lost its values." You assume that your readers are in search of clarity, that you have a loyal opposition consisting of the interested but uninformed. You have given your subject its edge; you have limited and organized it at a single stroke. Pick an *argument*, then, and you will automatically be defining and narrowing your subject and all the partitions that you don't need will fold up. Instead of dealing with things, subjects, and pieces of subjects, you will be dealing with an idea and its consequences.

## Sharpen Your Thesis

Come out with your subject pointed. You have chosen something that interests you, something you have thought about, read about, something preferably of which you have also had some experience—perhaps, let us say, seeing a friend loafing while cashing welfare checks. So take a stand. Make a judgment of value; make a *thesis*. Be reasonable, but don't be timid. It is helpful to think of your thesis, your main idea, as a debating question—"Resolved: Welfare payments must go"—taking out the

"Resolved" when you actually write your thesis down. But your resolution will be even stronger, your essay clearer and tighter, if you can sharpen your thesis even further—"Resolved: Welfare payments must go because _____." Fill in that blank, and your worries are practically over. The main idea is to put your whole argument into one sentence.

Try, for instance: "Welfare payments must go because they are making people irresponsible." I don't know at all if that is true, and neither will you until you write your way into it, considering probabilities, the alternatives and objections, and especially the underlying assumptions. In fact, no one, no master sociologist or future historian, can tell absolutely if it is true, so multiplex are the causes in human affairs, so endless and tangled the consequences. The basic assumption—that irresponsibility is growing—may be entirely false. No one, I repeat, can tell absolutely. But likewise, your guess may be as good as another's. At any rate, you are now ready to write. You have found your *logos*.

Now you can put your well-pointed thesis sentence on a card on the wall in front of you to keep from drifting off target. But you will now want to dress it for the public, to burnish it and make it comely. Suppose you try:

> **Welfare payments, perhaps more than anything else, are eroding personal initiative.**

But is this fully true? Perhaps you had better try something like:

> **Despite their immediate benefits, welfare payments may actually be eroding personal initiative and depriving society of needed workers.**

This is your full thesis. You have acknowledged the opposition ("immediate benefits"); you have spelled out your *because* (erosion, deprivation). This is your opinion, stated as certainty. But how do you know without all the facts? Well, no one knows everything. No one would write anything while still searching for the last fact. To a great extent, the writing of a thing is the learning of it—the discovery of truth. So make a desperate thesis and get into the arena. This is probably solution enough. If it becomes increasingly clear that your thesis is untrue, turn it around and use the other end. If your convictions have begun to falter with:

Despite their immediate benefits, welfare payments undermine initiative . . . .

try it the other way around, with something like:

Although welfare payments may offend the rugged individualist, they relieve much want and anxiety, and they enable many a family to maintain its integrity.

You will now have a beautiful command of the major objections to your new position, and you will have learned something about human fallibility and the nature of truth. You simply add enough evidence to persuade your reader that what you say is probably true, finding arguments that will stand up in the marketplace—public reasons for your private convictions.

## Look for the Fallacies

We saw the fallacies fade as we worked with "Welfare." Here are some further samples from students' papers that may help you improve your uncertain starts:

The answers to crime are longer sentences and more prisons.

Discussion soon showed that *crime* is too sweeping—everything from shoplifting to atrocious murder. The thesis also assumes that the death penalty no longer exists, even as a possibility. It needs more specifics:

Because the death penalty has proved both ineffective and, to many, repugnant, the only remaining answer to serious crimes is longer sentences and more prisons.

Your thesis, of course, may not always find its cure in covering neglected alternatives with a *Because, Although, Despite,* or the like. One student's thesis started:

Registration of guns will lead to confiscation of guns.

Classmates pointed out that registration merely validates ownership. Confiscation would ensue only from illegal ownership. In the end, the simplest way to revise this thesis was to reverse it and qualify *confiscation*:

> **Claims that registration of guns will lead to some universal confiscation are illogical and unfounded.**

Here are some theses, too narrow and too wide, and some suggested revisions.

> NARROW: **The tourist trade only brings financial gain to a few lucky landlords.**
>
> REVISED: **The tourist trade contributes significantly to the state's economy as it meets an essential need for recreation and natural beauty.**
>
> WIDE: **This campus is unique in many ways.**
>
> REVISED: **This campus is atrocious because economy has overruled beauty in several major decisions.**
>
> WIDE: **Abortion is a controversial problem that many people disagree on.**
>
> REVISED: **Laws prohibiting abortion to avoid unwanted births help to keep people from trying to play God for selfish reasons.**
>
> REVISED: **Laws prohibiting abortion to avoid unwanted births inhibit freedom of choice and endanger physical and mental health.**

The process of writing will usually discover the holes in a weak thesis and show the way to its, and the paper's, revision. But however it may work out in the end, get your thesis down, in one sentence, for a good beginning.

## Use Your Title

After your thesis, think of a title. A good title focuses your thinking even more sharply and catches your reader's thoughts on your finished paper. Your title is your opening opportunity. It is an integral part of your paper. Don't forget it.

Work up something from your thesis. It will be tentative, of course. Your thinking and your paper may change in the writing, and you will want to change your title to match. But a good title, like a good thesis, has a double advantage: (1) it helps you keep on track as you write; (2) it attracts and helps keep your reader on track. It is the first step in your persuasion. So try something attractive:

**Farewell to Welfare**
**The Sentence of Prisons**
**Check Your Guns**
**The Trade in Tourism**
**Ugly Building**
**Who's Right in Abortion?**

You can probably do better. You will do better when you finish your paper. But don't make it sound like a newspaper headline, and don't make it a complete statement. Don't forget your title is a starter, both for your writing and for your written paper. Capitalize all significant words (see pp. 227–228 for details). Titles do not take periods but do take question and exclamation marks if you need them. Your title and your opening sentence should be independent of each other. With a title like "Polluted Streams," for instance, don't begin with "*This* is a serious problem."

## SAMPLE: FROM SUBJECT TO THESIS

Now with the concepts in hand, we need a framework, a structure, to put them in. This we will look at in the next chapter. But let us close with a student's paper to illustrate the points of this chapter as it looks ahead to the structural points of the next one. In it, you can see the mechanics of typing, spacing, quoting, and so forth. The author has made a few small last-minute corrections in pencil, which are perfectly acceptable. Her writing is a little wordy and awkward. She is a little uncertain of her language. Her *one's*, for instance, seem far too stiff and insistent. This is her first paper, and she has not yet fully discovered her own written voice, but it is an excellent beginning. It shows well how a personal experience produces a publicly valid thesis and then turns around to give that thesis its most lively and specific illustration. The assignment had asked for a paper of about 500 words on a book (or movie, or TV program) that had proved personally meaningful. Even a memorable experience would do—fixing a car or building a boat or being arrested. The aim of the assignment was to generalize from a personally valuable experience and to explain to others how such an experience can be valuable to them.

## On Finding Oneself in New Guinea

Opposing View

*Reading for pleasure is not considered to be popular.* Young adults prefer the television set with which they have spent so many childhood hours. Too many attractions beckon them away from the books which the teacher recommended to the class for summer reading. One's friends come by in their automobiles to drive down for a coke. The kids go to the movies or to the beach, and the book one had intended to read remains on the shelf, or probably the library, where one has not yet been able to find the time to go. Nevertheless,

Thesis

*a book can furnish real enjoyment.*

Generalized Support

*The reader enjoys the experience of being in another world.* While one reads, one forgets that one is in one's own room. The book has served as a magic carpet to take one to India, or Africa, or Sweden, or even to the cities and areas of one's own country where one has never been. It has also transported one into the lives of people with different experiences and problems, from which one can learn to solve one's own problems of the future. The young person, in particular, can learn by the experience of reading what it is like to be a complete adult.

A book is able to help the young person to mature even further, and change one's whole point of view. *Growing up in New Guinea* by Margaret Mead is a valuable experience for this reason. *I found*

Personal Experience

*the book on our shelf, after having seen a TV program on Margaret Mead.* I was interested in her because the teacher had referred to her book entitled *Coming of Age in Samoa.* I was surprised to find this one about New Guinea. I thought it was a mistake. I opened it and read the first sentence:

Quotation

> The way in which each human infant is transformed into the finished adult, into the complicated individual version of his city and his century, is one of the most fascinating studies open to the curious minded.

The idea that the individual is a version of his city and his century was fascinating. I started reading and was surprised when I was called to dinner to learn that two hours had passed. I could hardly eat my dinner fast enough so that I could get back to New Guinea.

From this book I learned that different cultures have very different conceptions about what is right and wrong, in particular about the sex relations and the marriage ceremony, but that people have the same problems all over the world, namely the problem of finding

Thesis Restated

one's place in society. *I also learned that books can be more enjoyable than any other form of pleasure.* Books fascinate the reader because while one is learning about other people and their problems, particularly about the problem of becoming a full member of society, one is also learning about one's own problems.

## USING THE THESIS IN OTHER WAYS

Making a thesis can also help your reading and in all your courses. Therefore, at the end of each chapter or other reading, try to put down in one sentence (and right in your textbook) that chapter's point: not "This chapter discusses racial discrimination," but "Racial discrimination arises from powerful biological drives to seek one's own kind and to shun aliens." This practice strengthens your knowledge, aids your analysis—has your author said it anywhere as well as you have?—and develops your ability to generate theses for your own thoughts. It works equally well for poems, stories, and plays.

You can also cash in your thesis-making on your essay exams in any course. Here's the trick: MAKE YOURSELF ANSWER THE QUESTION IN ONE SENTENCE, and then just keep writing. This single opening sentence forces all you know on the question into its widest dimension. Everything you throw in after that will seem to illustrate your opening declaration, and your instructor will say, "Now *this* one is really organized—a real grasp of the subject." Next point, use the question's language in your thesis-sentence opener. This works even with the broadest kind of question:

1. Discuss the fall of the Roman Empire.
2. What is the most valuable thing you have learned in this course?
3. Demonstrate your knowledge of the materials of this course.

Your one-sentence openers might go like this:

1. The Roman Empire fell because of decay from within and attack from without.
2. The most valuable thing I have learned this semester is that people usually conceal their true motivations from themselves.
3. The materials of this course illustrate biological evolution, particularly the role of mutation in the survival of the fittest.

If you have time to jot down some points and quickly arrange them to save best for last, you are really off and running.

Be sure, first, to glance through the whole exam to get it and your time in perspective. Notice especially if you have choices. Many students run out of time writing pell-mell on both questions of an "either 1 or 2." Next, attend to your question's directive words like *summarize, consider, discuss, justify, enumerate, compare.* Then, again, using its language, ANSWER IT IN ONE SENTENCE and keep going.

## SUGGESTIONS FOR EXERCISE

1.  *(Best done in class, with comparisons and discussion.) Try a thesis off the top of your head. Put down quickly the first three or four subjects you can think of—anything like golf, knitting, canoes, nail polish, tomatoes. These must have interested you sometime, somewhere. Now take each one and say something about it, making a one-sentence argumentative thesis, filling it out, if appropriate, with reasons, as in "Although tennis _____, golf accomplishes more because _____."*

2.  *Write a thesis statement and a title for each of the following subjects:*

    1. Gun control
    2. Jogging (or some similar activity)
    3. The appearance of our campus
    4. A book you have read
    5. Pros and cons of marriage versus career

3.  *Now take one of these thesis statements and write it out into a paper about the length of the one on reading and New Guinea. First, introduce your thesis with a few remarks to get your reader acquainted with your subject; then write your paper straight through to illustrate your thesis as fully as you can. Then go back over this draft and make it publicly presentable. Think of yourself as a reader to be attracted and persuaded. Here, working in a group in class or with a friend or two after class is immensely helpful. Are your phrases really clear to someone else? Are your thoughts really explained? Let it rest awhile after consideration and discussion, and revise it up to its full potential.*

# 3
# Your Paper's Basic Structure

## ARGUMENT: BEGINNING, MIDDLE, END

As Aristotle long ago pointed out, works that spin their way through time need a beginning, a middle, and an end to be complete. You need a clear beginning to give your essay character and direction so that the reader can tell where he or she is going and can look forward with expectation. Your beginning, of course, will set forth your thesis. You need a middle to amplify and fulfill. This will be the body of your argument, the bulk of your essay. You need an end to let readers know that they have arrived. This will be your final paragraph, a summation and reassertion of your theme. So give your essay the three-part *feel* of completion, of beginning, middle, and end. Many a beginner's essay has no structure and leaves no impression. It is all chaotic middle. It has no beginning; it just starts. It has no end; it just stops, burned out at two in the morning.

The beginning must feel like a beginning, not like an accident. It should be at least a full paragraph that leads your reader into the subject and culminates with your thesis. The end, likewise, should be a full paragraph, one that drives the point home, pushes the implications wide, and brings the reader to rest, back on the fundamental thesis with a sense of completion. When we consider paragraphing in the next chapter, we will look more closely at beginning paragraphs and end paragraphs. But first let us look at the basic structural tactics that carry your reader from beginning to end.

## ARGUMENTATIVE TACTICS

## Arrange Your Points in Order of Increasing Interest

Once your thesis has sounded the challenge, your readers' interest is probably at its highest pitch. They want to see how you can prove so outrageous a thing or to see what the arguments are for this thing they have always believed but never tested. Each step of the way into your demonstration, they are learning more of what you have to say. But, unfortunately, their interest may be relaxing as it becomes satisfied: a reader's normal line of attention progressively declines, arching down like a wintry graph. Against this decline you must oppose your forces, making each successive point more interesting—and save your best till last. It is as simple as that.

Here, for example, is the middle of a short, three-paragraph essay on the thesis that "Working your way through college is valuable." The student's three points ascend in interest:

> The student who works finds that the experience is worth more than the money. He learns to budget his time. He now supports himself by using time he would otherwise waste, and he studies harder in the time he has left because he knows it is limited. He also makes real and lasting friends on the job, as compared to the other casual acquaintances around the campus. He has shared rush hours, and nighttime cleanups with the dishes piled high, and conversation and jokes when business is slow. Finally, he gains confidence in his ability to get along with all kinds of people and to make his own way. He sees how businesses operate and gains an insight into the real world, which is a good contrast to the more intellectual and idealistic world of the college student.

Again, make each successive item more interesting than the last, or you will suddenly seem anticlimactic. Actually, minor regressions of interest make no difference so long as the whole tendency is uphill and your last item clearly the best. Suppose, for example, you were to try a thesis about cats. You decide that four points would make up the case and that you might arrange them in the following order of increasing interest: (1) cats are affectionate but make few demands; (2) cats actually look out for themselves; (3) cats have, in fact, proved extremely useful to society throughout history in controlling mice and other plaguey rodents; (4) cats satisfy some human need for a touch of the jungle, savagery in repose, ferocity in silk, and have been worshiped for the exotic power they still seem to represent. It may be, as you write, that you will find Number 1 developing attractive or amusing instances and perhaps even virtually usurping the whole essay. Numbers 2, 3, and 4 should then be moved ahead as interesting but brief preliminaries.

Interests vary, of course—this is the point—and various subjects will suggest different kinds of importance: from small physical details to large, from incidental thought to basic principles. Sometimes, chronology will supply a naturally ascending order of interest, as in a tennis match or a hockey game or in any contest against natural hazards and time itself, like crossing a glacier with supplies and endurance dwindling. Space, too, may offer natural progressions of interest as you move from portico to inner shrine. But usually interest ascends in ideas, and these quite naturally ascend from your own interest in your subject, in which, with a little thought, you can tell which points to handle first and which to arrange for more and more importance, saving best till last. In short, your structure should range from least important to most important, from simple to complex, from narrow to broad, from pleasant to hilarious, from mundane to metaphysical—whatever "leasts" and "mosts" your subject suggests.

## ACKNOWLEDGING AND DISPOSING OF THE OPPOSITION

Your cat essay, because it is moderately playful, can proceed rather directly, throwing only an occasional bone of concession to the dogs; perhaps most of your essays, as you discuss the Constitutional Convention or explain a poem, will have no opposition to worry about. But a serious controversial argument demands one organizational consideration beyond the simple structure of ascending interest. Although you have taken your stand firmly as a *pro*, you will have to allow scope to the *cons*, or you will seem not to have thought much about your subject. The more opposition you can manage as you carry your point, the more triumphant you will seem, like a high-wire artist daring the impossible.

This balancing of *pros* against *cons* is one of the most fundamental orders of thought: the dialectic order, which is the order of argument, one side pitted against the other. Our minds naturally swing from side to side as we think. In dialectics, we simply give one side an argumentative edge, producing a thesis that cuts a clear line through any subject: "This is better than that." The basic organizing principle here is to get rid of the opposition first and to end on your own side. Probably you will have already organized your thesis sentence in a perfect pattern for your *con-pro* argument:

> **Despite their many advantages, welfare payments** ...
> **Although dogs are fine pets, cats** ...

The subordinate clause (see 95–96) states the subordinate part of your argument, which is your concession to the *con* viewpoint; your main clause states your main argument. As the subordinate clause comes first in your thesis sentence, so does the subordinate argument in your essay. Sentence and essay both reflect a natural psychological principle. You want, and your readers want, to get the opposition out of the way, and you want to end on your best foot. (You might try putting the opposition last, just to see how peculiarly the last word insists on seeming best, and how, when stated last by you, the opposition's case seems to be your own.)

Your opposition, of course, will vary. Some of your audience will agree with you but for different reasons. Others may disagree hotly. You need, then, to imagine what these varying objections might be, as if you were before a meeting in open discussion, giving the hottest as fair a hearing as possible. You probably would not persuade them, but you would ease the pressure and probably persuade the undecided by your reasonable stance. Asking what objections might arise will give you the opposing points that your essay must meet—and overcome.

GET RID OF THE OPPOSITION FIRST. This is the essential tactic of argumentation. You have introduced and stated your thesis in your beginning paragraph. Now start the middle with a paragraph of concession to the *cons:*

> **Dog lovers, of course, have tradition on their side. Dogs are** indeed affectionate and faithful . . . .

With that paragraph out of the way, go to bat for the cats, showing their superiority to dogs in every point.

Sometimes, as we have seen with the New Guinea essay, you can use the opposition itself to introduce your thesis in your first paragraph, getting some of it out of the way at the same time:

"Thou shalt not kill" is a basic commandment that applies to society as well as to individuals. The Constitution prohibits cruel and unusual punishment, and the death penalty now appears less frequently both in the statutes and in its execution. The penalty costs millions more in trials and appeals than straight life imprisonment. Nevertheless, simple justice for cruel and unusual antisocial behavior demands the death penalty.

But usually your beginning paragraph will lead down to your thesis somewhat neutrally, and you will attack your opposition head-on in paragraph two, as you launch into your argument.

If the opposing arguments seem relatively slight and brief, you can get rid of them neatly all together in one paragraph before you get down to your case. Immediately after your beginning, which has stated your thesis, you write a paragraph of concession—"Of course, security is a good thing. No one wants people begging"—and so on to the end of the paragraph, deflating every conceivable objection. Then back to the main line: "But the price in moral decay is too great." The structure of the essay, paragraph by paragraph, might be diagrammed something like the scheme shown in Diagram I:

Diagram I

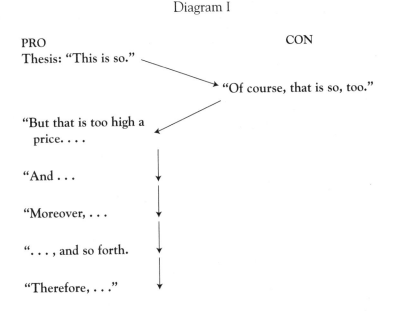

If the opposition is more considerable, demolish it point by point, using a series of *cons* and *pros,* in two or three paragraphs, before you steady down to your own side. Each paragraph can be a small argument that presents the opposition and then knocks it flat—a kind of Punch-and-Judy show: "We must admit that . . . . But . . . ."—and down goes the poor old opposition again. Or you can swing your argument through a number of alternating paragraphs: first your beginning (the thesis), then a paragraph to the opposition (*con*), then one for your side (*pro*), then another paragraph of *con,* and so on. The main point, again, is this: *get rid of the opposition first.* One paragraph of concession right after your thesis will probably handle most of your adversaries, and the more complicated argumentative swingers, like the ones shown in Diagram II, will develop naturally as you need them.

You will notice that *but* and *however* are always guides for the *pros,* serving as switches back to the main line. Indeed, *but, however,* and *nevertheless* are the basic *pros. But* always heads its turning sentence (not followed by a comma); *nevertheless* usually does (followed by a comma). I am sure, however, that *however* is always better buried in the sentence between commas. "However, . . ." at a sentence's beginning is the habit of heavy prose. *But* is for the quick turn; the inlaid *however* for the more elegant sweep.

The structural line of your arguments, then, might look like Diagram II:

### Diagram II: Controlling Handguns—Pro and Con

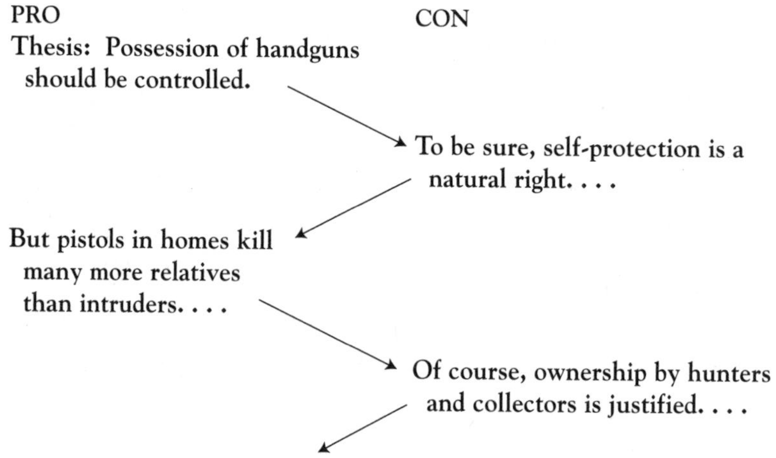

PRO                                    CON
**Thesis: Possession of handguns
    should be controlled.**

                                        **To be sure, self-protection is a
                                            natural right. . . .**

**But pistols in homes kill
many more relatives
than intruders. . . .**

                                        **Of course, ownership by hunters
                                            and collectors is justified. . . .**

Large numbers of weapons in
homes, however, give easy
access to theft. . . .

I concede that any restrictions
invade privacy and freedom. . . .

Nevertheless, the intrusion
is no more restrictive than
registering an automobile. . . .

Indeed, all arguments about
individual rights pale before
the crime rate and the annual
slaughter of individuals. . . .

Besides, handguns kill thousands
more in the United States than
in any other country.

Therefore, controlling handguns
is reasonable and neccessary.

## RUNNING COMPARISONS POINT BY POINT

After blasting the opposition first, only one argumentative principle
remains: *run your comparisons point by point*. This holds in any kind of comparison. Simply comparing and contrasting two poems, two stories, two
ball players, brings insight. It can illuminate the unfamiliar with the familiar or help you discover and convey to your readers new perspectives on
things well-known—two popular singers, two automobiles, two nursery
rhymes. But the principle is the same.

Compare point for point. Don't write all about sheep for three pages
and then all about goats. Every time you say something about a sheep, say
something about a goat, pelt for pelt, horn for horn, beard for beard.
Otherwise your essay will fall in two, and you will need to repeat all your
sheep points when you get down to goats and at last begin the comparison.
The tendency to organize comparisons by halves is so strong that you will
probably find that you have fallen into it unawares, and in revising you will
have to reorganize everything point for point—still arranging your pairs of

points from least important to most. Finally, the most effective comparison is one that aims to demonstrate a superiority, that is, one with an argumentative thesis—"Resolved: Sheep are more useful than goats."

Now you have almost finished your essay. You have found a thesis. You have worked it into a decent beginning. You have then worked out a convincing middle, with your arguments presented in a sequence of ascending interest. You have used up all your points and said your say. You and your argument are both exhausted. But don't stop. You need an end, or the whole thing will unravel in your readers' minds. You need to buttonhole them in a final paragraph, to imply "I told you so" without saying it, to hint at the whole round of experience and leave them convinced, satisfied, and admiring. One more paragraph will do it: beginning, middle, *and* end.

## SUGGESTIONS FOR EXERCISE

*1.* Warm up with two or three pro-and-con thesis sentences beginning "Although . . .".

*2.* For the following assertions, write one argument against and one argument for. Now combine your statements into one thesis sentence:

**EXAMPLE** Assertion: Movies should not be censored.

Con: *Children should not be exposed to obscene and explicitly sexual images on the screen.*

Pro: *Obscenity is far too subjective a thing for any person to define for anyone else.*

Thesis Statement: *Although young people probably should not be exposed to explicit sex in films, movies still should not be censored because obscenity is so subjective that no one can legitimately serve as censor for the rest of us.*

1. Assertion: Discussion classes are superior to lectures.
2. Assertion: Rapid and convenient transit systems must be built in our cities.
3. Assertion: The federal government should subsidize large companies forced near bankruptcy.
4. Assertion: Medical schools should reduce the time required for a degree in general medicine from four years to two.
5. Assertion: College degrees should require an apprenticeship away from the campus.

3.   *Here is a short concoction of what might be a first draft of a pro-con paper. See what you can do in rewriting it persuasively, rearranging the points, filling in with points and examples of your own, dropping what doesn't work, and supplying the missing* pro *and* con *switches:* But, however, nevertheless, of course, I admit, *and the like. Find a more persuasive title.*

### Public Transportation

To anyone who has spent a few hours in traffic jams, the need for public transportation is obvious. We waste hours stalled in one place. The pollution and smog are obvious. Public transportation has gone bankrupt because of the automobile. We must revive our systems of public transportation.

Public transportation is obsolescent because of the automobile. Rebuilding public transportation would be very expensive. It would save fuel and cut down pollution.

Our economy depends on the automobile. People need cars to get to work. The automobile industry generates a great many jobs and millions of dollars. Cars were once built to last. Now built-in obsolescence generates these jobs and dollars. For shopping and work, the car is a necessity. The freedom to go when and where one wants is part of the American way.

4.   *Write your own* pro-con *dialectical swinger, a good persuasive essay following Diagram I or II on pages 31–33.*

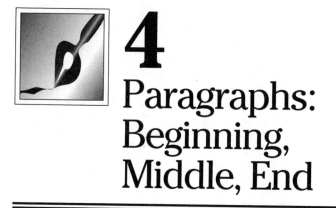

# 4
# Paragraphs: Beginning, Middle, End

## THE STANDARD PARAGRAPH

A paragraph is a structural convenience—a building block to get firmly in mind. I mean the standard, central paragraph, setting aside for the moment the climactic beginning paragraph and ending paragraph. You build the bulk of your essay with standard paragraphs, with blocks of concrete ideas, and they must fit smoothly. But they must also remain as perceptible parts to rest your reader's eye and mind. Indeed, the paragraph originated, among the Greeks, as a resting place and place finder, being first a mere mark (*graphos*) in the margin alongside (*para*) an unbroken sheet of handwriting—the proofreader's familiar ¶. You have heard that a paragraph is a single idea, and this is true. But so is a word, usually; and so is a sentence, sometimes. It seems best, after all, to think of a paragraph as something you use for your readers' convenience, rather than as some granitic form laid down by molten logic.

The medium determines the size of the paragraph. Your average longhand paragraph may look the same size as a typed one, much like a paragraph in a book. But the printed page would show your handwritten paragraph a short embarrassment, and your typed one barely long enough for decency. The beginner's insecurity produces inadequate paragraphs, often only a sentence each. Journalists, of course, are one-sentence paragraphers. The narrow newspaper column makes a sentence look like a paragraph, and narrow columns and short paragraphs serve the newspaper's rapid transit. A paragraph from a book might fill a whole newspaper column with solid lead. It would have to be broken—paragraphed—for the reader's convenience. A news story on the page of a book would look like a gap-toothed comb and would have to be consolidated for the reader's comfort. So make your paragraphs ample.

## Plan for the Big Paragraph

Imagine yourself writing for a book. Force yourself to write four or five sentences at least, visualizing your paragraphs as identical rectangular frames to be filled. This will allow you to build with orderly blocks, to strengthen your feel for structure. Because the beginner's problem is usually one of thinking of things to say rather than of trimming the overgrowth, you can do your filling out a unit at a time, always thinking up one or two sentences more to fill the customary space. You will probably be repetitive and wordy at first—this is our universal failing—but you will soon learn to fill your paragraph with interesting details. You will develop a constructional rhythm, coming to rest at the end of each paragraphic frame.

Once accustomed to a five-sentence frame, say, you can then begin to vary the length for emphasis, letting a good idea swell out beyond the norm or bringing a particular point home in a paragraph short and sharp—even in one sentence, like this.

The paragraph's structure, then, has its own rhetorical message. It tells the reader visually whether or not you are in charge of your subject. Tiny, ragged paragraphs display your hidden uncertainty, unless clearly placed among big ones for emphasis. Brief opening and closing paragraphs sometimes can emphasize your thesis effectively, but they usually make your beginning seem hasty and your ending perfunctory. So aim for the big paragraph all the way, and vary it only occasionally and knowingly for rhetorical emphasis.

## Find a Topic Sentence

Looked at as a convenient structural frame, the paragraph reveals a further advantage. Like the essay itself, it has a beginning, a middle, and an end. The beginning and the end are usually each one sentence long, and the middle gets you smoothly from one to the other. Because, like the essay, the paragraph flows through time, its last sentence is the most emphatic. This is your home punch. The first sentence holds the next most emphatic place. It will normally be your *topic sentence*, stating the paragraph's point like a small thesis of a miniature essay, something like this:

> *Jefferson believed in democracy because he firmly believed in reason.* He knew that reason was far from perfect, but he also knew that it was the best faculty we have. He knew that it was better than all the frightened and angry intolerances with which we fence off our own backyards at the cost of injustice. Thought must be free. Discussion must be free. Reason must be free to range among the widest possibilities. Even the opinion we hate and have reasons for believing wrong, we must leave free so that reason can operate on it, so that we advertise our belief in reason and demonstrate a faith unafraid of the consequences—because we know that the consequences will be right. Freedom is really not the aim and end of Jeffersonian democracy: freedom is the means by which democracy can rationally choose justice for all.

If your topic sentence covers everything within your paragraph, your paragraph is coherent, and you are using your paragraphs with maximum effect, leading your readers into your community block by block. If your end sentences bring them briefly to rest, they will know where they are and appreciate it.

This is the basic frame. As you write, you will discover your own variations: an occasional paragraph that illustrates its topic sentence with parallel items and no home punch at the end at all, or one beginning with a hint and ending with its topical idea in the most emphatic place, like the best beginning paragraphs.

## BEGINNING PARAGRAPHS: THE FUNNEL

### State Your Thesis at the END of Your Beginning Paragraph

Your beginning paragraph should contain your main idea, and present it to best advantage. Its topic sentence is also the *thesis sentence* of your entire essay. The clearest and most emphatic place for your thesis sentence is at the *end*—not at the beginning—of the beginning paragraph. Of course, many an essay begins with a subject-statement, a kind of open topic sentence for the whole essay, and unfolds amiably from there. But these are usually the more personal meditations of seasoned writers and established authorities. Bacon, for instance, usually steps off from a topical first sentence: "Studies serve for delight, for ornament, and for ability." Similarly,

A. A. Milne begins with "Of the fruits of the earth, I give my vote to the orange"—and just keeps going.

Some good beginnings run more than one paragraph before coming to rest on the thesis, and some only imply their thesis, as in E. B. White's "Farewell, My Lovely":

> I see by the new Sears Roebuck catalogue that it is still possible to buy an axle for a 1909 Model T Ford, but I am not deceived. The great days have faded, the end is in sight. Only one page in the current catalogue is devoted to parts and accessories for the Model T; yet everyone remembers springtimes when the Ford gadget section was larger than men's clothing, almost as large as household furnishings. The last Model T was build in 1927, and the car is fading from what scholars call the American scene—which is an understatement, because to a few million people who grew up with it, the old Ford practically *was* the American scene.
>
> It was a miracle God had wrought. And it was patently the sort of thing that could only happen once. Mechanically uncanny, it was like nothing that had ever come to the world before. Flourishing industries rose and fell with it. As a vehicle, it was hard-working, commonplace, heroic; and it often seemed to transmit those qualities to the persons who rode in it. My own generation identifies it with Youth, with its gaudy, irretrievable excitements; before it fades into the mist, I would like to pay it the tribute of the sigh that is not a sob, and set down random entries in a shape somewhat less cumbersome than a Sears Roebuck catalogue.*

We get White's point indirectly, but it is clearly there by the end of his second paragraph, which he concludes with an old-fashioned statement of intent. He might well have set an explicit thesis with little loss of his casual charm:

> The Model T caught the American heart and mind because it was unique, exciting, and heroically serviceable.

But for the less assured and the more structurally minded, the funnel is the reliable form, as the thesis sentence brings readers to rest for a moment at the end of the opening paragraph, with their bearings established. If you put your thesis sentence first, you may have to repeat some version of it as you bring your beginning paragraph to a close. If you put it

---

*© 1936, 1964, The New Yorker Magazine, Inc. From *Essays of E. B. White* (New York: Harper & Row, 1977): 162, originally published in *The New Yorker* in 1936 over the pseudonym "Lee Strout White." Richard L. Strout had submitted a manuscript on the Ford, and White, with his collaboration, rewrote it.

in the middle, readers will very likely take something else as your main point, probably whatever the last sentence contains. The inevitable psychology of interest, as you move your readers through your first paragraph and into your essay, urges you to put your thesis last—in the last sentence of your beginning paragraph.

Think of your beginning paragraph, then, not as the middle paragraph's frame to be filled but as a funnel. Start wide and end narrow:

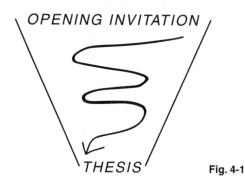

OPENING INVITATION

THESIS                    Fig. 4-1

If, for instance, you wished to show that "Learning to play the guitar pays off in friendship"—your thesis—you would start somewhere back from that thesis-idea with something more general—about music, about learning, about the pleasures of achievement, about guitars: "Playing the guitar looks easy," "Music can speak more directly than words," "Learning anything is a course in frustration." You can even open with something quite specific, *as long as it is more general than your thesis:* "Pick up a guitar, and you bump into people." A handy way to find an opener is to take one word from your thesis—*learning, play,* or *guitar,* for instance—and make a sentence out of it. Say something about it, and you are well on your way to your thesis, three or four sentences later.* Your opening line, in other words, should look forward to your thesis, should be something to engage interest easily, something to which most readers would assent without a rise in blood pressure. (Antagonize and startle if you wish, but beware of having the door slammed before you have a chance and of making your thesis an anticlimax.) Therefore, it should be broad and genial. From your opening geniality, you move progressively down to smaller particulars. You narrow down: from learning the guitar, to its musical and social complications, to its rewards in friendship (your thesis). Your paragraph might run, from broad to narrow, like this:

---

*I am grateful to James C. Raymond, of the University of Alabama, for this helpful idea.

Learning anything has unexpected rocks in its path, but the guitar seems particularly rocky. Playing it looks so simple. A few chords, you think, and you are on your way. Then you discover not only the musical and technical difficulties, but also a whole unexpected crowd of human complications. Your friends think you are showing off; the people you meet think you are a fake. Then the frustrations drive you to achievement. You learn to face the music and the people honestly. You finally learn to play a little, but you also discover something better. You have learned to make and keep some real friends because you have discovered a kind of ultimate friendship with yourself.

Now, that paragraph turned out a little different from what I anticipated. I used the informal *you*, and it seemed to suit the subject. I also overshot my original thesis, discovering, as I wrote, a thesis one step farther—an underlying cause—about coming to friendly terms with oneself. But it illustrates the funnel, from the broad and general to the one particular point that will be your essay's main idea, your thesis. Here is another example:

The environment is the world around us, and everyone agrees it needs a cleaning. Big corporations gobble up the countryside and disgorge what's left into the breeze and streams. Big trucks rumble by, trailing their fumes. A jet roars into the air, and its soot drifts over the trees. Everyone calls for massive action and then tosses away a cigarette butt or gum wrapper. The world around us is also a sidewalk, a lawn, a lounge, a hallway, a room right here. Cleaning the environment can begin by reaching for the scrap of paper at your feet.

In a more argumentative paper, you can sometimes set up your thesis effectively by opening with the opposition, as we have already noted (30–31):

Science is the twentieth century's answer to everything. We want the facts. We conduct statistical polls to measure the president's monthly popularity. We send spaceships to bring back pieces of the moon and send back data from the planets. We make babies in test tubes. We believe that eventually we will discover the chemical formula for life itself, creating a human being from the basic elements. Nevertheless, some vital element may be beyond the grasp of science and all human planning, as Michael Crichton's novel *The Lost World* suggests.

## MIDDLE PARAGRAPHS

### Make Your Middle Paragraphs Full, with Transitions

The middle paragraph is the standard paragraph, a little essay in itself, with its own little beginning and little end. Its beginning, its topic sentence, should carry forward the argument of the whole essay as projected in your thesis sentence. But it must also declare its allegiance to the paragraphs immediately before and after it. Each topic sentence must somehow hook onto the paragraph above it, must include some word or phrase to ease the reader's path: a transition. (1) You may simply repeat a word from the sentence that ended the paragraph just above. (2) You may bring down a thought generally developed or left slightly hanging in air: "Smith's idea is different" might be a tremendously economical topic sentence with automatic transition. (3) Or you may get from one paragraph to the next by the usual stepping-stones, like *But, however* (within the sentence), *Nevertheless, Therefore, Indeed, Of course.* One brief transitional touch in your topic sentence, your opening sentence, is usually sufficient.

The topic sentences in each of the following three paragraphs by Elizabeth Marshall Thomas contain clear transitions. I have just used an old standby myself: repeating the words *topic sentence* from the close of my preceding paragraph. Thomas has just commended a dozen scientists who have written for the public, wanting "to teach us something"—Rachel Carson, Jane Goodall, George Schaller, Loren Eisley. She now begins her next paragraph with a transitional reference to *this group.* In the next paragraph, *Dinosaurs*, reinforced with *stupid and slow,* does the trick; in the last, *this story* makes the transition and sets the contrast in a neat topic sentence. The paragraphs are nearly the same length, all cogent, clear, and full. No one-sentence paragraphing here, no gaps, but all a lively, orderly progression. Notice also how each end-sentence makes the paragraph's point:

> A prominent scientist belonging to this group is the controversial Robert T. Bakker, once known as the *enfant terrible* of paleontology. Before publishing his present novel, *Raptor Red* (Bantam, 1995), he published a very controversial nonfiction work, *The Dinosaur Heresies* (Morrow, 1986), in which he challenged the now antiquated view that, being Nature's first attempt at large animals, dinosaurs were for the most part badly designed hulks. A case in point was brontosaurus (now known as apatasaurus). Because its body was thought to be slung between its legs in lizard fashion, not set squarely above its legs in elephant style, it supposedly had to stand in water to support its huge weight.

Dinosaurs were supposed to be cold-blooded reptiles, stupid and slow, in contrast, as we fatuously saw it, to our own ancestors, the clever little mammals who preyed on the eggs carelessly dropped behind the poor, dumb, wandering monsters. Being warm-blooded, our furry little predecessors would have had no problem with the cooling climate that theoretically exterminated their reptilian over-lords. They fluffed out their fur, cuddled together in their burrows, and warmed one another up. The dinosaurs, in contrast, having been badly designed in the first place, wandered helplessly over the landscape, slowly getting colder and colder until they all fell down and died.

Much of this story was wrong. Mammals and dinosaurs diverged from a common ancestor about 260 million years ago. Dinosaurs subsequently evolved to fill every possible ecological niche, from which they ruled the earth for 160 million years and became the most successful vertebrates in the history of the planet. During all that time we mammals managed to evolve into nothing larger than a cat. When the dinosaurs vanished, the mammals final-ly took over, but they have not ruled nearly as long as the dinosaurs and, thanks to human activity, there seems a good possibility that they will not.*

## Check Your Paragraphs for Clarity and Coherence

Thomas's paragraphs run smoothly from first sentence to last. They are coherent. The *topic sentence* is the key. It assures that the subsequent sentences will fall into line, and it is the first point to check when you look back to see if they really do. Many a jumbled paragraph can be unified by writing a broader topic sentence. Consider this disjointed specimen:

Swimming is healthful. The first dive into the pool is always cold. Tennis takes a great deal of energy, especially under a hot sun. Team sports, like basketball, baseball, and volleyball, always make the awkward player miserable. Character and health go hand in hand.

What is all that about? From the last sentence, we can surmise what the writer intended. But the first sentence about swimming in no way covers

---

*Excerpt from "The First Fine Careless Raptor." Reprinted with permission from *The New York Review of Books*. Copyright © 1996 Nyrev, Inc.

the paragraph, which treats several sports not in the least like swimming, and seems to be driving at something other than health. The primary remedy is to find the paragraph's thesis and to devise a topic sentence that will state it, thus covering everything in the paragraph. Think of your topic sentence as a roof—covering your paragraph and pulling its contents together.

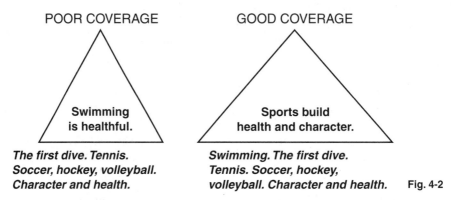

POOR COVERAGE

Swimming
is healthful.

*The first dive. Tennis.*
*Soccer, hockey, volleyball.*
*Character and health.*

GOOD COVERAGE

Sports build
health and character.

*Swimming. The first dive.*
*Tennis. Soccer, hockey,*
*volleyball. Character and health.*    **Fig. 4-2**

Suppose we add only a topic sentence, suggested by our right-hand diagram. It will indeed pull things together:

Topic Sentence    *Sports demand an effort of will and muscle that is healthful for the soul as well as the body.* Swimming is healthful. The first dive into the pool is always cold. Tennis takes a great deal of energy, especially under a hot sun. Team sports, like basketball, baseball, and volleyball, always make the awkward player miserable. Character and health go hand in hand.

But the paragraph is still far from an agreeable coherence. The islands of thought still need some bridges. Gaining coherence is primarily a filling in, or a spelling out, of submerged connections. You may fill in with (1) thought and (2) specific illustrative detail; you may spell out by tying your sentences together with (3) transitional tags and (4) repeated words or syntactical patterns. Let us see what we can do with our sample paragraph.

From the first, you probably noticed that the writer was thinking in pairs; the pleasure of sports is balanced off against their difficulty; the difficulty is physical as well as moral; character and health go hand in hand. We have already indicated this doubleness of idea in our topic sentence. Now to fill out the thought, we need merely expand each sentence so as to give each half of the double idea its due expression. We need also to qualify the thought here and there with *perhaps, often, some, sometimes, fre-*

*quently, all in all,* and the like. As we work through the possibilities, more specific detail will come to mind. We have already made the general ideas of *character* and *health* more specific with *will, muscle, soul,* and *body* in our topic sentence, and we shall add a touch or two more of illustration, almost automatically, as our imagination becomes more stimulated by the subject. We shall add a number of transitional ties like *but, and, of course, nevertheless,* and *similarly.* We shall look for chances to repeat key words, like *will,* if we can do so gracefully, and to repeat syntactical patterns if we can emphasize similar thoughts by doing so, as with *no matter how patient the teammates . . . no matter how heavy the heart,* toward the end of our revision below (the original phrases are in italics):

> *Sports demand an effort of will and muscle that is healthful for*         Topic Sentence
> *the soul as well as the body. Swimming is* physically *healthful,* of
> course, although it may seem undemanding and highly conducive to
> lying for hours inert on a deck chair in the sun. But *the first dive into*       Illustrative
> *the pool is always cold:* taking the plunge always requires some       Sentences with
> effort of will, and the swimmer soon summons the will to compete       Transitions
> for greater distances and greater speed, doing 20 laps where he or she
> used to do one. Similarly, *tennis takes* quantities *of energy,* physical
> and moral, *especially* when the competition stiffens *under a hot*
> *sun. Team sports, like basketball, baseball, and volleyball,* perhaps
> demand even more of the amateur. *The awkward player* is *miserable*
> when striking out or missing an easy fly or an easy basket, no mat-
> ter how patient the teammates. The player must drive to keep on try-
> ing, no matter how heavy the heart. Whatever the sport, a little
> determination can eventually conquer one's awkwardness and timid-
> ity, and the reward will be more than physical. *Character and health*      End Sentence:
> frequently *go hand in hand.*       The Point

Here we can see the essence of coherence: REPETITION, (1) repeating parallel examples, like *swimming, tennis, team sports,* as if stacking them up to support your topic sentence; or (2) stringing them along by idea and word, sentence by sentence, as in sports, *swimming, dive, tennis, team sports,* and so forth, as one thought suggests the next. Finally, TRANSITIONS *within* a paragraph contribute importantly to its coherence. Because beginners usually do not think of transitions, try to include a helpful *of course, but, and, similarly, perhaps, consequently, still,* and the like.

Here are the five points to remember about middle paragraphs. First, think of the middle paragraph as a miniature essay, with a beginning, a middle, and an end. Its beginning will normally be its topic sentence, the thesis of the miniature essay. Its middle will develop, explain, and illustrate your topic sentence. Its last sentence will drive home the idea. Second, remember that this kind of paragraph is the norm, which you may instinctively vary when your topic sentence requires only a series of parallel illustrations (*swimming, tennis, golf, basketball, hockey*) or when you open your paragraph with some hint to be fulfilled in a topical conclusive sentence (*Sports build body and soul*). Third, see that your paragraph is coherent, not only flowing smoothly but with nothing in it not covered by the topic sentence. Fourth, make your paragraphs full and well developed, with plenty of details, examples, and full explanations, or you will end up with a skeletal paper with very little meat on its bones. Fifth, remember transitions. Though each paragraph is a kind of miniature essay, it is also a part of a larger essay. Therefore, hook each paragraph smoothly to the paragraph preceding it with some transitional touch in each opening sentence.

## END PARAGRAPHS: THE INVERTED FUNNEL

### Reassert Your Thesis

If the beginning paragraph is a funnel, the end paragraph is a funnel upside down: the thought starts moderately narrow—it is more or less the thesis you have had all the time—and then pours out broader and broader implications and finer emphases. The end paragraph reiterates, summarizes, and emphasizes with decorous fervor. This is your last chance. This is what your readers will carry away—and if you can carry *them away*, so much the better—all within decent intellectual bounds, of course. You are the person of reason still, but the person of reason supercharged with conviction, sure of your idea and sure of its importance.

If your essay is anecdotal, however, largely narrative and descriptive, your ending may be no more than a sentence, or it may be a ruminative paragraph generalizing outward from the particulars to mirror your beginning paragraph, as in a more argumentative essay. The dramatic curve of your illustrative incident will tell you what to do. An essay illustrating how folly may lead to catastrophe—a friend dead from an overdose, or drowned by daring too far on thin ice—might end when a story has told itself out and made its point starkly: "The three of us walked numbly up the street toward home."

But the usual final paragraph conveys a sense of assurance and repose, of business completed. Its topic sentence is usually some version of the original thesis sentence, because the end paragraph is the exact structural opposite and complement of the beginning one. Its transitional word or phrase is often one of finality or summary—*then, finally, thus,* and *so:*

So, the guitar is a means to a finer end.
The environment, then, is in our lungs and at our fingertips.

The paragraph would then proceed to expand and elaborate this revived thesis. We would get a confident assertion that both the music and the friendships are really by-products of an inner alliance; we would get an urgent plea to clean up our personal environs and strengthen our convictions. One rule of thumb: the longer the paper, the more specific the summary of the points you have made. A short paper will need no specific summary of your points at all; the renewed thesis and its widening of implications are sufficient.

Here is an end paragraph by Sir James Jeans. His transitional phrase is *for a similar reason*. His thesis was that previous concepts of physical reality had mistaken surfaces for depths:

> The purely mechanical picture of visible nature fails for a similar reason. It proclaims that the ripples themselves direct the workings of the universe instead of being mere symptoms of occurrences below; in brief, it makes the mistake of thinking that the weathervane determines the direction from which the wind shall blow, or that the thermometer keeps the room hot.*

Here is an end paragraph of Professor Richard Hofstadter's. His transitional word is *intellectuals*, carried over from the preceding paragraphs. His thesis is that intellectuals should not abandon their defense of intellectual and spiritual freedom, as they have tended to do, under pressure to conform:

> This world will never be governed by intellectuals—it may rest assured. But we must be assured, too, that intellectuals will not be altogether governed by this world, that they maintain their piety, their longstanding allegiance to the world of spiritual values to which they should belong. Otherwise there will be no intellectuals, at least not above ground. And societies in which the intellectuals have been driven underground, as we have had occasion to see in our own time, are societies in which even the anti-intellectuals are unhappy.†

Remember a conclusion when you have used up all your points and had your say. One more paragraph will do it: beginning, middle, *and* end.

---

*The New Background of Science (Cambridge: Cambridge University Press, 1933): 261.
†"Democracy and Anti-intellectualism in America," Michigan Alumnus Quarterly Review, 59 (1953): 295.

## THE WHOLE ESSAY

You have now discovered the main ingredients of a good essay. You have learned to find and to sharpen your thesis in one sentence, to give your essay that all-important argumentative edge. You have learned to arrange your points in order of increasing interest, and you have practiced disposing of the opposition in a *pro-con* structure. You have seen that your beginning paragraph should seem like a funnel, working from broad generalization to thesis. You have tried your hand at middle paragraphs, which are almost like little essays with their own beginnings and ends. Finally, you have learned that your last paragraph should work like an inverted funnel, broadening and embellishing your thesis.

Some students have pictured the essay as a Greek column, with a narrowing beginning paragraph as its top, or capital, and a broadening end paragraph as its base. Others have seen it as a keyhole.* Picturing your structure like this is very handy. This is the basic pattern. You will probably find your own designs with your varying topics and audiences. Neverthless, keeping this basic pattern in mind helps you write. Checking your drafts against it will show you where you might amplify or rearrange. As you write more and more, you will discover new variations as each new subject pushes its way toward fulfillment, like a tree growing toward full light. But every tree is a tree. Each follows the general pattern, as if fulfilling some heavenly arboreal keyhole. Similarly, this essayistic one works out in convenient detail the inevitability of Aristotle's Beginning, Middle, and End.

The student's essay that follows illustrates this basic structure fairly well. He has picked from his own experience a topic meaningful to anyone.

### A Year to Learn

Broad Subject,
Illustration
         *Learning takes time.* **The year from first to second grade adds only the rudiments of reading. By high school, year after year, I thought I knew it all. Diving, with a great coach, took over. I won a scholarship. Then my classes caught fire. I learned that I wanted to know something, whatever that might be. I needed time to find out. I took a year off and learned again.** *I learned that the usual col-*

Narrowing
Thesis
*lege course needs more of this kind of time.*

---

*Mrs. Fran Measley of Santa Barbara, California, has devised for her students a mimeographed sheet to accompany my discussion of structure and paragraphing—to help them to visualize my points, through a keyhole, as it were. I am grateful to Mrs. Measley to be able to include it here.

## THE KEYHOLE

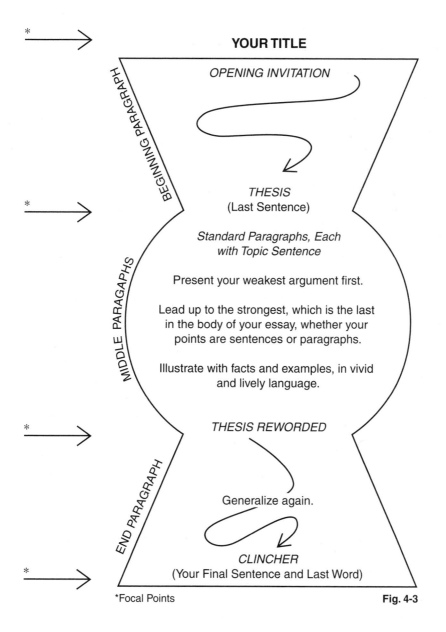

**YOUR TITLE**

*OPENING INVITATION*

*BEGINNING PARAGRAPH*

*THESIS*
(Last Sentence)

*Standard Paragraphs, Each
with Topic Sentence*

Present your weakest argument first.

Lead up to the strongest, which is the last
in the body of your essay, whether your
points are sentences or paragraphs.

Illustrate with facts and examples, in vivid
and lively language.

*MIDDLE PARAGAPHS*

*THESIS REWORDED*

*END PARAGRAPH*

Generalize again.

*CLINCHER*
(Your Final Sentence and Last Word)

*Focal Points                                                    **Fig. 4-3**

Topic Sentence,
Opposition

Of course, *getting through early gets the preliminary interviews*. You now know your field, as you hope. You now can write those applications for jobs. The competition is stiff, and you are in it from the first, meeting the people from the big companies, getting your name on their lists, hoping you have worn the right things, and said the right things.

Topic Sentence,
Pro Paragraph

*But a year off takes off the pressure of time.* Most of those first interviewees won't land in the land of dreams. They will face the inevitable rejections, the reapplications, the doubts, the changes of goal. A year away from the campus is a valuable step away from all this and into the real world, into learning about yourself and what you really want to know.

Thesis Restated

*Learning takes time.* I took that year off from financial necessity. I grew, physically, in fact, and learned. That early pressurized competition had evaporated. I discovered what I really wanted to know. Aside from meeting people and making yourself known to them and others, a required year off in a job or social service *would*

The Clincher

*mature every student for the courses and challenges ahead.*

## SUGGESTIONS FOR EXERCISE

**1.** *Below is a list of thesis sentences. Choose one (or its opposite), or make one of your own on the same pattern. Then back off from it at least four or five sentences, and write a funnellike beginning paragraph leading your readers down to it: your thesis, the last sentence of your beginning funnel.*

*EXAMPLE with thesis italicized:*

The coal operators will tell you that stripping is cheaper and more efficient than conventional mining. Their 250-cubic-yard draglines, their 200-cubic-yard shovels, their 50-ton trucks, can rip the top off a mountain and expose a whole seam of coal in a fraction of the time it takes to sink a shaft. "It is cheaper," they will say, "to bring the surface to the coal than to bring the coal to the surface." And of course they are right; in a sense it is cheaper. But visit eastern Kentucky and look at the real price we pay for stripped coal. Visit a stripped area and you will see that, no matter how low the price for a truckload of stripped coal, *the real price for strip-mining has to be reckoned in terms of blighted land, poisoned streams, and stunted human lives.*

1. Television should be cleaned up.
2. The computer has contributed to the modern sense of alienation.
3. If the filibuster is supposed to guarantee respect for minority opinion, it usually turns out to be a flagrant waste of time.
4. America's white workers think affirmative action threatens their material well-being.
5. If girls score lower than boys in Regents' tests, having them compete with boys for Regents' scholarships is unfair.

**2.** *Now try the inverted funnel for an end paragraph in which your topic sentence is some version of the thesis you used in Exercise 1, broadening its implications outward to leave the readers fully convinced and satisfied.*

> **EXAMPLE** *with the rephrased thesis (its topic sentence) italicized, and some of the evidence from the paper's middle summarized for emphasis:*
>
> *So, at last, we should add up the real costs of strip-mining; we should admit that the ultimate price of coal is far too high if we must rape the land, poison the streams, and wreck human lives to mine it.* For after the draglines have gone, even after the coal itself has been burned; the bills for strip-mining will keep coming in. So far, following the expedient path, we have laid bare more than 2,600 square miles of our land, and we show no signs of stopping. Every year we strip an additional 50,000 acres. Just as we cut down our forests in the nineteenth century and fouled our air in the twentieth, we still blunder along toward ecological and social disaster. Isn't it time to stop?

**3.** *Staying with the same topic sentence, develop a full middle paragraph, remembering the five points: (1) the miniature essay, with beginning, middle, and end; (2) coherence; (3) fullness; (4) transition; (5) repetition.*

> **EXAMPLE** *with transitional touches italicized:*
>
> The streams tell the story *as drearily as* the *eroded land.* In winter, *they* are red with running silt, and sometimes black with *coal* dust. *In summer, many* are no *streams* at all, merely gullies through which the *winter* rains have rushed. Before *the draglines stripped* the earth of its skin, the massed roots of grasses, shrubs, and trees held the soil in place and soaked up the *water,* easing it into the *streams* for a full year's run. Fish fed in pools below *grassy* banks and among

the weeds that slowed the *water* to a leisurely pace. Now the water is soon gone, if not *poisoned* with *industrial waste*, and the *land* is gone with it.

*Now you will have a three-paragraph essay that should convey a thorough sense of beginning, middle, end.* You might like to add another good middle paragraph or two of illustration, with transitions, for a richer essay, giving a stronger impetus to your end paragraph.

**4.**   *To strengthen your feel for coherence and transitional tags; take another look at pages 43–46 and see what you can do with this skeleton:*

Forest fires burn thousands of acres each year. Lodgepole pines release their seeds only when fire sears their cones. Aging and dead trees provide fuel for the fires. Most large animals, like elk and grizzly bears, reach unburned areas. Ashes fertilize seeds of grasses, wild flowers, and shrubs. Some seeds have lain dormant for a hundred years. Aspens spring up again from their roots.

# 5
# Middle Tactics: Description, Narration, Exposition

With the whole essay in mind, we will now look more closely at the possibilities in arranging those middle points—the descriptive, narrative, and expository orders that illustrate your argument and carry your ideas. Description talks about what we see; narration, about what we do. Exposition, which may include both, essentially follows modes of thought, the ancient *topoi* of comparison and contrast, cause and effect, classification, definition. All are tactics for arrangement and persuasion.

## DESCRIPTION

All of your essays partake of description as you bring some point before your readers' eyes: "Children play with tiny cars." Many will need whole paragraphs, and some may be purely descriptive as you persuade your reader that *This is beautiful.* Description tells your reader what you see:

> Almost everything in sight is black, from the tips of trees forty feet above the ground to the powdered ash blanketing the earth. The firestorm that raged through here in recent weeks was driven by sixty-mile-an-hour winds that fanned temperatures to more than

**1,600 degrees Fahrenheit. The fire was so intense that a gray shadow on the forest floor is all that remains of a fallen log.\***

Description is essentially *spatial*. Arranging details in some kind of tour through space is as natural as walking. You can frequently underline your argument with a brief visual tour. When your subject dwells in and upon physical space—the layout of a campus, for instance—you literally take your readers with you. You can sometimes organize by paragraphs as units of space, one for the gate, one for the first building, conducting your readers in an orderly progress down the mall or around the quadrangle; or you show them a rooming house floor by floor, from the apartment by the entry to the garret four flights up, where the graduate student lives on books and cheese. Within the paragraph, you similarly take your readers from one detail to the next in spatial order. Your topic sentence summarizes the total effect: "The Whistler Building was once elegant, three classic stories of brick with carved stoned pediments." Then your paragraph proceeds with noteworthy details in any convenient spatial order: first the sagging front door, then the windows to the left, then those to the right, then the second-floor windows, with their suggestion of dingy apartments, and then those of the third, which suggest only emptiness.

You describe what you see, but the other senses may aid your vision, as when Ian Frazier enters a church in a small town in North Dakota:

> **Inside, the silence teemed. There was a smell of polished wood, hymnals, and rubber floor mats. The empty air was still vibrating slightly with the suppressed fidgets of children. Except for the pews and the floors, almost every interior surface was covered with statues or pictures.†**

A city's slum or its crowded parking, a river's pollution, a mountain's trees from valley to timberline—any spatial subject will offer a convenient illustration of your argument, from bottom to top, or top to bottom, left to right, east to west, center to periphery. You will instinctively use a series of spatial signals: *on the right, above, next, across, down the slope.* Your concern is to keep your progress orderly to help your reader see what you are talking about, as in this view on the Tokaido Road in Japan:

---

\*Scott McMurray. *The Wall Street Journal*, 23 Sept. 1988: [A1].
†"Great Plains," *The New Yorker*, 20 Feb. 1989: 80.

At the highest point of the pass, where the path breaks out of the pines and into the open, there is a breath-taking view, and anyone who finds himself there must turn to drink it in. He faces the great sweep of Suruga Bay and the open Pacific beyond, while waves break into flowers on the rocks far beneath his feet. Yui lies on the shore to his left and Okitsu at his right. Beyond Yui, bathed in mist far off on the left, looms the mountainous coast of Izu. Beyond Okitsu, on the right, is one of the loveliest sights in Japan, for the harbor that lies there is protected by a long arm of curving black sand, covered with ancient and twisted pines. This is the fabled beach of Miho . . . .*

As you can *see*, literally, the best spatial description follows the perceptions of a person looking at or entering the space described, reporting the impressions, the colors, textures, sights, or sounds as they come, as again with the imaginary visitor in this description by Ruth Prawer Jhabvala of a modern house in India:

Our foreign visitor stands agape at the wonderful residence his second host has built for himself. No expense has been spared here, no decoration suggested by a vivid taste omitted. There are little Moorish balconies and Indian domes and squiggly lattice work and an air-conditioner in every window. Inside, all is marble flooring, and in the entrance hall there is a fountain lit up with green, yellow, and red bulbs. The curtains on the windows and in the doorways are of silk, the vast sofa-suites are upholstered in velvet, the telephone is red, and huge vases are filled with plastic flowers.†

Some novels proceed like this paragraph after paragraph, as in the beginning of Thomas Hardy's *The Return of the Native*, for instance, in which we are moved into the setting from a great distance, as if, years before moving pictures, we are riding a cameraman's dolly.

Description frequently blends time and space, picking out striking features then moving along. This is the usual way of describing people, as in this paragraph about an actual Englishman whose odd occupation is mending the broken eggs brought to him by bird's-egg collectors:

Colonel Prynne, who is sixty-seven, lives and carries on his singular pursuit in a rambling, thatch-roofed, five-hundred-year-old

---

*Oliver Statler, *Japanese Inn* (New York: Pyramid Books, Random House, 1962): 14–16. Copyright © 1961, Oliver Statler.
†*Encounter* 22 (1964): 42–43.

cottage in the tiny village of Spaxton, Somerset, and there, on a recent sunny afternoon, he received us. A man of medium build who retains a military carriage, he was sprucely turned out in a brown suit, a tan jersey vest, a green shirt and tie, and tan oxfords. He has a bald, distinctly egg-shaped head, wears a close-cropped mustache and black shell-rimmed glasses, and seems always to have his nose tilted slightly upward and the nostrils faintly distended, as if he were sniffing the air. After taking us on a rather cursory tour of his garden, which is as neat and well tended as its owner, he remarked crisply that it was time to get cracking, and we followed him indoors, past an enormous fireplace, which burns five-foot logs, and up a flight of stairs to a room that he calls his studio.*

## NARRATION

In contrast with description, narration is essentially *temporal*. Like space, time is a natural organizer. Hour follows hour, day follows day, year follows year, life follows life. Again, you illustrate your argument by taking your readers along the natural sequence of what happens—to us, to nations, or to any items in experience or experiment. We understand processes most clearly by tracking the way they move through time, even processes complicated by other, simultaneous events:

> And when this wheel turns, that lever tips the food into the trough.
> While this conveyor moves into the oven, the other one is bringing the chassis to point B.
> And all the time he talked, his hands were moving the shells and flicking the invisible pea.

Any event, whether a football game or the inauguration of a president, can be best perceived as you have perceived it—through time—and you can bring your reader to perceive it by following the sequence of things as they happened, stepping aside as necessary to explain background and simultaneous events, guiding your reader along with temporal signposts: *at the same time, now, when, while, then, before, after, next, all the time.*

---

*"Talk of the Town," *The New Yorker* (23 May 1964):37. © 1964, The New Yorker Magazine, Inc. Reprinted by permission.

As Audubon, the nineteenth-century naturalist, describes, in his *Ornithological Biography*, the passenger pigeon and its astounding flights in masses a mile wide and 180 long, he naturally gives us his observations through the order of time. I have italicized the temporal words in one of his paragraphs:

> *As soon as* the pigeons discover a sufficiency of food to entice them to alight, they fly round in circles, reviewing the country below. *During* their evolutions, *on such occasions*, the dense mass which they form exhibits a beautiful appearance, *as it changes direction, now* displaying a glistening sheet of azure, *when* the backs of the birds come *simultaneously* into view, *and anon, suddenly* presenting a mass of rich deep purple. They *then* pass lower, over the woods, and *for a moment* are lost among the foliage, *but again* emerge, and are seen gliding aloft. They *now* alight, but *the next moment*, as if *suddenly* alarmed, they take to wing, producing by the flappings of their wings a noise like the roar of distant thunder, and sweep through the forests to see if danger is near. Hunger, however, *soon* brings them to the ground. *When* alighted, they are seen industriously throwing up the withered leaves. . . .

Sometimes an argumentative essay will give over its entire middle to a narrative of some event that illustrates its thesis, as in George Orwell's great "Shooting an Elephant." Let us look at one of his crucial narrative paragraphs. Notice how he mixes external events and snippets of conversation with his inner thoughts, pegging all perfectly with a topic sentence:

> But I did not want to shoot the elephant. I watched him beating his bunch of grass against his knees, with that preoccupied grandmotherly air that elephants have. It seemed to me that it would be murder to shoot him. At that age, I was not squeamish about killing animals, but I had never shot an elephant and never wanted to. (Somehow it always seems worse to kill a *large* animal.) Besides, there was the beast's owner to be considered. Alive, the elephant was worth at least a hundred pounds; dead, he would only be worth the value of his tusks, five pounds, possibly. But I had got to act quickly. I turned to some experienced-looking Burmans who had been there when we arrived, and asked them how the elephant had been behaving. They all said the same thing: he took no notice of you if you left him alone, but he might charge if you went too close to him.

Orwell is simply recounting events and his thoughts as they happened, one after the other. Almost any kind of essay could use a similar paragraph of narrative to illustrate a point.

# EXPOSITION

Exposition is a setting forth, an explaining, which naturally may include both description and narration. But it also includes some essential modes of thought: comparison and contrast, cause and effect, classification, definition. Good exposition depends on specific details to illustrate its general point.

Loren Eiseley, for instance, illustrates his generalization "these apes are not similar" not only with comparative contrasts but with particularized specifics, as he upholds Alfred Russel Wallace's view against Charles Darwin's as to the evolution of the human brain from that of the humanoid ape:

> These apes are not all similar in type or appearance. They are men and yet not men. Some are frailer-bodied, some have great, bone-cracking jaws and massive gorilloid crests atop their skulls. The fact leads us to another of Wallace's remarkable perceptions of long ago. With the rise of the truly human brain, Wallace saw that man had transferred to his machines and tools many of the alterations of parts that in animals take place through evolution of the body. Unwittingly, man had assigned to his machines the selective evolution which in the animal changes the nature of its bodily structure through the ages. Man of today, the atomic manipulator, the aeronaut who flies faster than sound, has precisely the same brain and body as his ancestors of twenty thousand years ago who painted the last Ice Age mammoths on the walls of caves in France.*

Notice how he spells out the specifics of bodies, jaws, and skulls. He does not say *aeronauts*, plural, but *the* single and specific *aeronaut*, adding the further specific *who flies faster than sound*, letting that single specific person illustrate the whole general range of what people can do with machines.

---

*"The Real Secret of Piltdown," in *The Immense Journey* (New York: Random House, Inc., 1955). © Copyright 1955 by Loren C. Eiseley.

He does not say merely "ancestors," but ancestors of specifically *twenty thousand years ago*; not merely "lived," but *who painted*, and not merely "pictures," but *the last Ice Age mammoths*, and specifically on *walls* in specific *caves* in one specific country, *France*. The point is to try to extend each of your generalizations by adding some specific detail to illustrate it. Don't stop with *awkward player*: go on to *when striking out, or missing an easy fly, or an easy basket*. Your illustration may also be hypothetical, as it frequently is in scientific explanation. With a thesis like *Relativity is not so inscrutable as many think*, you might illustrate with a paragraph something like this:

> Suppose someone riding in a car drops a ball. We see it fall straight down to the floor. But the ball also traces a long line slanting downward relative to the rapidly receding highway beneath the car. If the highway curves, the ball also traces an invisible curve. Adding the ball's drop relative to the Earth's movement around the sun may be hard to imagine, but calculations of such relative motion are what send our rockets to their meetings with the moon or Mars.

## Comparison and Contrast: Run Contrasts Side by Side

Comparison and contrast is a natural mode of thought, a natural organizer of exposition, making two specifics vivid by bringing them side by side. It may be the very basis of thought itself, as it certainly is of dialectic persuasion. All knowledge involves comparing things for their similarities and noticing their contrasting differences. We group all people as people and then tell them apart as individuals.

We instinctively know our friends in this way, for instance. Two of them drift side by side in our thoughts. We are comparing them. They are both boys; they are the same age and stature; we like them both. But one bubbles up like a mountain spring, and the other runs deep. Their appearances, mannerisms, and tastes match their contrasting personalities. One's room is messy; the other's is neat. One races his car; the other collects stamps. We compare the similar categories—looks, habits, hobbies, goals—and contrast the difference. Your thesis might be something neutrally expository like "*Differences make life interesting*," or it may affirm what makes a better person.

Your topic sentence sets the comparison and makes the contrast:

Contrast    Opposites seem to attract. *My father, a lawyer, is quiet and stu-dious, a music lover. My mother, a clinical psychologist, is vivacious and gregarious.* She loves a party, a play, a crowd of friends, seeing and being seen in the social whirl. Dad, though good with people, would probably just as soon stay home with a book and a symphony on the stereo. He builds model airplanes. Mom plays bridge almost at the master's level. But when they come in from their different days, they grin and compare notes, she taking in some calm, he some zest for human involvements. They obviously still find each other attractive.

## Comparison and Contrast: Illustrate by Analogy

An analogy points up similarities between things otherwise dissimilar. With an analogy, you help your reader grasp your subject by showing how it is like something familiar. Your topic sentence asserts the comparison, and then your paragraph unfolds the comparison in detail:

School spirit is like patriotism. Students take their school's fortunes as their own, defending and promoting them against those of another school, as citizens champion their country, right or wrong. Their school is not only their alma mater but their fatherland as well. Like soldiers, they will give their utmost strength in field games and intellectual contests for both personal glory and the greater glory of the domain they represent. And, in defeat, they will mourn as if dragged in chains through the streets of Rome.

Here is E. B. White describing Thoreau's *Walden*. His comparison shows that analogy is really a form of extended metaphor:

Topic Sentence
with Analogy

Analogy
Extended

Analogy
Extended

Thoreau's assault on the Concord society of the mid-nine-teenth century has the quality of a modern Western: he rides into the subject at top speed, shooting in all directions. Many of his shots ricochet and nick him on the rebound, and throughout the melee there is a horrendous cloud of inconsistencies and contradictions, and when the shooting dies down and the air clears, one is impressed chiefly by the courage of the rider and by how splendid it was that somebody should have ridden in there and raised all that ruckus.*

---

*From "A Slight Sound at Evening," *The Essays of E. B. White* (New York: Harper & Row, 1982): 235–36. Copyright 1954, © 1982 by E. B. White. Reprinted by permission of Harper & Row, Publishers, Inc.

That is probably as long as an analogy can run effectively. One paragraph is about the limit. Beyond that, the reader may tire of it.

## Comparison Versus Contrast

Comparison illuminates the unknown with the known, emphasizing similarities:

> **This year's team has all the makings of last year's champions.**
> **Clark has the virtuosity of a Horowitz.**
> **Throstle is a twentieth-century Wordsworth.**

The essays under these theses would then favor these unknowns, point by point, with their similarities to the paragons. Contrasts, on the other hand, compare similar things to emphasize their differences—formal gardens as against natural gardens, for example—usually to persuade the readers that one is in some or most ways better than the other.

Remember to keep both sides before the readers. You may do this in one of two ways: (1) by making a topic sentence to cover one point—gardens, let us say—and then continuing your paragraph in paired sentences, one for the formal, one for the natural, another for the formal, another for the natural, and so on; or (2) by writing your paragraphs in pairs, one paragraph for the formal, one for the natural, using the topic sentence of the first paragraph to govern the second, something like this:

> *The formal garden still holds a certain edge over the natural garden that overtook it in the eighteenth century.* Small box hedges, cut squarely and sharply in geometrical lines and orderly arabesques, contain glories of bright begonias, sweet williams, and violas. Sharp cones of yews punctuate the expanding order of smooth lawns. . . .
> *In the natural garden, unkempt hedges wander off.* Flowering trees bloom wildly for a week. Yews sprawl along extending meadows . . . .

In an extended contrast, you will probably want to contrast some things sentence against sentence, within single paragraphs, and to contrast others by giving a paragraph to each. Remember only to keep your readers sufficiently in touch with both sides.

Here are two paragraphs from a student's paper neatly contrasted without losing touch:

Topic Sentence

First Subject

The Contrast

*In fact, in some respects the commercials are really better than the shows they sponsor. The commercials are carefully rehearsed, expertly photographed, highly edited and polished.* They are made with absolute attention to detail and to the clock. One split-second over time, one bad note, one slightly wrinkled dress, and they are done over again. Weeks, even months, go into the production of a single sixty-second commercial.

*The shows, on the other hand, are slapped together hastily by writers and performers who have less than a week to put together an hour show.* Actors have little time to rehearse, and often the pieces of a show are put together for the first time in front of the camera. Lighting, sound reproduction, and editing are workmanlike but unpolished; a shadow from an overhead microphone on an actor's face causes no real concern in the control room. A blown line or a muffed cue is "just one of those things that happen." In all, it often takes less time and money to do an hour show than to do the four sixty-second commercials that sponsor it.

Contrasts done sentence by sentence, or by clauses hinged on a semicolon, are also effective:

The most essential distinction between athletics and education lies in the institution's own interest in the athlete as distinguished from its interest in its other students. Universities attract students in order to teach them what they do not already know; they recruit athletes only when they are already proficient. Students are educated for something which will be useful to them and to society after graduation; athletes are required to spend their time on activities the usefulness of which disappears upon graduation or soon thereafter. Universities exist to do what they can for students; athletes are recruited for what they can do for the universities. This makes the operation of the athletic program in which recruited players are used basically different from any educational interest of colleges and universities.*

---

*Harold W. Stoke, "College Athletics: Education or Show Business?" *Atlantic Monthly* (March 1954): 46–50. Copyright © 1954 by Harold W. Stoke. Reprinted by permission.

# Cause and Effect: Trace Back or Look Ahead

*Because* is the impulse here: "Such and such is so *because* . . . ." You think back through a train of causes, each one the effect of something prior, or you think your way into the future, speculating about the possible effects of some present cause. In other words, you organize your paragraph in one of two ways:

1. You state a general effect and then deal with its several causes.
2. You state a general cause and then deal with its possible effects.

In Arrangement 1, you know the effect (a lost football game or the solar system, let us say), and you speculate as to causes. In Arrangement 2, you know the cause (a new restriction or abolishing nuclear weapons, let us say), and you speculate as to the effects.

## *Arrangement 1: Effect Followed by Causes*

An unusual cluster of bad luck lost the game. Many blamed Fraser's failure to block the tackler who caused the fumble that produced the winning touchdown. But even here, bad weather and bad luck shared the blame. Both teams faced a slippery field, of course. But Fraser was standing in a virtual bog when he lunged for the block and slipped. Moreover, the storm had delayed the bus for hours, tiring and frustrating the team, leaving them short of sleep and with no chance to practice. Furthermore, Hunter's throwing arm was still not back in shape from his early injury. Finally, one must admit, the Acorns were simply heavier and stronger, which is the real luck of the game.

You will probably notice, as you try to explain causes and effects, that they do not always run in a simple linear sequence, one thing following another, like a row of falling dominoes. Indeed, mere sequence is so famously untrustworthy in tracing causes that one of the classical errors of thought is named *post hoc, ergo propter hoc* ("after this, therefore because of this"). In other words, we cannot reasonably suppose that A caused B simply because A preceded B. The two may have been entirely unrelated. But the greatest danger in identifying causes is to fasten upon a single cause while ignoring others of equal significance. Both your paragraph and your persuasiveness will be better if you do not insist, as some did, that only Fraser's failure to block the tackler lost the game.

In the lost ball game, you were interested in explaining causes, but sometimes your interest will lie with effects. When describing a slum problem, for instance, your topic sentence might be *The downtown slum is a screaming disgrace* (the effect), and you might then in a single sentence set aside the causes as irrelevant, as water over the dam, as so much spilt milk: "perhaps caused by inefficiency, perhaps by avarice, perhaps by the indifference of Mayor Richman." Your interests will dictate your proportions of cause and effect. You might well write an entire essay that balances the slum's causes and effects in equal proportions: a paragraph each on inefficiency, avarice, and the mayor's indifference, and then a paragraph each on ill health, poor education, and hopelessness.

Here is how a brief essay, in three paragraphs, can deal with cause and effect alone. I have begun and ended with the effect (the peculiar layout of a town). First, I located the *immediate cause* (cattle) as my thesis, and then, in the middle paragraph, I moved through the cause and its *conditions* up to the *effect* again—the town as it stands today:

### North of the Tracks

Effect    If you drive out west from Chicago, you will notice something happening to the towns. *After the country levels into Nebraska, the smaller towns are built only on one side of the road.* When you stop for a rest, and look south across the broad main street, you will see the railroad immediately beyond. *All of these towns spread north-* Effect    *ward from the tracks.* Why? As you munch your hamburger and look at the restaurant's murals, *you will realize that the answer is* Thesis    *cattle.*

Cause   *These towns were the destinations of the great cattle drives* Conditions  *from Texas.* They probably had begun at the scattered watering places in the dry land. Then *the wagon trails and,* finally, *the* Causes   *transcontinental railroad had strung them together.* Once the railroad came, the whole Southwest could raise cattle for the slaughter- Effect    houses of Chicago. The droves of cattle came up from the south, and *all of these towns reflect the traffic:* corrals beside the tracks to the south, the road for passengers and wagons paralleling the tracks on the northern side; then, along the road, the row of hotels, saloons, and businesses, with the town spreading northward behind the businesses.

*The cattle-business itself shaped these one-sided Nebraska* Cause    *towns.* The conditions in which this immediate cause took root were the growing population in the East and the railroad that connected the plains of the West, and Southwest, with the tables of New York. The towns took their hopeful being north of the rails, on the leeward side of the vast cattle drives from the south. The trade in cattle has

now changed, all the way from Miami to Sacramento. But *the great
herds of the old Southwest, together with the transcontinental railroad and man's need to make a living, plotted these Western towns
north of the tracks.*                                             Effect

## *Arrangement 2: Cause Followed by Probable Effects*

Arrangement 2 is the staple of deliberative rhetoric, of all political and
economic forecasting, for instance. Your order of presenting cause and
effect is reversed. You are looking to the future. You state a known cause
(a new restriction on dormitory hours) or a hypothetical cause ("If this
restriction is passed"), and then you speculate about the possible, or probable, effects. Your procedure will then be much the same as before. But, for
maximum persuasiveness, try to keep your supposed effects, which no one
can really foresee, as nearly probable as you can.

Lending Students Debt

With costs for education rising annually, more and more

students must supplement their family's funds or miss col-

lege completely. Some manage to work their way through col-

lege on their own. Many work during summers and find

part-time jobs for the academic year. Many also still need

loans, particularly for advanced degrees in fields such as

medicine. But a recent proposal for guaranteed federal loans          Thesis:
                                                                      Cause with
to students carries more burdens than benefits.                       Effects

On the surface, the proposal promises entrance to col-         Effects: Con

lege to many students otherwise unable to attend. Some

areas of the nation, it claims, have few local funds available

for loans, and local attitudes might militate against help for

students from various minority backgrounds. A governmen-

tal program of loans would promise equal opportunity for all

qualified students.

Actually, however, most colleges do have loans available          Pro: Factual

for needy and worthy students. Many colleges, like this one,

have fellowships that go unclaimed because no one applies          Effects: Pro for them. But the temptation of an easy loan against paying as you go with extra work is the essential defect of the federal proposal.

Effects: Con    To be sure, concentrating on one's studies without the drain on time and energy from extra work and long hours would seem a distinct advantage. But if we honestly look at

Effects: Pro    our schedules and what we do with the hours in a week, we can see much more free time than one might suppose, and a great deal of it spent in nonacademic activities, to say the least. A few hours of work actually budgets one's time and concentrates the hours of study.

Effects: Con    If federal supervision would spread opportunity for all,

Effects: Pro    it would also spread bureaucracy, with new agencies to set loans up and track them down, in a government already operating with greater deficits each year. Loans to students are now managed by local deans and staffs already there and effectively doing other things too.

Effects: Pro    But the cost to individual students is probably the biggest burden. Instead of paying as they go, perhaps with some short-term local help, perhaps even by working for a year, they would be tempted to borrow more than they can afford and would then have to face payroll deductions and the Internal Revenue Service for years to come.

This student's projected effects hold fairly well to the probable. Occasionally, of course, you may put an improbable hypothetical cause to good use in a satiric essay, reducing some proposal to absurdity: "If all restrictions were abolished . . . ." "If no one wore clothes . . . ." Or the improbable *if* may even help clarify a straightforward explanation of real relationships, as in the following excerpt from *Time* magazine's report on Fred Hoyle, the British astronomer and mathematician who has been modifying Newton's gravity and Einstein's relativity. The paragraph states the general condition, proposes its hypothetical cause with an *if*, then moves to the effects, first in temporal order and then in order of human interest:

> The masses, and therefore the gravity, of the sun and the earth are partly due to each other, partly to more distant objects such as the stars and galaxies. According to Hoyle, if the universe were to be cut in half, local solar-system gravitation would double, drawing the earth closer to the sun. The pressure in the sun's center would increase, thus raising its temperature, its generation of energy, and its brightness. Before being seared into a lump of charcoal, a man on earth would find his weight increasing from 150 to 300 lbs.*

## Classification: Use the Natural Divisions

Many subjects fall into natural or customary classifications, as if they were blandly jointed, like a good roast of pork ready for carving, contrasting one joint with the next: freshman, sophomore, junior, senior; Republicans, Democrats; right, middle, left; legislative, executive, judicial. You can easily follow these divisions in organizing a paragraph, or you can write one paragraph for each division and attain a nicely coherent essay. Similarly, any manufacturing process, or any machine, will already have distinct steps and parts. These customary divisions will help your readers because they know something of them already. Describe the Democratic position on inflation, and they will naturally expect your description of the Republican position to follow. If no other divisions suggest themselves, you can often organize your paragraph—or your essay—into a consistent series of parallel answers, or "reasons for," or "reasons against," something like this:

> A broad liberal education is best:
> 1. It prepares you for a world of changing employment.
> 2. It enables you to function well as a citizen.
> 3. It enables you to make the most of your life.

Many problems present natural classifying joints. Take the Panama Canal, for instance. Its construction divides into three nicely jointed problems—political, geological, and biological—each with its solutions, as the following paragraph shows:

---

*June 26, 1964: 63.

Problem 1

Solution 1

Problem(s) 2

Solution to 2

Problem 3

Solution to 3

Building the Panama Canal posed problems of politics, geology, and human survival from the beginning. *A French company, organized in 1880 to dig the canal, repeatedly had to extend its treaties at higher and higher prices as the work dragged on.* Uneasy about the French, *the United States made treaties with Nicaragua and Costa Rica* to dig along the other most feasible route. *This political threat,* together with the failure of the French and the revolt of Panama from Colombia, *finally enabled the United States to buy the French rights and negotiate new treaties,* which, nevertheless, continue to cause political trouble to this day. *Geology also posed its ancient problems:* how to manage torrential rivers and inland lakes; whether to build a longer but more enduring canal at sea level, or *a shorter, cheaper, and safer canal with locks.* Economy eventually won, but the problem of *yellow fever and malaria,* which had plagued the French, remained. *By detecting and combating the fever-carrying mosquito, William Gorgas solved these ancient tropical problems.* Without him, the political and geological solutions would have come to nothing.

You could easily organize this into three paragraphs of problem and solution, with topic sentences like these:

> The Panama Canal posed three major problems, the first of which was political.
> The second problem was geological, a massive problem of engineering.
> The third problem, that of human survival, proved the most stubborn of all.

Any problem and its solution can produce a neatly ordered paragraph—or essay, for that matter: choosing a college, or something to wear (if you want to be light-hearted), making an apartment or a commune work, building the Eiffel Tower or the pyramids. You can often similarly classify sets of comparisons and contrasts, causes and effects, combining your tactics with magnified force.

In the following paper, a student has nicely amalgamated description, narration, and the classification implied in a problem and its solution to analyze a fascinating process.

### Nothing Primitive About It

Stonehenge, the gigantic prehistoric construction on Salisbury Plain in England, cannot fail to fascinate us with a number of nearly unanswerable questions. How long has it been there? Who built it? Why? But of all the questions Stonehenge raises, none is more intriguing than *"How was it built?" How did these primitive people,* whose only tools were rock, bone, or crudely fashioned sticks, who had not yet even discovered the wheel, *manage to transport the huge rocks,* most of them more than twenty feet in length and weighing over thirty tons, *more than twenty miles overland? And by what ingenuity did they manage,* having transported the rocks, *to stand them on end and support them so that now,* thousands of years later, *most of them still stand?* What primitive engineering geniuses were these?

    *Transporting the stones from their original site at Marlborough Downs, some twenty miles to the north of Stonehenge, must have been, by any of the possible means, a very slow process.* One possibility is that *hundreds of people,* some pulling on the rock, some cutting down trees and filling in holes as they went, *simply dragged the stones over the bare ground. Or perhaps they used snow or mud to "grease" the path.* Foot by foot, and day by day, they may have dragged the rocks all the way from Marlborough Downs to Stonehenge. *Another guess is that these primitive people,* even though they had not yet invented the wheel, *knew about using logs as rollers.* If so, perhaps they mounted each stone on a sledge, and rolled the sledge slowly forward, workmen placing logs in its path as it moved. Such a method, while a good deal easier than dragging the rock along the ground, would still have required as many as seven or eight hundred people, and perhaps as much as a decade to move all the stones. *A third possibility is that the stones were moved along riverbeds,* the shallow water helping to buoy the weight, and the muddy banks helping to slide the weight along. Though much less direct than the overland route, the riverbed route would have provided these primitive people with a relatively clear path that ran approximately halfway from the stones' point of origin to their final location. Of course, the point is that any of these three means of transporting the stones must have been an incredibly laborious task, occupying as many as a thousand people, year after year after year.

    *Lifting the stones into an upright position,* once they had been transported, *was another triumph of ingenuity and brute strength.* Apparently, the workers dug closely fitted holes where they wanted the stones eventually to stand. Probably they cut away one side of the hole, the side nearest the stone, to form a ramp. Perhaps they also lined the hole with wooden skids. Then gradually they eased the stone down the ramp until it rested in a tilted position at the bottom of the hole. Next, they used brute strength, some people pushing, some pulling on primitive ropes, to raise the rock into a vertical position. If we suppose each person lifted 150 pounds, it might have

*Margin annotations:*

Thesis

Problem 1

Description and Narration

Problem 2

Narrating the Process

Solutions to 1

First Classification

Second Classification

Narrating and Describing the Process

Third Classification

Solutions to 2

Describing and Narrating the Process

taken as many as 400 workers to stand the stones upright. Finally, while some workers held the rock in position, others quickly filled in the excavation left by the ramp. For many months afterward, they probably refilled and pounded the dirt until it was completely firm. They probably placed the huge transverse pieces across the tops of columns by similarly dragging them up long earthen ramps. The fact that most of the rocks are still standing after thousands of years is testimony of their planning and workmanship.

*Thesis Restated*

We may never know quite why these primitive people chose to build Stonehenge, or who they were. We may never know where they came from, or where they went. *In Stonehenge, however, they have left a testament to their perseverance and their ingenuity. Clearly, they rivaled any of the builders of the ancient world.*

## Definition: Clear Up Your Terms

Definition is another mode of classification, in which we clear away hidden assumptions along with unwanted categories. What the Russians and Chinese call a People's Democracy is the very opposite of what the Americans and British call democracy, assumed also to be of and for and by the people. Ideally, your running prose should make your terms clear to your reader, avoiding those definitions that seem too stiff and stuffy, and especially avoid quoting the dictionary: "As *Webster's* says . . . ." Nevertheless, what we mean by *egotism, superiority, education,* or *character* may need laying on the table.

Richard Hofstadter, for instance, found it necessary in his essay "Democracy and Anti-Intellectualism in America" to devote a number of paragraphs to defining both *democracy* and *intellectual,* each paragraph examining the evidence and clarifying one aspect of his term. Coming early in his essay, after he has set his thesis and surveyed his subject, his section of definition begins with the following paragraph:

*Topic Sentence as Question*

*What It Is Not*

**But what is an intellectual, really?** This is a problem of definition that I found, when I came to it, far more elusive than I had anticipated. *A great deal of what might be called the journeyman's work of our culture*—the work of engineers, physicians, newspapermen, and indeed of most professors—does not strike me as distinctively intellectual, although it is certainly work based in an important sense on ideas. *The distinction that we must recognize,* then, *is one*

*What It Is*
*Con: Examples*

originally made by Max Weber *between living for ideas and living off ideas. The intellectual lives for ideas; the journeyman lives off them. The engineer or the physician—I don't mean here to be invidious—*

*needs to have a pretty considerable capital stock in frozen ideas* to do his work; but they *serve for him a purely instrumental purpose: he lives off them, not for them.* Of course *he may also be, in his private role and his personal ways of thought, an intellectual,* but it is not necessary for him to be in order to work at his profession. **There is in fact no profession which demands that one be an intellectual.** *There do seem to be vocations, however, which almost demand that one be an anti-intellectual,* in which those who live off ideas seem to have implacable hatred for those who live for them. The marginal intellectual workers and the unfrocked intellectuals who work in journalism, advertising, and mass communication are the bitterest and most powerful among those who work at such vocations.*

Pro: Examples

Con: Detailed Opposition

Your subject will prompt you in one of two ways, toward inclusiveness or toward exclusiveness. Hofstadter found that he needed to be inclusive about the several essentials in *democracy* and *intellectual*—terms used commonly and often loosely. Inclusiveness is the usual need, as you will find in trying to define *love* or *loyalty* or *education.* But you may sometimes need to move in the opposite direction, toward exclusiveness, as in sociological, philosophical, or scientific discussion, when you need to nail your terms firmly to single meanings: "By *reality,* I mean only that which exists in the physical world, excluding our ideas about it."

Such exclusive defining is called *stipulative* because you stipulate the precise meaning you want. But you should avoid the danger of trying to exclude more than the word will allow. If you try to limit the meaning of the term *course* to "three hours a week a semester," your discussion will soon encounter courses with different hours, or you may find yourself inadvertently drifting to another meaning, as you mention something about graduating from an "engineering course." At any rate, if you can avoid the sound of dogmatism in your stipulation, so much the better. You may well practice some disguise, as with *properly speaking* and *only* in the following stipulative definition: "Properly speaking, the *structure* of any literary work is only that framelike quality we can picture in two, or three, dimensions."

Definitions frequently seem to develop into paragraphs, almost by second nature. A sentence of definition is usually short and crisp, seeming to demand some explanation, some illustration and sociability. The definition, in other words, is a natural topic sentence. Here are three classic single-sentence kinds of definition that will serve well as topics for your paragraphs:

---

*\*The Michigan Alumnus Quarterly Review 59 (1953): 282. Copyright © 1953 by the University of Michigan.*

1. DEFINITION BY SYNONYM.  A quick way to stipulate the single meaning you want: "Virtue means moral rectitude."

2. DEFINITION BY FUNCTION.  "A barometer measures atmospheric pressure"—"A social barometer measures human pressures"—"A good quarterback calls the signals and sparks the whole team's spirits."

3. DEFINITION BY SYNTHESIS.  A placing of your term in striking (and not necessarily logical) relationship to its whole class, usually for the purpose of wit: "The fox is the craftiest of beasts"—"A sheep is a friendlier form of goat"—"A lexicographer is a harmless drudge"—"A sophomore is a sophisticated moron."

Three more of the classic kinds of definition follow, of broader dimensions than the single-sentence kinds above, but also ready-made for a paragraph apiece or for several. Actually, in making paragraphs from your single-sentence definitions, you have undoubtedly used at least one of these three kinds or a mixture of them all. They are no more than the natural ways we define our meanings.

4. DEFINITION BY EXAMPLE.  The opposite of *definition by synthesis*. You start with the class ("crafty beasts") and then name a member or two ("fox—plus monkey and raccoon"). But of course you would go on to give further examples or illustrations—accounts of how the bacon was snitched through the screen—that broaden your definition beyond the mere naming of class and members.

5. DEFINITION BY COMPARISON.  You just use a paragraph of comparison to expand and explain your definition. Begin with a topic sentence something like: "Love is like the sun." Then extend your comparison on to the end of the paragraph (or even separate it, if your cup runneth over, into several paragraphs) as you develop the idea: "Love is like the sun because it too gives out warmth, makes everything bright, shines even when it is not seen, and is indeed the center of our lives."

6. DEFINITION BY ANALYSIS.  This is Hofstadter's way, a searching out and explaining of the essentials in terms used generally, loosely, and often in ways that emphasize incidentals for biased reasons, as when it is said that an *intellectual* is a manipulator of ideas.

Here are four good steps to take in reaching a thorough definition of something, assuring that you have covered all the angles. Consider:

1. What it *is not like*.
2. What it *is like*.
3. What it *is not*.
4. What it *is*.

This program can produce a good paragraph of definition:

> Love may be many things to many people, but, all in all, we
> agree on its essentials. *Love is not like a rummage sale,* in which     1
> many people try to grab what they want. *It is more like a Christmas,*     2
> in which gifts and thoughtfulness come just a little unexpectedly,
> even from routine directions. *Love, in short, is not a matter of*
> *seeking self-satisfaction; it is first a matter of giving and then dis-*     3
> *covering,* as an unexpected gift, *the deepest satisfaction one can*     4
> *know.*

The four steps above can also furnish four effective paragraphs, which
you would present in the same order of ascending interest and climax. But,
finally, the point is simply to consider that the advantage of the dialectic
*is not* in highlighting the *is* in your definitions.

## Avoid the Pitfalls

1. Avoid echoing the term you are defining. Do not write "Courtesy
is being courteous" or "Freedom is feeling free." Look around for synonyms:
"Courtesy is being polite, being attentive to others' needs, making them
feel at ease, using what society accepts as good manners." You can go
against this rule to great advantage, however, if you repeat the *root* of the
word meaningfully: "Courtesy is treating your girlfriend like a princess in
her *court.*"

2. Don't make your definitions too narrow—except for humor
("Professors are only disappointed students"). Do not write: "Communism
is subversive totalitarianism." Obviously, your definition needs more
breadth, something about sharing property, and so forth.

3. Don't make your definition too broad. Do not go uphill in your
terms, as in "Vanity is pride" or "Affection is love." Bring the definers down
to the same level: "Vanity is a kind of frivolous personal pride"—"Affection
is a mild and chronic case of love."

## SUGGESTIONS FOR EXERCISE

1.  *Write a paragraph describing a unit of space, taking your readers from the outside to the inside of your own home, for instance, or dealing with some interesting spatial unit, as in the following paragraph from a student's paper.*

> The courtyard of the hotel at Uxmal was a wonderfully cool and welcome surprise after the sweaty bus trip out from Mérida. Surrounding the whole yard was a large *galeria*, its ceiling blocking out the few rays of the sun that managed to filter through the heavy plantings that filled the yard. Overhead, along the *galeria*, ceiling fans quietly turned, and underfoot the glazed tile floors felt smooth and delightfully cool even though the temperature on the road had pushed up past 100 degrees. Airy wicker chairs lined the railing, and just a few feet away, flowering jungle plants rose almost to the top of the stone arches on the second floor. Under the branches of a tall tree in the middle of the courtyard, out beyond the rail and the thick plantings, raised tile walkways crisscrossed the yard, bordered all along by neatly cultivated jungle flowers. And right in the middle of the yard, at the base of the big tree, a small waterfall splashed down over mossy rocks into a tiny bathing pool. The splashing water, the shade, the cool tile—all made the road outside seem very far off indeed.

2.  *Write a narrative paragraph in which you blend the incidents and thoughts of a crucial moment, as in Orwell's paragraph on 57.*
3.  *Write a paragraph comparing two people—like the one on 60.*
4.  *(a) Write a paragraph developed by contrasts, running them point by point, as in the paragraph contrasting "students" and "athletes" on 62. (b) Write two paragraphs contrasting something like high school and college, small town and city, football and baseball, men and women— the first paragraph describing one, the second the other, and the two using parallel contrasting terms, as in the examples contrasting the two kinds of garden or the television commercials and shows on 61–62.*
5.  *Write a paragraph of effect followed by causes like that on 63, Arrangement 1.*
6.  *Write a paragraph about some cause followed by its probable effects, Arrangement 2. See 65–67. Work in a hypothetical effect if you can.*
7.  *Here are some topics that fall conveniently into natural divisions. For each topic, list the divisions that occur to you.*

1. Causes affecting the rate at which a population grows.
2. Levels of government.
3. Undersea exploration.
4. Geological eras.
5. Mathematics in public schools.

**8.**  *Write a paragraph using one of the topics and the divisions you have worked out in Exercise 7.*

**9.**  *Using the classifications of problem and solution, write a three- or four-paragraph paper in which you describe the process behind some particularly interesting architectural or engineering accomplishment. Choose any topic you wish. For example, how did architects design the high-rise buildings in San Francisco so that they would withstand the shock of severe earthquakes? Or how did medieval blacksmiths make a suit of armor? Or how do you plan to convert your minibus into a camper that will sleep four people? In the first paragraph, state the problem as your thesis sentence. Then go on to describe how the problem could be or was solved.*

**10.**  *Work out a paragraph defining a term such as* barometer, computer, class, humanities, intelligence. *Avoid sounding like a dictionary. Consider and use if possible: (1) what it is not like, (2) what it is like, (3) what it is not, and, finally, (4) what it is. See 73.*

# 6

# Straight and Crooked Thinking: Working with Evidence

All along, you have been working to support your thesis and persuade your readers with evidence. Evidence is an example or several examples. Your thesis has, in fact, emerged from the evidence, from thinking about the specific things you have experienced, seen, heard, in person, in reading, or on TV. To support that thesis, you have simply turned the process around, bringing in those same specific things, and others, as evidence— descriptive, narrative, and expository. You have been deciding logically on the weight and shape of that evidence, comparing, working out causes and effects, classifying, defining. But your evidence and its connections are always exposed to certain logical fallacies that may defeat its persuasiveness.

## DEGREES OF EVIDENCE

### Write as Close to the Facts as Possible

The nature of *fact*, and of *belief*, *opinion*, and *preference* poses some problems for the writer. You cannot really present the "hard facts" themselves. You cannot reach through the page to hand out actual lumps of coal and bags of wheat. You can only tell *about* these things and then persuade your readers to see them as you believe they should be seen. Facts are the firmest kind of thought, but they are *thoughts* nevertheless—verifiable thoughts about the coal and wheat and other entities of our experience. The whole question of fact comes down to verifiability: things not susceptible of verification leave the realm of factuality. Fact is limited, therefore, to the kinds of things that can be tested by the senses (verified empirically, as the philosophers say) or by inferences from physical data so strong as to allow no other explanation. "Statements of fact" are assertions of a kind provable by referring to experience. The simplest physical facts—that a stone is a stone and that it exists—are so bound into our elementary perceptions of the world that we never think to verify them, and indeed could not verify them beyond gathering testimonials from the group. With less tangible facts, verification is simply doing enough to persuade any reasonable person that the assertion of fact is true, beginning with what our senses can in some way check.

Measuring, weighing, and counting are the strongest empirical verifiers; assertions capable of such verification are the most firmly and quickly demonstrated as factual:

> **Smith is 5 feet high and 4 feet wide.**
> **The car weighs 2,300 pounds.**
> **Three members voted for beer.**

In the last assertion, we have moved from what we call physical fact to historical fact—that which can be verified by its signs: we have the ballots. Events in history are verified the same way, although the evidence is scarcer the farther back we go.

So facts are those things, states, or events of a kind susceptible to verification. Notice: *of a kind* susceptible to verification. Some perfectly solid facts we may never verify. The place, date, and manner of Catullus's death; whether a person is guilty as accused or innocent as claimed—these we may never know, may never establish as facts, because we lack the evidence to verify them. But we would not want to remove them from the realm of factuality: they are the *kind* of thing that *could* be verified, if only we could get at the evidence. They are valid grounds for speculation from the facts we have. Book after book has speculated about who Jack the Ripper was or how the universe began.

## BELIEVE WHAT YOU WRITE—BUT BELIEF NEEDS ARGUMENT

Facts, then, are things susceptible to verification. Belief presents an entirely different kind of knowledge: things believed true but yet beyond the reach of sensory verification—a belief in God, for instance. We may infer a Creator from the creation, a Beginning from the beginnings we see around us. But a doubting Thomas will have nothing to touch or see; judging our inferences wrongly drawn, the doubting Thomas may prefer to believe in a physical accident or in a flux with neither beginning nor end. The point is that although beliefs are unprovable, they are not necessarily untrue, and they are not unusable as you discourse with your readers. Many beliefs, of course, have proved false as new evidence turns up—new sensory verification such as sailing around the world believed flat—and many beliefs have proved true, like Galileo's belief that the world moved.

But empirical verification is surprisingly far from reach. We take almost all our knowledge, even factual knowledge, from the reports of others, who have it from others. Even pictures give us, secondhand, only one partial view. Karl Popper suggests persuasively that the only way toward truth and our belief in it is through *Conjectures and Refutations*,* as his title says. We can come no closer to truth than conjectures as to probability established by argument over time against the widest range of refutations. We conjecture our beliefs and hold them more firmly or revise them as we must, under the battering of refutations, as the pre-Socratic philosophers and Plato demonstrated and Popper has shown.

So the dialectic process of argument serves our highest quest for knowledge and our firmest beliefs, both in the laboratory and out in the realms of value. Assert your belief. This is your thesis, your *pro* conjecture about the truth. Then look around for the evidence and the reasons to support it against the refuting *cons* as they rise. Make your belief stick. But for politeness and persuasion, you may wish to qualify your least demonstrable convictions with a judicious "I believe," "we may reasonably suppose," "perhaps," "from one point of view," and the like—unless the power of your conviction moves you beyond the gentilities and you are writing heart to heart.

---

*London: Routlege, 1969.

## Handle Your Opinions with Care

Opinion is a kind of lesser—or more immediate—belief, another candidate for truth, to be verified by the outcome or left to haunt the probabilities. One horse, one team, one candidate, will win, or the social impact of working mothers will await the verdict of centuries. Opinions are the daily bread of our editorial pages, our sports sections, our books of ideas, our reviews of novels, films, concerts, exhibits, fashions, diets, and social habits.

As with belief, the testing of opinions to discover the truth is the central business of argumentation. When you assert something as fact, you indicate (1) that you assume it true and easily verified and (2) that its truth is generally acknowledged. When you assert something as opinion, you imply some uncertainty about both these things. Here are two opinions that seem to persist in spite of social change and that will probably remain opinions exactly because of fervid disagreement:

> **Girls are brighter than boys.**
> **Men are superior to women.**

We know that the terms *brighter* and *superior* have a range of meaning hard to pin down. Superior in what way? Even when agreeing upon the tests for numerical and verbal abilities, for memory and ingenuity, for health and strength of character, we cannot be sure that we will not miss other kinds of brightness and superiority or that our tests will measure these things in any thorough way. The range of meaning in our four other terms, moreover, is so wide as virtually to defy verification. We need only ask "At what age?" to illustrate how broad they are. So in these slippery regions of opinion, keep your assertions tentative with *may* and *might* and *perhaps*.

## Be Even More Careful with Preferences

Preferences are something else again. They are farther from proof than opinions—indeed, beyond the pale of proof—and yet they are more firmly held than opinions because they are primarily subjective, sweetening our palates and warming our hearts. *De gustibus non est disputandum:* tastes are not to be disputed. So goes the medieval epigram from the age that refined the arts of logic. You can't argue successfully about tastes, empirical though they be, the logicians say, because they are beyond empirical demonstration. Are peaches better than pears? Whichever you choose, your choice is probably neither logically defensible nor logically vulnerable. The writer's responsibility is to recognize the logical immunity of preferences and to qualify them politely with "I think," "many believe," "some may prefer," and so forth.

So go ahead, dispute over tastes, and you may find some solid grounds for them. Shakespeare is greater than Ben Jonson. Subjective tastes have moved all the way up beside fact: the grounds for Shakespeare's margin of greatness have been exhibited, argued, and explored over the centuries until we accept his superiority as if empirically verified. Actually, the questions that most commonly concern us are beyond scientific verification. But you can frequently establish your preferences as testable opinions by asserting them reasonably and without unwholesome prejudice and by using the secondary evidence that other reasonable people agree with you in persuasive strength and number.

## ASSESSING THE EVIDENCE

### Logical Fallacies

From the first, in talking about a valid thesis, about proof, about assumptions and implications and definition, we have been facing logical fallacies—that is, flaws in thought, things that do not add up. Evidence itself raises the biggest question of logic. Presenting any evidence at all faces a logical fallacy that can never be surmounted: no amount of evidence can *logically* prove an assertion because *one* and *some* can never equal *all*. Because the sun has gotten up on time every morning so far is—the logicians tell us—no logical assurance that it will do so tomorrow. Actually, we can take comfort in that fallacy. Because we can never *logically* produce enough evidence for certitude, we can settle for a reasonable amount and call it quits. One piece of evidence all by itself tempts us to cry, "Fallacy! *One* isn't *all* or *every*." But three or four pieces will probably suit our common sense and calm us into agreement.

### Cite Authorities Reasonably

An appeal to some authority to prove your point is really an appeal beyond logic but not necessarily beyond reason. We naturally turn to authorities to confirm our ideas. "Einstein said" can silence many an objection. But appeals to authority risk four common fallacies. The first is in appealing to the authority outside of his field, even if his field is the universe. After all, the good doctor of the wispy hair and frayed sweater was little known for understanding money too.

The second fallacy is in misunderstanding or misrepresenting what the authority really says. Sir Arthur Eddington, if I may appeal to an authority myself, puts the case: "It is a common mistake to suppose that Einstein's theory of relativity asserts that everything is relative. Actually it says, 'There are absolute things in the world but you must look deeply for them. The things that first present themselves to your notice are for the most part relative.'"* If you appeal loosely to Einstein to authenticate an assertion that everything is "relative," you may appeal in vain—because *relative* means relative to something else, eventually to some absolute.

The third fallacy is in assuming that one instance from an authority represents him or her accurately. Arguments for admitting the split infinitive (see 195–196, 263–264) to equal status with the unsplit, for instance, often present split constructions from prominent writers. But they do not tell us how many splits the writers avoided or how they themselves feel about the construction. A friend once showed me a split infinitive in the late Walter Lippmann's column after I had boldly asserted that careful writers like Lippmann never split them. Out of curiosity, I wrote Mr. Lippmann: after all, he might have changed his tune. He wrote back that he had slipped, that he disliked the thing and tried to revise it out whenever it crept in.

The fourth fallacy is deepest: the authority may have faded. New facts have generated new ideas. Einstein has limited Newton's authority. Geology and radioactive carbon have challenged the literal authority of Genesis. Jung has challenged Freud; and Keynes, Marx.

The more eminent the authority, the easier the fallacy. Ask these four questions:

1. Am I citing him (or her) outside his (or her) field?
2. Am I presenting him (or her) accurately?
3. Is this instance really representative?
4. Is he (or she) still fully authoritative?

Do not claim too much for your authority, and add other kinds of proof or other authorities. In short, don't put all your eggs in one basket.

---

*The Nature of the Physical World (Ann Arbor: University of Michigan Press. 1958): 23.

## Handle Persistences as You Would Authorities

That an idea's persistence constitutes a kind of unwritten or cumulative authority is also open to logical challenge. Because a belief has persisted, the appeal goes, it must be true. Since earliest times, for example, man has believed in some kind of supernatural beings or Being. Something must be there, the persistence seems to suggest. But the appeal is not logical; the belief could have persisted from causes other than the actuality of divine existence, perhaps only from the human being's psychological need. As with authority, new facts may vanquish persistent beliefs. The belief that the world was a pancake, persistent though it had been, simply had to give way to Columbus and Magellan. For all this, however, persistence does have considerable strength as an *indication* of validity, to be supported by other reasons.

## Inspect Your Documentary Evidence

Documents are both authoritative and persistent. They provide the only evidence, aside from oral testimony, for all that we know beyond the immediate presence of our physical universe, with its physical remains of the past. Documents point to what has happened as long ago as Nineveh and Egypt and as recently as the tracings on last hour's blackboard. But documents vary in reliability. You must consider a document's historical context because factuality may have been of little concern, as with stories of heroes and saints or with propaganda. You must allow, as with newspapers, for the effects of haste and limited facts. You should consider all aspects of a document's author, including background, range of knowledge and belief, assumptions, prejudices, probable motives, and possible tendencies to suppress or slant the facts.

Finally, you should consider the document's data. Are the facts of a kind easily verifiable or easily collected? Indeed, can you present other verification? For example, numerical reports of population can be no more than approximations, and they are hazier the farther back you go in history, as statistical methods slacken. Because the data must have been selected from almost infinite possibilities, does the selection seem reasonably representative? Are your source's conclusions right for the data? Might not the data produce other conclusions? Your own data and conclusions, of course, must also face questioning.

Statistics are particularly persuasive evidence, and because of their psychological appeal, they can be devilishly misleading. To reduce things to numbers seems scientific, incontrovertible, final. But each "1" represents a slightly different quantity, as one glance around a class of 20 students will make clear. Each student is the same and yet entirely different. The "20" is a broad generalization convenient for certain kinds of information: how many seats the instructor will need, how many people are absent, how much the instruction costs per head, and so forth. But clearly the "20" will tell nothing about the varying characteristics of the students or the education. So present your statistics with some caution so that they will honestly show what you want them to show and will not mislead your readers. Averages and percentages can be especially misleading, carrying the numerical generalization one step farther from the physical facts. The truth behind a statement that the average student earns $10 a week could be that 9 students earn nothing and one earns $100.

## SOME INDUCTIVE TRAPS

### Keep Your Hypothesis Hypothetical

Induction and deduction are the two paths of reasoning. Induction is "leading into" (*in ducere*, "to lead in"), thinking through the evidence to some general conclusion. Deduction is "leading away from" some general precept to its particular parts and consequences. All along, you have been *thinking inductively* to find your thesis, and then you have turned the process around, *writing deductively* when you present your thesis and support it with your evidence. Both modes have their uses, and their fallacies.

Induction is the way of science: one collects the facts and sees what they come to. Sir Francis Bacon laid down in 1620 the inductive program in his famous *Novum Organum, sive indicia vera de interpretatione naturae* ("The New Instrument, or true evidence concerning the interpretation of nature"). Bacon was at war with the syllogism; its abstract deductions seemed too rigid to measure nature's subtlety. His new instrument changed the entire course of thought. Before Bacon, the world had deduced the consequences of its general ideas; after Bacon, the world looked around and induced new generalizations from what it saw. Observed facts called the old ideas into question, and theories replaced "truths." As you may know, Bacon died from a cold caught while stuffing a chicken's carcass with snow for an inductive test of refrigeration.

Induction has great strength, but it also has a basic fallacy. The strength is in taking nothing on faith, in having no ideas at all until the facts have suggested them. The fallacy is in assuming that the mind can start blank. Theoretically, Bacon had no previous ideas about refrigeration. Theoretically, he would experiment aimlessly until he noticed consistencies that would lead to the icebox. Actually, from experience, one would already have a hunch, a half-formed theory, that would suggest the experimental tests. Induction, in other words, is always well mixed with deduction. The major difference is in the tentative frame of mind: in making an hypothesis instead of merely borrowing an honored assumption, and in keeping the hypothesis hypothetical, even after the facts seem to have supported it.

## Use Analogies to Clarify, Not to Prove

In logic, the simplest kind of induction is analogy: because this tree is much like that oak, it too must be some kind of oak. Figurative analogies couple dissimilar things in metaphors on the strength of a striking similarity—death and a shadow, the heart and a pump. But logically, you identify the unknown by its likeness to the known. Inductively, you look over the similarities until you conclude that the trees are very similar and therefore of the same kind. You see that a large number of details agree, that they are salient and typical, and that the exceptions are unimportant.

Analogies are tremendously useful indications of likeness. They are virtually our only means of classifying things, putting things into groups, and handling them by naming them. Analogy also illustrates the logical weakness of induction: assuming that *all* characteristics are analogous after finding one or two analogous. We check a few symptoms against what we know of colds and flu and conclude that we have a cold and flu, but the doctor will add to these a few more symptoms and conclude that we have a virulent pneumonia.

Similarity does not mean total identity, and analogies must always make that shaky assumption. In your writing, you may use analogy with tremendous effect, as we saw when E. B. White compares Thoreau to a gun-slinging cowboy (60). But again, watch out for the logical gap between *some* and *all*. If the brain seems in some ways like a computer, be careful not to assume it is in all ways like a computer. Keep the analogy figurative: as a metaphor, it can serve you well, illustrating the unknown with the known. It is helpful evidence but not conclusive proof.

## Look Before You Leap

The hypothetical frame of mind is the essence of the inductive method because it acknowledges the logical flaw of induction, namely, the *inductive leap*. No matter how many the facts or how carefully weighed, a time comes when thought must abandon the details and leap to the conclusion. We leap from the knowledge that *some* apples are good to the conclusion: "[All] apples are good." This leap, say the logicians, crosses an abyss no logic can bridge because *some* can never guarantee *all*, or even *most*, except as a general *probability*. The major lesson of induction is that *nothing* can be proved, except as a probability. The best we can manage is an *hypothesis*, while maintaining a perpetual hospitality to new facts. This is the scientific frame of mind; it gets as close to substantive truth as we can come, and it keeps us healthily humble about our theories.

Probability underscores the generalizations to which we must eventually leap. You know that bad apples are neither so numerous nor so strongly typical that you must conclude: "Apples are unfit for human consumption." You also know what causes the bad ones. Therefore, to justify your leap and strengthen your generalization, make sure that:

1. Your samples are reasonably numerous.
2. Your samples are truly typical.
3. You can explain the atypical exceptions.

The inductive leap might also be in the wrong direction: the same evidence may prompt more than one conclusion. Here, again, the inductive frame of mind can help. It can teach you always to check your conclusions by asking if another answer might not do just as well. Some linguists have concluded that speech is superior to writing because speech has many more "signals" than writing. But from the same facts one might declare writing superior: it conveys the same message more economically.

The lesson of induction is the lesson of caution. Logically, induction is shot full of holes and human error. But it makes as firm a statement as we can expect about the physical universe and our experience in it. It keeps our feet on the ground while we make sense of our evidence. It keeps the mind open for new hypotheses, reminding us that no explanation is absolute.

## The Common Logical Fallacies: Trust Your Common Sense

All in all, most fallacies in writing—our own and others'—we can uncover simply by knowing they lurk and by using our heads. We must constantly ask if our words are meaning what they say and saying what we mean. We must check our assumptions. Then we must ask if we are inadvertently taking *some* for *all* or making that inductive leap too soon or in an errant direction. Common sense will tell you that something is wrong.

But here is a list of the classic common fallacies. Being wary of them will help protect your flanks as you advance your ideas. Recognizing them in your opponents and naming them will give you a nice argumentative edge.

1. EITHER–OR. You assume only two opposing possibilities: "Either we abolish requirements or education is finished." Education will probably amble on, somewhere in between. Similarly, IF–THEN: "If I work harder on the next paper, then I'll get a better grade." You have overlooked differences in subject, knowledge, involvement, inspiration. A president said: "If the Senate behaves irresponsibly on this entirely reasonable nomination, how can I go forward with compromise and cooperation?" The president was simply putting the ball in the Senate's court with the old "either-or" twist. Actually, he could, and did, continue to compromise and angle for cooperation.

2. OVERSIMPLIFICATION. As with *either-or*, you ignore alternatives. "A student learns only what he wants to learn" ignores all the pressures from parents and society, which in fact account for a good deal of learning. Like most mass demonstrations, "Ban Abortion" rallies vastly oversimplify a complex social and moral issue and its many varied consequences.

3. BEGGING THE QUESTION. An unhandy term, arising in Shakespeare's day, perhaps as a poor translation of the Medieval Latin *petitio principi* ("the claim of the beginning"), because *petere* also means "to request, to beg." At any rate, the Latin phrase and our "begging the question" both mean taking for granted something that really needs proving. "Free all political prisoners" begs the question of whether some of those concerned have committed an actual crime, like blowing up the chemistry building in a political protest.

Edmund Wilson, in the "Ambiguity of Henry James" (1934), asserted of *The Turn of the Screw* that "the whole story has been primarily intended as a characterization of the governess"—who tells the story and whom he considers one of James's sexually repressed spinsters, so haunted that she sees nonexistent ghosts. Wilson has begged the question of James's intention, assuming it without proving it. An author's intention is notoriously elusive, even if he states it, as many have pointed out.

4. IGNORING THE QUESTION.  The question of whether it is right for a neighborhood to organize against a newcomer shifts to prices of property and taxes. Someone is convicted of murder: the question of innocence or guilt shifts to the numbers who escape conviction or get lighter sentences.

5. NON SEQUITUR ("it does not follow").  "He's certainly sincere; he must be right." "He's the most popular; he should be president." The conclusions do not reasonably follow from sincerity and popularity. Aristotle cites the conclusion that Prince Paris had a lofty soul because he shunned society and lived "loftily" on Mt. Ida. Or someone says, "He planned carefully; it's not his fault the meeting failed." That may be true, of course, but it is a non sequitur if his plans overlooked some crucial possibilities.

6. POST HOC, ERGO PROPTER HOC ("after this, therefore because of this").  The non sequitur of events: "He stayed up late and therefore won the race." He probably won in spite of late hours and for other reasons. This is the politician's favorite fallacy. "Democratic presidents get us into war"— because America has entered World Wars I and II, Korea, and Vietnam during Democratic presidencies. But Lincoln was a Republican, and many forces, both prior and contemporary, have involved us in wars. Conversely, presidents and governors invariably claim the prosperity already in motion before their election and blame setbacks on their predecessors. Most fallacies, like this one, are also oversimplifications.

7. ARGUMENTUM AD HOMINEM ("argument toward the man").  Using unfavorable personal traits to attack a work of art, an accomplishment, an ability, a precept—this is also a species of ignoring the question. "He walked out on his wife and children: his sculpture is terrible." His sculpture is what it is, apart from his personal conduct. When someone complained of Grant's drinking, Lincoln wryly remarked he wished he had more generals like him, exposing the *ad hominem* fallacy. Political campaigning is frequently *ad hominem*. In 64 B.C., when Cicero was running for the Roman consulate against Catiline, his brother Quintus advised: "Contrive to get some new scandal aired against your rivals for crime, corruption, or immorality." Although Quintus seems to recommend cooking up new dirt, *ad hominem* attacks are not always fallacious, as Cicero's exposure of Catiline's crimes demonstrated. Conversely, attorneys introduce testimony of good citizenship to defend their clients: "How could a loving father rob a bank?"

8. ARGUMENTUM AD MISERICORDIUM ("argument toward pity"). A kind of reverse *ad hominem*, which also ignores the question. The lawyer appeals to the starving family to evade the question of guilt. Appeals to pity, of course, are far from illogical concerning support for the poor, the bereft, the victims of disaster.

9. ARGUMENTUM AD POPULUM ("argument toward the people"). The *ad hominem* shifts to a social type or group of people, appealing to prejudices about race, sex, religion, class, or the like. Stereotyping appeals *ad populum*. The United States interned thousands of west-coast Japanese Americans as untrustworthy enemies after Japan attacked Pearl Harbor. Edmund Wilson's "spinster" for a 20-year-old unmarried woman is a loaded *ad populum*, as is his assuming that all such women are sexually obsessed. Frequent *ad populum* fallacies are appeals to one's birthplace as a guarantee of excellence ("I was born in the cradle of democracy"—a physical impossibility to boot) or to social class as bad ("His immense wealth is entirely in wildcat oil").

10. GUILT BY ASSOCIATION. A form of *ad populum*. The reasoning is that of a false syllogism:

**X votes against criminalizing the possession of marijuana.**
**Medpot holds rallies against restrictions on possession.**
**X is a member of Medpot.**

Because X and Medpot concur on one point does not mean they concur on all. This is our old *one* and *all* again, in formal logic called "the fallacy of the undistributed middle term." It is all too frequent in political infighting, easily recognized as unfair, and, unfortunately, easily accepted by proponents.

11. ARGUMENTUM AD IGNORANTUM ("argument toward ignorance"). Assuming that lack of evidence proves its opposite: UFOs exist because no one has proved that they don't, or ghosts do not exist because no one has proved that they do. For years, the tobacco industry argued that smoking was not a cause of cancer because no one had yet shown that it was.

12. THE BANDWAGON. "Everyone does it, so it must be OK." Slavery held sway on "bandwagon" grounds, as have smoking and drinking and a great deal of our behavior at the polls.

13. THE COMPLEX QUESTION. "Have you stopped beating your spouse?" is the classic example. Either "yes" or "no" traps the answerer—if guiltless. "Yes" says that the person has beaten the spouse. "No" says that the person has been doing this and continues. The only escape is to answer, "No—because I never started." Political questions take subtler form: "Jones opposes these nuclear plants and promoting the industry and jobs they

would create." To defend Jones, you would point to Jones's opposition to radiation and unnecessary hazards and show that other means of generating electricity would also promote industry and jobs.

## SUGGESTIONS FOR EXERCISE

**1.** *After each of the following assertions, write two or three short questions that will challenge its assumptions, questions like "Good for what? Throwing? Fertilizer?" For example: Girls are brighter than boys. "At what age? All girls? In chess? In physics?" In the questions, probe and distinguish among your facts, opinions, beliefs, and preferences.*

1. Men are superior to women.
2. The backfield made some mistakes.
3. Communism means violent repression.
4. Don't trust anyone over 30.
5. All people are equal.
6. The big companies are ruining the environment.
7. Travel is educational.
8. Our brand of cigarette is free of tar.
9. The right will prevail.
10. A long run is good for you.

**2.** *Each of the following statements contains at least one fallacious citation of authority. Identify it, and explain how it involves one or several of these reasons: "Outside Field," "Not Accurately Presented," "Not Representative," "Out of Date."*

1. According to Charles Morton, a distinguished seventeenth-century theologian and schoolmaster, the swallows of England disappear to the dark side of the moon in winter.
2. Einstein states that everything is relative.
3. War between capitalists and communists is inevitable, as Karl Marx shows.
4. Government should legalize drugs; after all, neuroscientist Michael Gazzaniga recommends legalization.
5. "Fluff is America's finest bubble bath," says Michael Jordan.

**3.** *Each of the following statistical statements is fallacious in one or several ways, either omitting something necessary for full understanding or generalizing in unsupported ways. Identify and explain the statistical fallacies.*

1. This car gets 35 miles per gallon.

2. Fifty percent of his snapshots are poor.
3. Twenty-nine persons were injured when a local bus skidded on an icy road near Weston and overturned. Two were hospitalized. Twenty-seven were treated and released.
4. Women support this book 100 percent, but 50 percent of American males are drug addicts. (In a class of five women and ten men, all the women and five of the men vote to write about a book entitled *Say "No" to Drugs.*)

**4.** *If baseball is in season, go to the sports page and write a brief explanation of the statistics on batting averages, RBIs, and so forth. Can you find any fallacies—things the statistics do not tell? You might instead do the same with another sport or subject where statistics are common.*

**5.** *Explain the following fallacious analogies and inductive leaps.*

1. The brain is like a computer. Scientists have demonstrated that, like the computer, the brain works through electrical impulses.
2. This woman has ten sweaters; that woman has ten sweaters. They are equally rich in sweaters.
3. At 60, Ethel retires with investments and savings worth more than $500,000. She has nothing to worry about for the rest of her life.
4. Every time the Boilers play a postseason game, they lose. They will lose this one.
5. English majors are poor mathematicians.
6. I studied hard. I answered every question. None of my answers was wrong. I have read my exam over again and again and can still see no reason for getting only a C.

**6.** *Name and explain the fallacy in each of the following:*

1. Jones is rich. He must be dishonest.
2. She either worked hard for her money, or she is just plain lucky.
3. The best things in life are free, like free love.
4. Sunshine breeds flies because when the sun shines the flies come out.
5. If they have no bread, let them eat cake. Cake is both tastier and richer in calories.
6. This is another example of American imperialism.
7. Smith's canned-soup empire reaches farther than the Roman Empire.
8. *Dallas* is America's most popular soap. It is clearly the best.
9. He is innocent. His record is spotless. The jury found him not guilty.
10. Women are the most exploited people in the history of the world.

# 7
# Writing Good
# Sentences

All this time you have been writing sentences, as naturally as breathing and perhaps with as little variation. Now for a close look at the varieties of the sentence. Some varieties can be shaggy and tangled indeed. But they are all offshoots of the simple active sentence, the basic English genus *John hits Joe*, with action moving straight from subject through verb to object.

This subject-verb-object sentence can be infinitely grafted and contorted, but it really has only two general varieties: (1) the "loose, or strung-along," in Aristotle's phrase, and (2) the periodic. English naturally runs "loose," or "cumulative." Our thoughts are naturally strung along from subject through verb to object, with whatever comes to mind added as it comes. The loose sentence puts its subject and verb early. But we can also use the periodic sentence characteristic of our Latin and Germanic ancestry, where ideas hang in the air like girders until all interconnections are locked by the final word, at the period: *John, the best student in the class, the tallest and most handsome, hits Joe*. A periodic sentence, in other words, is one that suspends its meaning until the end, usually with subject and verb widely separated and the verb as near the end as possible.

So we have two varieties of the English sentence. The piece-by-piece and the periodic species represent two ways of thought: the first, the natural stringing of thoughts as they come; the second, the more careful contrivance of emphasis and suspense.

## THE SIMPLE SENTENCE

### Use the Simple Active Sentence, Loosely Periodic

Your best sentences will be hybrids of the loose and the periodic. First, learn to use active verbs (*John* HITS *Joe*), which will keep you within the simple active pattern with all parts showing (subject-verb-object), as opposed to a verb in the passive voice (*Joe* IS HIT *by John*), which puts everything backwards and uses more words. Then learn to give your native strung-along sentence a touch of periodicity and suspense.

Any change in normal order can give you unusual emphasis, as when you move the object ahead of the subject:

> That I like.
> The house itself she hated, but the yard was grand.
> Nature I loved; and next to Nature, Art.

Most often, we expect our ideas one at a time, in normal succession—*John hits Joe*—and with anything further added, in proper sequence, at the end—*a real haymaker*. Change this fixed way of thinking, and you immediately put your readers on the alert for a pleasant surprise. Consequently, some of your best sentences will be simple, active ones sprung wide with phrases coloring subject, verb, object, or all three, in various ways. You may, for instance, effectively complicate the subject:

> King Lear, proud, old, and childish, probably aware that his grip on the kingdom is beginning to slip, devises a foolish plan.

Or the verb:

> A good speech usually begins quietly, proceeds sensibly, gathers momentum, and finally moves even the most indifferent audience.

Or the object:

> Her notebooks contain marvelous comments on the turtle in the backyard, the flowers and weeds, the great elm by the drive, the road, the earth, the stars, and the men and women of the village.

# COMPOUND AND COMPLEX SENTENCES

## Learn the Difference Between Compound and Complex Sentences

You make a compound sentence by linking together simple sentences with a coordinating conjunction (*and, but, or, nor, yet, still, for, so*) or with a colon or a semicolon. You make a complex one by hooking lesser sentences onto the main sentence with *that, which, who,* or one of the many other subordinating connectives like *although, because, where, when, after, if.* The compound sentence *coordinates,* treating everything on the same level; the complex *subordinates,* putting everything else somewhere below its one main self-sufficient idea. The compound links ideas one after the other, as in the basic simple sentence; the complex is a simple sentence elaborated by clauses instead of merely by phrases. The compound represents the strung-along way of thinking; the complex usually represents the periodic.

## Avoid Simple-Minded Compounds

Essentially the compound sentence is simple-minded, a set of clauses on a string—a child's description of a birthday party, for instance: "We got paper hats and we pinned the tail on the donkey and we had chocolate ice cream and Randy sat on a piece of cake and I won third prize." *And . . . and . . . and.*

But this way of thinking is always useful for pacing off related thoughts, and for breaking the staccato of simple statement. It often briskly connects cause and effect: "The clock struck one, and down he run." "The solipsist relates all knowledge to his own being, and the demonstrable commonwealth of human nature dissolves before his dogged timidity." The compound sentence is built on the most enduring of colloquial patterns—the simple sequence of things said as they occur to the mind—it has the pace, the immediacy, and the dramatic effect of talk. Hemingway, for instance, often gets all the numb tension of a shell-shocked mind by reducing his character's thoughts all to one level, in compound sentences something like this: "It was a good night and I sat at a table and . . . and . . . and . . . ."

Think of the compound sentence in terms of its conjunctions—the words that yoke its clauses—and of the accompanying punctuation. Here are three basic groups of conjunctions that will help you sort out and punctuate your compound thoughts.

### Group I

*The three common coordinating conjunctions:* and, but, *and* or (nor). *Put a comma before each.*

> I like her, and I don't mind saying so.
> Art is long, but life is short.
> Win this point, or the game is lost.

### Group II

*Conjunctive adverbs:* therefore, moreover, however, nevertheless, consequently, furthermore. *Put a semicolon before, and a comma after, each.*

> Nations indeed seem to have a kind of biological span like human life, from rebellious youth, through caution, to decay; consequently, predictions of doom are not uncommon.

### Group III

*Some in-betweeners—*yet, still, so*—which sometimes take a comma, sometimes a semicolon, depending on your pace and emphasis.*

> We long for the good old days, yet we never include the disadvantages.
> People long for the good old days; yet they rarely take into account the inaccuracy of human memory.
> The preparation had been halfhearted and hasty, so the meeting was wretched.
> Rome declined into the pleasures of its circuses and couches; so the tough barbarians conquered.

## Try Compounding Without Conjunctions

Though the conjunction usually governs its compound sentence, two powerful coordinators remain—the semicolon and the colon alone. For contrasts, the semicolon is the prince of coordinators:

The novel concentrates on character; the film intensifies the vio-     Semicolon
  lence.
Golf demands the best of time and space; tennis, the best of personal
  energy.
The government tries to get the most out of taxes; the individual
  tries to get out of the most taxes.

The colon similarly pulls two "sentences" together without the blessing of conjunction, period, or capital. But it signals amplification, not contrast: the second clause explains the first.

A house with an aging furnace costs more than the asking price suggests: $40 more a month in fuel means about $320 more a     Colon
  year.
Each year, thousands of acres of forest vanish: vanishing forests
  mean more carbon dioxide and less oxygen.
Sports at any age are beneficial: they keep your pulses hopping.

## Learn to Subordinate

You probably write compound sentences almost without thinking. But the subordinations of the complex usually require some thought. Indeed, you are ranking closely related thoughts, arranging the lesser ones so that they bear effectively on your main thought. You must first pick your most important idea. You must then change mere sequence into subordination— ordering your lesser thoughts "sub," or below, the main idea. The childish birthday sentence, then, might come out something like this:

After we got paper hats and ate chocolate ice cream, after
Randy sat on a piece of cake and everyone pinned the tail on the donkey, I WON THIRD PRIZE.

You do the trick with connectives—with any word, like *after* in the sentence above, indicating time, place, cause, or other qualification.

*If* they try, *if* they fail, THEY ARE STILL GREAT *because* their
spirit is unbeaten.

You daily achieve subtler levels of subordination with the three relative pronouns *that, which, who,* and with the conjunction *that. That, which,* and *who* connect thoughts so closely related as to seem almost equal, but actually each tucks a clause (subject-and-verb) into some larger idea:

Relative Pronoun    The car, *which* runs perfectly, is not worth selling.
The car *that* runs perfectly is worth keeping.

Subordinating      He thought *that* the car would run forever.
Conjunctions      He thought [*that* omitted but understood] the car would run forever.

But the subordinating conjunctions and adverbs (*although, if, because, since, until, where, when, as if, so that*) really put subordinates in their places. Look at *when* in this sentence of E. B. White's from *Charlotte's Web:*

Adverbs          Next morning *when* the first light came into the sky and the
sparrows stirred in the trees, *when* the cows rattled their chains and
the rooster crowed and the early automobiles went whispering along
the road, Wilbur awoke and looked for Charlotte.

Here the simple *when*, used only twice, has regimented five subordinate clauses, all of equal rank, into their proper station below that of the main clause, "Wilbur awoke and looked for Charlotte." You can vary the ranking intricately and still keep it straight:

Subordinating      *Although* some claim *that* time is an illusion *because* we have
Conjunctions      no absolute chronometer, *although* the mind cannot effectively grasp
time *because* the mind itself is a kind of timeless presence almost
oblivious to seconds and hours, *although* the time of our solar system may be only an instant in the universe at large, WE STILL CAN-
NOT QUITE DENY *that* some progression of universal time is passing
over us, *if* only we could measure it.

Complex sentences are, at their best, really simple sentences gloriously delayed and elaborated with subordinate thoughts. The following beautiful and elaborate sentence from the Book of Common Prayer is all built on the simple sentence "draw near":

Ye who do truly and earnestly repent you of your sins, and are
in love and charity with your neighbors, and intend to lead a new
life, following the commandments of God, and walking from hence-
forth in his holy ways, draw near with faith, and take this holy
sacrament to your comfort, and make your humble confession to
Almighty God, devoutly kneeling.

Even a short sentence may be complex, attaining a remarkably varied suspense. Notice how the simple statement "I allowed myself" is skillfully elaborated in this sentence by the late Wolcott Gibbs of *The New Yorker:*

> **Twice in my life, for reasons that escape me now, though I'm
> sure they were discreditable, I allowed myself to be persuaded that
> I ought to take a hand in turning out a musical comedy.**

## Try for Still Closer Connections: Modify

Your subordinating *ifs* and *whens* have really been modifying—that is, limiting—the things you have attached them to. But there is a smoother way. It is an adjectival sort of thing, a shoulder-to-shoulder operation, a neat trick with no need for shouting, a stone to a stone with no need for mortar. You simply put clauses and phrases up against a noun instead of attaching them with a subordinator. This sort of modification includes the following constructions, all using the same close masonry: (1) appositives, (2) relatives understood, (3) adjectives-with-phrase, (4) participles, (5) absolutes.

### Appositives

Those phrases about shoulders and tricks and stones, above, are all in apposition with *sort of thing*, and they are grammatically subordinate to it. *Apposition* means "put to" or "add to"—putting an equivalent beside, like two peas in a pod—hence, these phrases are nearly coordinate and interchangeable. They are compressions of a series of sentences ("It is an adjectival sort of thing. It is a neat trick . . . ," and so forth) set side by side, "stone to stone." Mere contact does the work of the verb *is* and its subject *it*. English often does the same with subordinate clauses, omitting the *who is* or *that is* and putting the rest directly into apposition. "The William who is the Conqueror" becomes "William the Conqueror." "The Jack who is the heavy hitter" becomes "Jack the heavy hitter." These, incidentally, are called "restrictive" appositions because they restrict to a particular designation the nouns they modify, setting this William and this Jack apart from all others (with no separating commas). Similarly, you can make nonrestrictive appositives from nonrestrictive clauses, clauses that simply add information (between commas). "Smith, who is a woman to be reckoned with, . . ." becomes "Smith, a woman to be reckoned with, . . ." "Jones, who is our manager in Liverpool, . . ." becomes "Jones, our manager in Liverpool, . . ." Restrictive or nonrestrictive, close contact neatly makes your point.

## *Relatives Understood*

You can often achieve the same economy, as I have already hinted, by omitting the relative pronouns *that*, *which*, and *who* with their verbs, thus gaining a compression both colloquial and classic:

> A compression [that is] both colloquial and classic . . .
> The house, [which was] facing north, had a superb view.
> The specimens [that] she had collected . . .
> The friends [whom] he [had] left behind . . .

## *Adjectives-with-Phrase*

This construction is also appositive and adjectival. It is neat and useful:

> The law was passed, *thick with provisions and codicils, heavy with implications.*
> There was the lake, *smooth in the morning air.*

## *Participles*

Participles—when acting as adjectives—are extremely supple subordinators. Consider this sequence of six simple sentences:

> He had been thrown.
> He had accepted.
> He felt a need.
> He demanded money.
> He failed.
> He chose not to struggle.

Now see how Richard Wright, in *Native Son*, subordinates the first five of these to the sixth with participles. He elaborates the complete thought into a forceful sentence that runs for 89 words with perfect clarity:

> *Having been thrown* by an accidental murder into a position where he had sensed a possible order and meaning in his relations with the people about him; *having accepted* the moral guilt and responsibility for that murder because it had made him feel free for the first time in his life; *having felt* in his heart some obscure need to be at home with people and *having demanded* ransom money to enable him to do it— *having* done all this and *failed,* he chose not to struggle any more.

These participles have the same adjectival force:

> Dead to the world, *wrapped* in sweet dreams, *untroubled* by bills, he slept till noon.

Notiçe that the participles operate exactly as the adjective *dead* does.

Beware of dangling participles. They may trip you, as they have tripped others. The participle, with its adjectival urge, may grab the first noun that comes along, with shocking results:

> Bowing to the crowd, the bull caught him unawares.
> Observing quietly from the bank, the beavers made several errors in judgment.
> Squandering everything at the track, the money was never repaid.
> What we need is a list of teachers broken down alphabetically.

Move the participle next to its intended noun or pronoun; you will have to supply this word if inadvertence or the passive voice has omitted it entirely. Recast the sentence for good alignment when necessary. You may also save the day by changing a present participle to a past, as in the third example below, or, perhaps better, by activating the sentence, as in the fourth example:

> The bull caught him unawares as he bowed to the crowd.
> Observing quietly from the bank, they saw the beavers make several errors in judgment.
> Squandered at the track, the money was never repaid.
> Having squandered everything at the track, she never repaid the money.
> What we need is an alphabetical list of teachers.

*Gerunds*, which look like present participles but act as nouns, are also good economizers. The two sentences "He had been thrown" and "It was unpleasant" can become one with a gerund as subject: "*Having been thrown* was unpleasant." Gerunds also serve as objects of verbs and prepositions:

> She hated *going* home.
> By *driving* carefully, they increased their mileage.

*Absolutes*

The absolute phrase has a great potential of polished economy. It stands grammatically "absolute" or alone, modifying only through proximity, like an apposition. Many an absolute is simply a prepositional phrase with the preposition dropped:

> **He ran up the stairs, [with]** *a bouquet of roses under his arm,* **and rang the bell.**
> **She walked slowly, [with]** *her camera ready.*

But the ablative absolute (*ablative* means "removed") is absolutely removed from the main clause, modifying only by proximity. If you have had some Latin, you will probably remember this construction as some kind of brusque condensation, something like "*The road completed,* Caesar moved his camp." But it survives in the best of circles. Somewhere, E. B. White admits to feeling particularly good one morning, just having brought off an especially fine ablative absolute. And it is actually more common than you may suppose. A recent newspaper article stated that "the Prince had fled the country, *his hopes of a negotiated peace shattered.*" The *hopes shattered* pattern (noun plus participle) marks the ablative absolute (also called, because of the noun, a "nominative absolute"). The idea might have been more conventionally subordinated: "because his hopes were shattered" or "with his hopes shattered." But the ablative absolute accomplishes the subordination with economy and style.

Take a regular subordinate clause: "*When* the road *was* completed." Cut the subordinator and reduce the verb. You now have an ablative absolute, a phrase that stands absolutely alone, shorn of both its connective *when* and its full predication: "*The road completed,* Caesar moved his camp." Basically a noun and a participle, or noun and adjective, it is a kind of grammatical shorthand, a telegram: *ROAD COMPLETED CAESAR MOVED*—most said in fewest words, speed with high compression. This is its appeal and its power:

> **The cat froze,** *its back arched, its eyes frantic.*
> *All things considered,* **the plan would work.**
> **The** *dishes washed,* **the** *baby bathed* **and** *asleep,* **the last** *ashtray emptied,* **they could at last relax.**

# PARALLEL CONSTRUCTION

## Use Parallels to Strengthen Equivalent Ideas

No long complex sentence will hold up without parallel construction. Paralleling can be very simple. Any word will seek its own kind, noun to noun, adjective to adjective, infinitive to infinitive. The simplest series of things automatically runs parallel:

> shoes and ships and sealing wax
> I came, I saw, I conquered
> to be or not to be
> a dull, dark, and soundless day
> mediocre work, cowardly work, disastrous work

But they very easily run out of parallel too, and this you must learn to prevent. The last item especially may slip out of line, as in this series: "friendly, kind, unobtrusive, and _a bore_" (boring). The noun _bore_ has jumped off the track laid by the preceding parallel adjectives. Your train of equivalent ideas should all be of the same grammatical kind to carry their equivalence clearly—to strengthen it: either parallel adjectives, _friendly, kind, unobtrusive_, and _boring_, or all nouns, _a friend, a saint, a diplomat_, and _a bore_. Your paralleling articles and prepositions should govern a series as a whole or should accompany _every_ item:

> a hat, cane, pair of gloves, and mustache
> a hat, a cane, a pair of gloves, and a mustache
> by land, sea, or air
> by land, by sea, or by air

Verbs also frequently intrude to throw a series of adjectives (or nouns) out of parallel:

> FAULTY: The woman was _attractive, intelligent_, and _knew_ how to express her ideas.
> IMPROVED: The woman was _attractive, intelligent_, and _articulate_, knowing how to express her ideas.

## Watch the Paralleling of Pairs

Pairs should be pairs, not odds and ends. Notice how the faulty pairs in these sentences have been corrected:

> ✓She liked *the theater and dancing* (the theater and the dance).
> — They were *all athletic or leaders on campus* (athletes or leaders on campus).
> They wanted *peace without being disgraced* (peace without dishonor).
> ✓He was *shy but a creative man* (shy but creative).

Check your terms on both sides of your coordinating conjunctions (*and, but, or*) and see that they match:

> Orientation week seems both worthwhile [adjective] and
>     necessary [adj.]
>     ~~a necessity~~ [noun].
>                    ∧
>                              that
> He prayed that they would leave and ∧ the telephone would
>     not ring.

## Learn to Use Paralleling Coordinators

The sentence above about "orientation week" has used one of a number of useful (and tricky) parallel constructions: *both–and; either–or; not only–but also; not–but; first–second–third; as well as*. This last one is similar to *and*, a simple link between two equivalents, but it often goes wrong:

> One should take care of one's physical self [noun] *as well as*
> being [participle] able to read and write.

Again, the pair should be matched: "one's *physical self* as well as one's *intellectual self*," or "one's physical *self* as well as one's *ability* to read and write"— though this second is still slightly unbalanced, in rhetoric if not in grammar. The best cure would probably extend the underlying antithesis, the basic parallel:

One should take care of one's physical self as well as one's intellectual self, of one's ability to survive as well as to read and write.

With the *either–ors* and the *not only–but alsos*, you continue the principle of pairing. The *either* and the *not only* are merely signposts of what is coming: two equivalents linked by a coordinating conjunction (*or* or *but*). Beware of putting the signs in the wrong place—too soon for the turn:

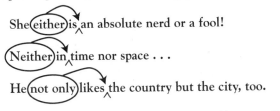

She either is an absolute nerd or a fool!

Neither in time nor space . . .

He not only likes the country but the city, too.

In these examples, the thought got ahead of itself, as in talk. Just make sure that the word following each of the two coordinators is of the same kind, preposition for preposition, article for article, adjective for adjective—for even with signs well placed, the parallel can skid:

> The students are not only organizing [present participle]
> discussing
> social activities, but also are ~~interested~~ [passive
> construction] ~~in~~ political questions.

Put identical parts in parallel places; fill in the blanks with the same parts of speech: "not only _____, but also _____."

Beginning with *Not only*, a common habit, always takes more words as it duplicates subject and verb, inviting a comma splice and frequently misaligning a parallel:

POOR: **Not only** are human beings limited in their minds and in their position in the universe, they are also limited in their physical powers.

IMPROVED: Human beings are limited *not only* in their minds and in their position in the universe, *but also* in their physical powers. [*22 words for 24*]

The following sentence avoids the comma splice but still must duplicate subject and verb:

POOR: *Not only* are the names similar, but the two men share some similarities of character.

IMPROVED: The two men share similarities *not only* in name *but* in character. [*12 words for 15*]

The following experienced writer avoids the usual comma splice with a semicolon but makes a dubious parallel:

POOR: *Not only* was the right badly splintered into traditional conservatives, economic liberals, and several other factions; the left made its weakest showing in half a century.

IMPROVED: The right was badly splintered . . . , and the left . . . .

You similarly parallel the words following numerical coordinators:

Numerical  
Coordinates

However variously he expressed himself, he unquestionably thought, first, *that* everyone could get ahead; second, *that* workers generally were paid more than they earned; and, third, *that* laws enforcing a minimum wage were positively undemocratic.

For a number of reasons, he decided (1) *that* she did not like it, (2) *that* he would not like it, (3) *that* they would be better off without it. [Note that the parentheses around the numbers operate exactly as any parentheses and need no additional punctuation, even if you omit the first half of the parenthesis: "3) *that* they . . . ."]

My objections are obvious: (1) *it* is unnecessary, (2) *it* costs too much, and (3) *it* won't work.

In parallels of this kind, *that* is usually the problem because you may easily, and properly, omit it when there is only one clause and no confusion:

. . . he unquestionably thought everyone could get ahead.

If second and third clauses occur, as your thought moves along, you may have to go back and put up the first signpost:

. . . he unquestionably thought that everyone could get ahead, that workers . . . , and that laws . . . .

Enough of *that*. Remember simply that equivalent thoughts demand parallel constructions. Notice the clear and massive strategy in the following sentence from the concluding chapter of Freud's last book, *An Outline of Psychoanalysis*. Freud is not only summing up the previous discussion, but also expressing the quintessence of his life's work. He is pulling everything together in a single sentence. Each of the parallel *which* clauses gathers up, in proper order, an entire chapter of his book (notice the parallel force in repeating *picture,* and the summarizing dash):

> The picture of an ego which mediates between the id and the external world, which takes over the instinctual demands of the former in order to bring them to satisfaction, which perceives things in the latter and uses them as memories, which, intent upon its self-preservation, is on guard against excessive claims from both directions, and which is governed in all its decisions by the injunctions of a modified pleasure principle—this picture actually applies to the ego only up to the end of the first period of childhood, till about the age of five.

Such precision is hard to match. This is what parallel thinking brings—balance and control and an eye for sentences that seem intellectual totalities, as if struck out all at once from the uncut rock. Francis Bacon's sentences can seem like this (notice how he drops the verb after establishing his pattern):

> For a crowd is not company, and faces are but a gallery of pictures,
>      and talk but a tinkling cymbal, where there is no love.
> Reading maketh a full man; conference a ready man; and writing an
>      exact man.

Commas would work well in the second example (see 212):

> Reading maketh a full man; conference, a ready man; and writing,
> an exact man.

## THE LONG AND SHORT OF IT

Your style will emerge once you can manage some length of sentence, some intricacy of subordination, some vigor of parallel, and some play of long against short, of amplitude against brevity. Try the very long sentence, and the very short. Short sentences are meatiest:

Money talks.
The mass of men lead lives of quiet desperation.
The more selfish the man, the more anguished the failure.

## Experiment with the Fragment

The fragment is close to conversation. It is the laconic reply, the pointed afterthought, the quiet exclamation, the telling question. Try to cut and place it clearly (usually at beginnings and ends of paragraphs) so as not to lead your reader to expect a full sentence or to suspect a poor writer:

Not at all.
First, a look behind the scenes.
Expert within limits, that is.
Enough of that.

The fragment, of course, usually counts as an error. The reader expects a sentence and gets only a fragment of one: you leave him hanging in air, waiting for the second shoe to fall or the voice to drop, with the thought completed, at the period. The *rhetorical* fragment—the effective and persuasive one—leaves him satisfied: *Of course.* The *grammatical* fragment leaves him unsatisfied: *When the vote was counted.* A question hangs in the air: *What* happened? Who won? Who got mad? Each of the following typical grammatical fragments—italicized—could be cured by attaching it, with a comma, to its governing sentence:

He dropped his teeth. *Which had cost five hundred dollars.*
A good example is Hawthorne. *A writer who could dramatize abstract moral theories.*
Cleopatra is the stronger. *Trying to create Antony in her own Egyptian image.*

The grammatical, or *accidental*, fragment usually follows its governing sentence, as in the examples above.

Here is a paragraph with rhetorical fragments placed at the surest and most emphatic places, beginning and end, with a faulty grammatical fragment, to illustrate the difference, still wandering in the middle (all fragments in italics):

*Not quite.* The battle, as it proved, still had two bloody hours to run. B Company, presumed lost by allies and enemy alike, had finally worked through the jungle and flanking outposts, virtually intact. *Tired but fully equipped.* They now brought the full force of surprise and weaponry to bear on the attackers' weakened right flank. The attack turned to meet the surprise. The defenders, heartened, increased their pressure. Reinforcements by helicopter completed the flaming drama. *Curtains for the assault on Won Thang.*

That floating fragment in the middle needs to be attached to the sentence of which it is really a part, either the one before or the one following.

> EITHER: B Company, presumed lost by allies and enemy alike, had finally worked through the jungle and flanking outposts, virtually intact, tired but fully equipped.
> OR: Tired but fully equipped, they now brought the full force . . . .

But the point here about rhetorical fragments is to use their short, conversational staccato as one of your means to vary the rhythm of your long and longer sentences, playing long against short.

## Develop a Rhythm of Long and Short

The conversational flow between long and short makes a passage move. Study the subordinations, the parallels, and the play of short and long in this elegant passage of Virginia Woolf's—after you have read it once for sheer enjoyment. She is writing of Lord Chesterfield's famous letters to Philip Stanhope, his illegitimate son:

But while we amuse ourselves with this brilliant nobleman and his views on life we are aware, and the letters owe much of their fascination to this consciousness, of a dumb yet substantial figure on the farther side of the page. Philip Stanhope is always there. It is true that he says nothing, but we feel his presence in Dresden, in Berlin, in Paris, opening the letters and pouring over them and looking dolefully at the thick packets which have been accumulating year after year since he was a child of seven. He had grown into a rather serious, rather stout, rather short young man. He had a taste for foreign politics. A little serious reading was rather to his liking. And by every post the letters came—urbane, polished, brilliant, imploring and commanding him to learn to dance, to learn to carve, to consider the management of his legs, and to seduce a lady of fashion. He did his best. He worked very hard in the school of the Graces, but their service was too exacting. He sat down halfway up the steep stairs which lead to the glittering hall with all the mirrors. He could

*(margin notes:)*
Subordinate, Long

Short, Long

Short, Shorter; Longer, Long

Short; Longer

Short Parallels   not do it. He failed in the House of Commons; he subsided into some
Long   small post in Ratisbon; he died untimely. He left it to his widow to
break the news which he had lacked the heart or the courage to tell
his father—that he had been married all these years to a lady of low
birth, who had borne him children.

Short; Longer   The Earl took the blow like a gentleman. His letter to his
daughter-in-law is a model of urbanity. He began the education of his
grandsons . . . .*

Those are some sentences to copy. We immediately feel the rhythmic play
of periodic and loose, parallel and simple, long and short. Such orchestra-
tion takes years of practice, but you can always begin.

## SUGGESTIONS FOR EXERCISE

*These work best in short spurts in the classroom.*

1. *Warm up by writing two or three sentences that differ from your usual
   style. Try:*

   1. A simple sentence elaborated—as much as possible, even ridicu-
      lously—by interruptive words or phrases, or by modifying the
      subject, the verb, or the object, or all three. See who can write the
      longest coherent sentence.
   2. A compound sentence balanced for contrast on a semicolon.
   3. A compound sentence with colon pointing to its explanatory sec-
      ond half.
   4. A compound sentence with conjunctive adverb (*therefore, how-
      ever, moreover* . . . ), punctuated with semicolon and comma.
   5. Now write a usual complex sentence with a subordinating clause
      beginning *who* or *which* ("Tim Shields, who . . ."; "The course,
      which . . ."). Then revise that clause into an appositive phrase (see
      97–98).
   6. A sentence modified by adjective-with-phrase ("The law passed,
      thick with provisions . . .").

---

*From *The Second Common Reader* by Virginia Woolf, copyright 1932 by Harcourt Brace Jovanovich, Inc.;
renewed 1960 by Leonard Woolf. Reprinted by permission of the publisher.

7. A sentence with an absolute ("The Prince fled, his hopes shattered . . .").

*2.* *Here is a chance for some fun with what may be the best exercise in parallels ever devised. Write a 100-word sentence!—yes, you can do it—with only one independent clause and with everything else subordinated. You can get started with a string of parallel clauses: "When I get up in the morning, when I look at my bleary eyes in the mirror, when I think of the paper still to be done . . . ," or "After . . . , after . . . , after . . . ." See how far you can run before you must bring in your main subject and verb.*

*3.* *Write a sentence beginning* Not only. *Then revise it by moving the* not only *along into the sentence to make the best parallel.*

*4.* *Correct the faulty parallelism in the following sentences from students' papers, and clean up any wordiness you find.*

1. A student follows not only a special course of training, but among the studies and social activities finds a liberal education.
2. Either the critics attacked the book for its triteness, or it was criticized for its lack of organization.
3. This is not only the case with the young voters of the United States but also of the adult ones.
4. Certain things are not actually taught in the classroom. They are learning how to get along with others, to depend on oneself, and managing one's own affairs.
5. Knowing Greek and Roman antiquity is not just learning to speak their language but also their culture.

*5.* *In the following famous sentence of Bacon's, straighten the faulty parallels and fill out all the phrasing implied by them:*

> Histories make men wise; poets witty; the mathematics subtle; natural philosophy deep; moral grave; logic and rhetoric able to contend.

*6.* *To discover how far parallelism might take you, write a parody of the following passage from Samuel Johnson, matching him phrase for phrase and sentence for sentence. Pick out two ball players, two TV actresses, two rock stars, or the like, and have some fun. You simply substitute your terms for Johnson's, leaving everything else as it is, where it fits. ("Of genius, that power that constitutes a ball player, that quality without which fielding is cold and batting is inert. . . ." "Of glamour, that power which constitutes an actress. . . .")*

> Of genius, that power which constitutes a poet; that quality without which judgement is cold and knowledge is

inert; that energy which collects, combines, amplifies, and animates—the superiority must, with some hesitation, be allowed to Dryden. It is not to be inferred that of this poetical vigour Pope had only a little, because Dryden had more, for every other writer since Milton must give place to Pope; and even of Dryden it must be said that if he has brighter paragraphs, he has not better poems. Dryden's performances were always hasty, either excited by some external occasion, or extorted by domestick necessity; he composed without consideration, and published without correction. What his mind could supply at call, or gather in one excursion, was all that he sought, and all that he gave. The dilatory caution of Pope enabled him to condense his sentiments, to multiply his images, and to accumulate all that study might produce, or chance might supply. If the flights of Dryden therefore are higher, Pope continues longer on the wing. If of Dryden's fire the blaze is brighter, of Pope's the heat is more regular and constant. Dryden often surpasses expectation, and Pope never falls below it. Dryden is read with frequent astonishment, and Pope with perpetual delight.

7.  Write a paragraph beginning and ending with a deliberate rhetorical fragment.

8.  Write an imitation of the passage from Virginia Woolf on 107-108, choosing your own subject but matching the pattern, lengths, and rhythms of her sentences, sentence for sentence, if you can. At any rate, aim toward effective rhythms of long and short.

# 8

## Correcting Wordy Sentences

Now let us contemplate evil—or at least the innocently awful, the bad habits that waste our words, fog our thoughts, and wreck our delivery. Our thoughts are naturally roundabout, our phrases naturally secondhand. Our satisfaction in merely getting something down on paper naturally blinds us to our errors and ineptitudes. It hypnotizes us into believing we have said what we meant, when our words actually say something else: "Every seat in the house was filled to capacity." Two ways of expressing your thought, two clichés, have collided: *every seat was taken* and *the house was filled to capacity*. Cut the excess wordage, and the absurd accident vanishes. *Every seat was taken*. Good sentences come from constant practice in correcting the bad.

## COUNT YOUR WORDS

Writing is devilish; the general sin is wordiness. We put down the first thought that comes, we miss the best order, and we then need lengths of *is's, ofs, bys*, and *whichs*—words virtually meaningless in themselves—to wire our meaningful words together again. Look for the two or three words that carry your meaning; then see if you can rearrange them to speak for themselves, cutting out all the little useless wirings:

> This is the young woman who was elected to be president by the class. [This is the young woman the class elected president. *Or:* The class elected this young woman president. *9 words, or 7 words, for 14*]

**111**

See if you can't promote a noun into a verb and cut overlaps in meaning:

> **Last week, the gold stampede in Europe reached near panic proportions.** [Last week, Europe's gold speculators almost *stampeded*. 7 *words for 11*]

When you convert the noun, *stampede*, into a verb, *stampeded*, you suddenly discover you have already said "near panic proportions," and you can drop it entirely: stampedes *are* panics. That ungrammatical and inaccurate *near* is usually a symptom of wordiness, probably because it reveals a general inattention to meanings: the writer is not, as the word seems to say, visualizing a hand reaching near something called "panic." A "near miss" says what it means: the opposite of a far or wide one. But what is a far panic? That awful *near* has driven *almost* and *nearly* from our daily papers and weekly magazines. Use them, and you will save some words and seem remarkably fresh. A *virtual* or *virtually* also comes in handy. Stop splitting hairs with "a near-mystical experience" and risk a little hyperbole: "a mystical experience"—that *-al* handles the approximation, and your readers will admire your verve.

You can frequently also reduce other tautologies, those useless repetitions of the same idea in different words (see 118–119):

| | |
|---|---|
| each separate incident | each incident |
| many different ways | many ways |
| dash quickly | dash |

As these examples show, the basic cure for wordiness is to count the words in any suspected sentence or phrase—and to make each word count. If you can rephrase to save even one word, your sentence will be clearer. And seek the active verb: *John* HITS *Joe*.

## SHUN THE PASSIVE VOICE

The passive voice is more wordy and deadly than most people imagine, or it would not be so persistent.

> **It was voted that there would be a drive for the cleaning up of the people's park.** [*passive voice—17 words*]
> **We** [the town, the council] **voted a drive to clean up the people's park.** [*active voice—10 or 11 words, depending on subject*]

The passive voice puts the cart before the horse: the object of the action first, then the harnessing verb, running backwards, then the driver forgotten, and the whole contraption at a standstill. The passive voice is simply "passive" action, the normal action backwards: object-verb-subject (with the true subject usually forgotten) instead of subject-verb-object—*Joe is hit by John* instead of *John hits Joe*.

The passive voice liquidates and buries the active individual, along with most of the awful truth. Our massed, scientific, and bureaucratic society is so addicted to it that you must constantly alert yourself against its drowsy, impersonal pomp. The simple English sentence is active; it *moves* from subject through verb to object: "The dean's office has turned down your proposal." But the impersonal bureau emits instead a passive smoke-screen, and the student sees no one at all to help him:

> **It has been decided that your proposal for independent study is not sufficiently in line with the prescribed qualifications as outlined by the college in the catalog.**

Committees always write this way, and the effect on academic writing, as the professor goes from committee to desk to classroom, is astounding. "It was moved that a meeting would be held," the secretary writes, to avoid pinning the rap on anybody. So writes the professor; so writes the student.

I reluctantly admit that the passive voice has certain uses. In fact, your meaning sometimes demands the passive voice; the agent may be better under cover—insignificant, or unknown, or mysterious. The active "Shrapnel hit him" seems to belie the uncanny impersonality of "He was hit by shrapnel." The broad forces of history similarly demand the passive: "The West was opened in 1848." Moreover, you may sometimes need the passive voice to place your true subject, the hero of the piece, where you can modify him conveniently: "Joe was hit by John, who, in spite of all . . . ." And sometimes it simply is more convenient: "This subject-verb-object sentence can be infinitely contorted." You can, of course, find a number of passive constructions in this book, which preaches against them, because they can also space out a thought that comes too fast and thick. In trying to describe periodic sentences, for instance (91), I changed "until all interconnections lock in the final word" (active) to ". . . are locked by the final word" (passive). The *lock* seemed too tight, especially with *in*, and the locking seemed contrary to the ways buildings *are built*. Yes, the passive has its uses.

But it is wordy. It puts useless words in a sentence. Its dullness derives as much from its extra wordage as from its impersonality. The best way to prune is with the active voice, cutting the passive and its fungus as you go. Notice the effect on these typical and real samples:

PASSIVE: Public concern *has also been given* a tremendous impetus *by* the findings of the HUD commission on public housing, and similar commissions to survey the structure and functions of many state organizations concerned with public housing *have been established.*

ACTIVE: The HUD commission's findings on public housing *have* also aroused public concern, and many states have *established* commissions to survey their housing organizations. *[23 words for 39]*

PASSIVE: The algal mats *are made up of* the interwoven filaments of several genera.

ACTIVE: The interwoven filaments of several genera *make up* the algal mats. *[11 words for 13]*

PASSIVE: Many of the remedies *would* probably *be shown to be* faith cures.

ACTIVE: Many of the remedies were probably faith cures. *[8 words for 12]*

PASSIVE: Anxiety and emotional conflict *are lessened* when latency sets in. The total personality *is oriented* in a repressive, inhibitory fashion so as to maintain the barriers, and what Freud has called "psychic dams," against psychosexual impulses.

ACTIVE: When latency sets in, anxiety and emotional conflict *lessen.* The personality *inhibits* itself, maintaining its barriers— Freud's "psychic dams"—against psychosexual impulses. *[22 words for 36]*

## CHECK THE STRETCHERS

*To be,* itself, frequently ought not to be:

He seems [to be] upset about something.
She considered him [to be] perfect.
This appears [to be] difficult.

Above all, keep your sentences awake by not putting them into those favorite stretchers of the passivists, *There is . . . which, It is . . . that,* and the like:

Moreover, [there is] one segment of the population [which] never
   seeks employment.
[There are] many women [who] never marry.
[There] is nothing wrong with it. [Nothing is . . . .]
[It is] his last book [that] shows his genius best.
[It is] this [that] is important.

Cut every *it* not referring to something. Next to activating your passive
verbs, and cutting the passive *there is*'s and *it is*'s, perhaps nothing so
improves your prose as to go through it systematically also deleting every
*to be*, every *which, that, who,* and *whom* not needed for utter clarity or for
spacing out a thought. All your sentences will feel better.

Cut every *is when*, a common habit in defining something:

Paranoia *is when* you think everything is hostile.
Good communication *is when* both speaker and audience understand each other.

Recast these, with an active verb if possible:

Paranoia puts everything in a threatening gloom.
Good communication connects speaker and audience with understanding.

## BEWARE THE OF-AND-WHICH DISEASE

The passive sentence frequently breaks out in a rash of *of*s and *which*s, and
even the active sentence may suffer. Diagnosis: something like sleeping
sickness. *Withs, ins, to*'s, and *bys* also inflamed. Surgery imperative. Here
is an actual case:

Many biological journals, especially those *which* regularly publish new scientific names, now state *in* each issue the exact date *of*
publication *of* the preceding issue. *In* dealing *with* journals *which* do
not follow this practice, or *with* volumes *which* are issued individually, the biologist often needs *to* resort *to* indexes . . . *in order to*
determine the actual date *of* publication *of* a particular name.

Note *of publication of* twice over, and the three *which*s. The passage is a
sleeping beauty. The longer you look at it, the more useless little attendants

you see. Note the inevitable passive voice (*which are issued*) in spite of the author's active efforts. The *of*s accompany extra nouns, *publication* repeating *publish*, for instance. Remedy: (1) eliminate *of*s and their nouns, (2) change *which* clauses into participles, and (3) change nouns into verbs. You can cut more than a third of this passage without touching the sense(39 words for 63):

> **Many biological journals, especially those regularly *publishing* new scientific names, now give the date of each preceding issue. With journals not *following* this practice, and with some books, the biologist must turn to indexes . . . *to date* a particular name.**

I repeat: you can cut most *which*s one way or another with no loss of blood. Participles can modify their antecedents directly because they are verbal adjectives, without an intervening *which*: "a car *which was* going south" is "a car going south"; "a train *which is* moving" is "a moving train." Similarly with the adjective itself: "a song *which was* popular last year" is "a song popular last year"; "a person *who is* attractive" is "an attractive person." Beware of this whole crowd: *who are, that was, which are.*

I had opened my Preface, after several castings, with:

> **This new edition of *The Practical Stylist* continues to lay out, step by step, the simple poetics of the persuasive essay, the processes of argumentation, which is the essence of our attitudes, our thinking, our conversation, our writing.**

That night I luckily awoke to my *of*-ing-and-*which*-ing. Next morning I gave it the pencil:

> **This new edition of *The Practical Stylist* continues to lay out, step by step, the simple poetics of ~~the~~ persuasi̶v̶e̶ ̶e̶s̶s̶a̶y̶,͏ the processes of argumenta̶t̶i̶o̶n̶, ̶w̶h̶i̶c̶h̶ ̶i̶s̶ the essence of . . .**

If you need a relative clause, remember *that*. *Which* has almost completely displaced it in labored writing. *That* is still best for restrictive clauses, those necessary to definition: "A house that faces north is cool" (a participle would save a word: "A house facing north is cool"). *That* is tolerable; *which* is downright oppressive. *Which* should signal the nonrestrictive clause (the afterthought): "The house, which faces north, is a good buy." Here you need *which*. Even restrictive clauses must turn to *which* when complicated parallels arise. "He preaches the fellowship of humanity *that* everyone affirms" elaborates like this: "He preaches the fellowship of humanity *which* everyone affirms, *which* all the great philosophies support, but *for which* few can make any immediate concession." Nevertheless, if you need relatives, a *that* will often ease your sentence and save you from the *whichs*.

Verbs and their derivatives, especially present participles and gerunds, can also help to cure a string of *of*s. Alfred North Whitehead, usually of clear mind, once produced this linked sausage: "Education is the acquisition *of* the art *of* the utilization *of* knowledge." Anything to get around the three *of*s and the three heavy nouns would have been better: "Education instills the art of using knowledge"—"Education teaches us to use knowledge well." Find an active verb for *is the acquisition of*, and shift *the utilization of* into some verbal form: the gerund *using*, or the infinitive *to use*. Shun the *-tions*! Simply change your surplus *-tions* and *of*s—along with your *which* phrases—into verbs, or verbals (*to use, learning*). You will save words and activate your sentences.

## AVOID "THE USE OF"

In fact, both *use* as a noun and *use* as a verb are dangerously wordy words. Because *using* is one of our most basic concepts, other words in your sentence will already contain it.

> He uses rationalization. [He rationalizes.]
> She used the device of foreshadowing. [She foreshadows.]
> Through [the use of] logic, he persuades.
> His [use of] dialogue is effective.

The *utilization of* and *utilize* are only horrendous extremes of the same pestilence, to be stamped out completely.

## BREAK THE NOUN HABIT

Passive writing adores the noun, modifying nouns with nouns in pairs, and even in denser clusters—which then become official jargon. Break up these logjams, let the language flow, and make one noun of the pair an adjective:

*Air pollution* is not as marked in Portland. [*Air* is not *so pol-luted* in Portland. *7 words for 8*]

Or convert one noun to a verb:

*Consumer demand* is falling in the area of services. [Consumers *are demanding* fewer services. *5 words for 9*]

Of course, nouns have long served English as adjectives: as in "rail-road," "*railroad* station," "*court*house," and "*noun* habit." But modern prose has aggravated the tendency beyond belief, and we get such monstrosities as *child sex education course* and *child sex education curriculum publication deadline reminder*—whole strings of nothing but nouns. Education, sociol-ogy, and psychology produce the worst noun stringers, the hardest for you not to copy if you take these courses. But we have all caught the habit. The nouns *level* and *quality*, used as adjectives, have produced a rash of redun-dancies. A meeting of "high officials" has now unfortunately become a meeting of "high-*level* officials." The "finest cloth" these days is always "finest-*quality* cloth." Drop those two redundant nouns and you will make a good start and will sound surprisingly original. In fact, using the noun *quality* as an adjective has become almost obsessive—*quality food, quality wine, quality service, quality entertainment, high-quality drilling equipment*—blurring all distinctions of *good, fine, excellent, superb,* and *superior* in one dull and inaccurate cliché. A good rule is: DON'T USE NOUNS AS ADJECTIVES. You can drop many an excess noun:

| WORDY | DIRECT |
|---|---|
| advance notice | notice |
| long in size | long |
| puzzling in nature | puzzling |
| of an indefinite nature | indefinite |
| of a peculiar kind | peculiar |
| in order to | to |
| by means of | by |
| in relation to | with |
| in connection with | with |
| 1991-model car | 1991 car |
| at this point in time | at this time; now |

Wherever possible, find the equivalent adjective:

| | |
|---|---|
| of great importance | important |
| highest significance level | highest significant level |
| government spending | governmental spending |
| reaction fixation | reactional fixation |
| teaching excellence | excellent teaching |
| encourage teaching quality | encourage good teaching |

Or change the noun to its related participle:

| | |
|---|---|
| advance placement | advanced placement |
| uniform police | uniformed police |
| poison arrow | poisoned arrow |

Or make the noun possessive:

| | |
|---|---|
| reader interest | reader's interest |
| veterans insurance | veterans' insurance |

Or try a cautious *of*:

| | |
|---|---|
| color lipstick | color of lipstick |
| significance level | level of significance |

Of our many misused nouns, *type* often uselessly intrudes. Advertisers talk of *detergent-type cleansers* instead of *detergents*; educators, of *apprentice-type situations* instead of *apprenticeships*; journalists, of *fascist-type organizations* instead of *fascistic organizations*. We have forgotten that making the individual stand for the type is the simplest and oldest of metaphors: "Give us this day our daily bread." A twentieth-century supplicant might have written "bread-type food."

The active sentence transmits the message by putting each word unmistakably in its place, a noun as a noun, an adjective as an adjective, with the verb—no stationary *is*—really carrying the mail. Recently, after a flood, a newspaper produced this apparently succinct and dramatic sentence: **Dead animals cause water pollution.** (The word *cause*, incidentally, indicates wasted words.) That noun water as an adjective throws the meaning off and takes 25 percent more words than the essential active message: **Dead animals pollute water.** As you read your way into the sentence, it seems to say *dead animals cause water* (which is true enough), and then you must readjust your thoughts to accommodate *pollution*. The simplest change is from *water pollution* (noun–noun) to *polluted water* (adjective–noun), clarifying each word's function. But the supreme solution is to make *pollute* the verb it is, and the sentence a simple active message in which no word misspeaks itself. Here are the possibilities, in a scale from most active and clearest to most passive and wordiest, which may serve to chart your troubles if you become tangled in causes and nouns:

> Dead animals pollute water.
> Dead animals cause polluted water.
> Dead animals cause water pollution.
> Dead animals are a factor in causing the pollution of water.
> Dead animals are a serious factor in causing the water pollution situation.
> Dead farm-type animals are a danger factor in causing the post-flood clearance and water pollution situation.

So the message should now be clear. Write simple active sentences, outmaneuvering all passive eddies, all shallow *is*'s, *ofs*, *whichs*, and *thats*, all overlappings, all rocky clusters of nouns: they take you off your course, delay your delivery, and wreck many a straight and gallant thought.

## AVOID EXCESSIVE DISTINCTIONS AND DEFINITIONS

Too many distinctions, too many nouns, and too much Latin make pea soup:

> Reading is a processing skill of symbolic reasoning sustained by the interfacilitation of an intricate hierarchy of substrata factors that have been mobilized as a psychological working system and pressed into service in accordance with the purpose of the reader.

This comes from an educator with the wrong kind of education. He is saying:

> Reading is a process of symbolic reasoning aided by an intricate network of ideas and motives. [16 *words for* 40]

Except with crucial assumptions and implications (see 70–73), try *not* to define your terms. If you do, you are probably either evading the toil of finding the right word, or defining the obvious:

> Let us agree to use the word *signal* as an abbreviation for the phrase "the simplest kind of sign." (This agrees fairly well with the customary meaning of the word *signal*.)

That came from a renowned semanticist, an authority on the meanings of words. The customary meaning of a word *is* its meaning, and uncustomary meanings come only from careful punning. Don't underestimate your readers, as this semanticist did.

The definer of words is usually a bad writer. Our semanticist continues, trying to get his signals straight and grinding out about three parts sawdust to every one of meat. In the following excerpt, I have bracketed his sawdust. Read the sentence first as he wrote it: then read it again, omitting the bracketed words:

> The moral of such examples is that all intelligent criticism [of any instance] of language [in use] must begin with understanding [of] the motives [and purposes] of the speaker [in that situation].

Here, each of the bracketed phrases is already implied in the others. Attempting to be precise, the writer has beclouded himself. Naturally, the speaker would be "in that situation;" naturally, a sampling of language would be "an instance" of language "in use." *Motives* may not be *purposes*, but the difference here is insignificant. Our semanticist's next sentence deserves some kind of immortality. He means "Muddy language makes trouble":

> Unfortunately, the type of case that causes trouble in practice is that in which the kind of use made of language is not transparently clear
> . . . .

Clearly, transparency is hard. Writing is hard. It requires constant attention to meanings, and constant pruning. Count your words, and make your words count.

## SUGGESTIONS FOR EXERCISE

   ***1.*** *Clear up the blurred ideas and grammar in these sentences from students' papers and official prose, making each word say what it means and counting your words to make sure your version has fewer.*

   1. Tree pruning may be done in any season of the year. [11 words]
   2. After reading a dozen books, the subject is still as puzzling as ever. [13]
   3. They were unable to locate my check, as well as their cashier department. [13]

4. The courses listed herein are those which meet the college-level requirements which were stated above. [16]
5. Tapes can be used in the Audio Room by individual students for their suggested listening assignments. [16]
6. My counter was for refunds for which the customer had already paid for. [13]
7. Entrance was gained by means of the skylight. [8]
8. The reason we give this test is because we are anxious to know whether or not you have reflexes that are sufficiently fast to allow you to be a safe worker. [31]
9. Spring thaw makes roads most susceptible to pavement breakup. [9].

2. *If you happen to find in your textbooks, or elsewhere, a passage suffering from the passive voice, the of-and-which disease, the the-use-of contagion, and the noun habit (e.g., "which shows the effect of age and intelligence level upon the use of the reflexes and the emergence of child behavior difficulties"), rewrite it in clear English.*

3. *Recast these sentences in the active voice, clearing out all passive constructions, saving as many words as you can, and indicating the number saved:*

1. The particular topic chosen by the instructor for study in his section of English 2 must be approved by the Steering Committee. [Start with "The Steering Committee," and don't forget the economy of an apostrophe-*s*. I managed 14 words for 22.]
2. Avoidance of such blunders should not be considered a virtue for which the student is to be commended, any more than the student would be praised for not wiping his hands on the tablecloth or polishing his shoes with the guest towels. [Begin "We should not"; try *avoiding* for *avoidance*. I dropped *virtue* as redundant and scored 27 for 41.]
3. The first respect in which too much variation seems to exist is in the care with which writing assignments are made. ["First, care in assigning"—8 for 21.]
4. The remaining variations that will be mentioned are concerned not with the assignment of papers but with the marking and grading of them. ["Finally, I shall mention"—14 for 23.]
5. The difference between restrictives and nonrestrictives can also be better approached through a study of the different contours that mark the utterance of the two kinds of elements than through confusing attempts to differentiate the two by meaning. ["One can differentiate restrictives"—I managed 13 for 38. The writer is dead wrong, incidentally: meaning is the true differentiator. See 203–205.]

4.  *Eliminate the italicized words in the following passages, together with all their accompanying wordiness, and indicate the number of words saved (my figures again are merely guides; other solutions that come close are quite good).*

> 1.  *There is* a certain tendency to defend one's own position *which* will cause the opponent's argument *to be* ignored. [13 for 19]
> 2.  *It is* the other requirements *that* present obstacles, some *of which* may prove insurmountable in the teaching *of* certain subjects. [11 for 20]
> 3.  In the sort of literature-centered course being discussed here, *there is* usually a general understanding *that* themes will be based on the various literary works *that* are studied, the theory being *that* both the instruction in literature and *that* in writing will be made more effective by this interrelationship. [21 for 50]
> 4.  The person *whom* he met was an expert *who was* able to teach the fundamentals quickly. [13 for 16]
> 5.  They will take a pride *which is* wholly justifiable in being able to command a prose style *that is* lucid and supple. [13 for 22]

5.  *To culminate this chapter, clear up the wordiness, especially the italicized patches, in these two official statements, one from an eminent linguist and one from an eminent publisher.*

> 1.  The work *which is* reported *in this* study *is* an investigation *of* language *within* the social context *of the* community *in which it is* spoken. *It is* a study *of* a linguistic structure *which is* unusually complex, but no more than the social structure of the city *in which it* functions. [I tried two versions, as I chased out the *whichs*; 29 for 51, and 22 for 51.]
> 2.  Methods *which are* unique to the historian *are illustrated* throughout the volume *in order* to show how history *is written* and how historians work. The historian's approach to his subject, *which* leads to the asking of provocative questions and to a new understanding of complex events, situations, and personalities, *is probed.* The manner *in which* the historian reduces masses of chaotic fact—and occasional fancy—to reliable meaning, and the way *in which* he formulates explanations and tests them *is examined* and *clarified* for the student. *It is its* emphasis on historical method *which* distinguishes this book from other source readings in western civilization. The problems *which are examined* concern *themselves with* subjects *which are dealt with by* most courses in western civilization. [66 for 123. The all-time winner from a student is 45 words.]

# 9
## Words

Here is the word. Sesquipedalian or short, magniloquent or low, Latin or Anglo-Saxon, Celtic, Danish, French, Spanish, Indian, Hindustani, Dutch, Italian, Portuguese, Choctaw, Swahili, Chinese, Hebrew, Turkish, Greek—English contains them all, a million words at our disposal, if we are disposed to use them. No language is richer than English. But our spoken vocabularies average only about 2,800 words; our expository vocabularies probably fewer than 8,000. We all have a way to go to possess our heritage.

## VOCABULARY

### Build Your Stock Systematically

If you can increase your hoard, you increase your chances of finding the right word when you need it. Read as widely as you can, and look words up the second or third time you meet them. I once knew a man who swore he learned three new words a day from his reading by using each at least once in conversation. I didn't ask him about *polyphiloprogenitive* or *antidisestablishmentarianism*. It depends a little on the crowd. But the idea is sound. The bigger the vocabulary, the more various the ideas one can get across with it—the more the shades and intensities of meaning.

The big vocabulary also needs the little word. The vocabularian often stands on a Latin cloud and forgets the Anglo-Saxon ground—the common ground between writer and audience. So do not forget the little things, the *stuff, lint, get, twig, snap, go, mud, coax*. Hundreds of small words not in immediate vogue can refresh your vocabulary. The Norse and Anglo-Saxon adjectives in -y (*muggy, scrawny, drowsy*), for instance, rarely appear in sober print. The minute the beginner tries to sound dignified, in comes a misty layer of words a few feet off the ground and nowhere near heaven, the same two dozen or so, most of them verbs. One or two will do no harm, but any accumulation is fatal—words like *depart* instead of *go*. Avoid the big ones; go for the little ones after the dash:

| | |
|---|---|
| accompany—go with | place—put |
| appeared—looked *or* seemed | possess—have |
| arrive—come | prepare—get ready |
| become—get | questioned—asked |
| cause—make | receive—get |
| cease—stop | relate—tell |
| complete—finish | remain—stay |
| continue—keep on | remove—take off |
| delve—dig | retire—go to bed |
| discover—find | return—go back |
| indicate—say | secure—get |
| individual—person | transform—change |
| locate—find | verify—check |

*Persons* for *people* is also faintly stuffy. I add one treasured noun: *manner* for *way*. The question, as always, is one of meaning. *Manner* is something with a flourish; *way* is the usual way. But the beginner makes no distinction, losing the normal *way* and the meaning in a false flourish of *manners*. Similarly, "She *placed* her keys on the table" is usually not what the writer means (*place* connotes *arrange*). *Delve* is something that happens only when students try to dig. *Get* and *got* may be too colloquial for constant use, but a discreet one or two can limber many a stiff sentence. Therefore, use the elegant Latin along with the commonplace Anglo-Saxon, but shun the frayed gentility of *secure* and *place* and *remain*.

Through the centuries, English has added Latin derivatives alongside the Anglo-Saxon words already there, keeping the old with the new: after the Anglo-Saxon *deor* (now *deer*) came the *beast* and then the *brute*, both from Latin through French, and the *animal* straight from Rome. We have the Anglo-Saxon *cow*, *sheep*, and *pig* alongside Latin (through French) *beef*, *mutton*, and *pork*. Although we use more Anglo-Saxon in assembling our sentences (*to*, *by*, *with*, *though*, *is*), well over half our total vocabulary comes one way or another from Latin. The things of this world tend to be Anglo-Saxon (*man*, *house*, *stone*, *wind*, *rain*); the abstract qualities, Latin and French (*value*, *duty*, *contemplation*).

Most of our big words are Latin and Greek. Your reading acquaints you with them; your dictionary will show you their prefixes and roots. Learn the common prefixes and roots (see Exercise 3 at the end of this chapter), and you can handle all kinds of foreigners at first encounter: *con-cession* (going along with), *ex-clude* (lock out), *pre-fer* (carry before), *sub-version* (turning under), *trans-late* (carry across), *claustro-phobia* (dread of being locked in), *hydro-phobia* (dread of water), *ailuro-philia* (love of cats), *megalo-cephalic* (big-headed), *micro-meter* (little measurer). You can even, for fun, coin a word to suit the occasion: *megalopede* (big-footed). You can remember that *intramural* means "within the (college) walls," and that "intermural sports," which is the frequent mispronunciation and misspelling, would mean something like "wall battling wall," a physical absurdity.

Besides owning a good dictionary, you should refer, with caution, to a thesaurus, a treasury of synonyms ("together-names"), in which you can find the word you couldn't think of; the danger lies in raiding this treasury too enthusiastically. Checking for meaning in a dictionary will help assure that you have expanded, not distorted, your vocabulary.

## ABSTRACT AND CONCRETE

### Learn Their Powers, Separate and Combined

Every good stylist has perceived, in one way or another, the distinction between the abstract and the concrete. Tangible things—things we can touch—are "concrete"; their qualities, along with all our emotional, intellectual, and spiritual states, are "abstract." The rule for a good style is to be as concrete as you can, to illustrate tangibly your general propositions, to use *shoes* and *ships* and *sealing wax* instead of *commercial concomitants*.

But abstraction, a "drawing out from," is the very nature of thought. Thought moves from concrete to abstract. In fact, *all* words are abstractions. *Stick* is a generalization of all sticks, the crooked and the straight, the long and the short, the peeled and the shaggy. No word fits its object like a glove because words are not things: words represent ideas of things. They are the means by which we class eggs and tents and trees so that we can handle them as ideas—not as actual things but as *kinds* or *classes* of things.

Abstract words can attain a power of their own, as the rhetorician heightens attention to their meanings. This ability, of course, does not come easily or soon. I repeat, you need to be as concrete as you can, to illustrate tangibly, and to pin your abstractions down to specifics. But once you have learned this, you can move on to the rhetoric of abstraction, which is a kind of squeezing of abstract words for their specific juice.

Lincoln does exactly this when he concentrates on *dedication* six times within the ten sentences of his dedication at Gettysburg: "We have come to *dedicate*. . . . It is rather for us to be here *dedicated*. . . ." Similarly,

Eliot refers to "faces / Distracted from distraction by distraction" (*Four Quartets*). Abstractions can, in fact, operate beautifully as specifics: "As a knight, Richard the Lion-Hearted was a *triumph*; as a king, he was a *disaster*." Many rhetorical patterns likewise concentrate on abstract essences:

> . . . tribulation works patience, and patience experience, and experience hope. (Rom. 5.3–4)
> The humble are proud of their humility.
> Care in your youth so you may live without care.

An able writer like Samuel Johnson can make a virtual poetry of abstractions as he alliterates and balances them against each other (I have capitalized the alliterations and italicized the balances):

> Dryden's performances were always hasty, either *Excited* by some *External occasion*, or *Extorted* by some *domestic necessity*; he *ComPosed without Consideration* and *Published without Correction*.

Notice especially how *excited* ("called forth") and *extorted* ("twisted out"), so alike in sound and form, so alike in making Dryden write, nevertheless contrast their opposite essential meanings. So before we disparage abstraction, we should acknowledge its rhetorical power, and we should understand that it is an essential distillation, a primary and natural and continual mental process. Without it, we could not make four of two and two. So we make abstractions of abstractions to handle bigger and bigger groups of ideas. *Egg* becomes *food*, and *food* becomes *nourishment*. We also classify all the psychic and physical qualities we can recognize: *candor, truth, anger, beauty, negligence, temperament*. But because our thoughts drift upward, we need always to look for the word that will bring them nearer earth, that will make our abstractions seem visible and tangible, that will make them graspable—mentioning a *handle*, or a *pin*, or an *egg*, alongside our abstraction, for instance.

But the writer's ultimate skill perhaps lies in making a single object represent its whole abstract class. I have paired each abstraction below with its concrete translation:

> *Friendliness* is the salesperson's best asset.
> A *smile* is the salesperson's best asset.
> *Administration of proper proteins* might have saved John Keats.
> A *good steak* might have saved John Keats.
> To *understand* the world by *observing all of its geological details* . . .
> To *see* the world in *a grain of sand* . . .

## DENOTATION AND CONNOTATION

Denotation is the concrete shade of meaning for the general abstract con-notation. When we look up synonyms in our dictionary—*shake, tremble, quake, quiver, shiver, shudder, wobble*—we see that all of them specify, or *denote*, the same thing: a shaking motion. But each also *connotes* a differ-ent kind of shake. We move from the *denotation*, "a shaking," to the *con-notations* of different shakings. These connotations have certain emotional attachments: *tremble* (fear), *quiver* (excitement), *shiver* (coldness), *shudder* (horror), *wobble* (imbalance). In short, words *denote* things, acts, moods, whatever: *tree, house, running, anger*. But they also *connote* an attitude toward these things. *Tree* is a purely neutral denotation, but *oak* connotes sturdiness and *willow* sadness, in addition to denoting different trees. Contexts also add connotations. *Christ died on the tree*, for instance, con-notes the whole expanse of agony and sacrifice with which medieval Christianity endowed the word. *A House Is Not a Home*, wrote a certain lady, playing on the warm connotation of *home* and a specific denotation: a house of prostitution. *Woman* and *lady* both denote the human female, but also carry connotations awakened in differing contexts:

> A *woman* usually outlives a man. (Denotation)
> She is a very able *woman*. (Connotation positive)
> She is his *woman*. (Connotation negative)
> She acts more like a *lady* than a *lady* of pleasure. (Connotations plus and minus)

Usage changes denotations: *a gay party* changes from a festive to a homo-sexual gathering. Usage and contexts also change connotations. *Negro*, once polite and then taboo for the once impolite *black*, is now moving again toward acceptance. *Chairman*, once a neutral denoter, now has acquired enough negative connotations to change a number of letterheads and signatures to *chairperson*. Even the denotative *chairwoman* has picked up negative connotations.

## EUPHEMISM

Substituting positive for negative connotations is *euphemism* ("good speak-ing"). Ironically, it is an effective kind of understatement: "She drove *a lit-tle fast*"; "He *imbibed occasionally*." But it also grows straight and unadorned from our social tact as we avoid hurting others and from our private defenses as we sugarcoat our shortcomings. We constantly say *passed away* for *died* and, with our pets, *put to sleep* for *killed*. A cripple is a *handicapped person*. Dull children go to classes for *exceptional students*. Politics, as George Orwell points out, is a constant game of euphemism to cover mistakes and atrocities:

> Things like the continuance of British rule in India, the Russian purges and deportations, the dropping of the atomic bombs on Japan, can indeed be defended, but only by arguments which are too brutal for most people to face, and which do not square with the professed aims of political parties. Thus political language has to consist largely of euphemism, question-begging, and sheer cloudy vagueness. Defenceless villages are bombarded from the air, the inhabitants driven out into the countryside, the cattle machine-gunned, the huts set on fire with incendiary bullets: this is called *pacification*. Millions of peasants are robbed of their farms and sent trudging along the roads with no more than they can carry: this is called *transfer of population* or *rectification of frontiers*. People are imprisoned for years without trial, or shot in the back of the neck, or sent to die of scurvy in Arctic lumber camps: this is called *elimination of unreliable elements*.*

Because euphemism veils stark particulars in generality, we should steer clear of euphemisms if we can, except for irony. Give the particulars as clearly as possible without hurting or antagonizing your readers. Your writing, as Orwell suggests, will be livelier and truer.

## METAPHOR

### Bring Your Words to Life

As you have probably noticed, I frequently use metaphors—the most useful way of making our abstractions concrete. The word is Greek for "transfer" (*meta* equals *trans* equals *across*; *phor* equals *fer* equals *ferry*). Metaphors illustrate our general ideas at a single stroke. Many of our common words are metaphors, *grasp* for "understanding," for instance, which compares the mind to something with hands, *transferring* the physical picture of the clutching hand to the invisible mental act.

---

*From "Politics and the English Language" from *Shooting an Elephant and Other Essays*. Copyright 1950 by Sonia Brownell Orwell, renewed © 1978 by Sonia Pitt-Rivers.

Metaphor seems to work at about four levels, each with a different clarity and force. Suppose you wrote "he swelled and displayed his finery." You have transferred to a man the qualities of a peacock to make his appearance and personality vivid. You have chosen one of the four ways to make this transfer (I italicize the distinguishing signals):

|  |  |
|---|---|
| I. SIMILE | He was *like* a peacock. |
|  | He displayed himself *as* a peacock does. |
|  | He displayed himself *as if* he were a peacock. |
| II. PLAIN METAPHOR: | He *was* a peacock. |
| III. IMPLIED METAPHOR: | He swelled and displayed his finery. |
|  | He swelled, and ruffled his plumage. |
|  | He swelled, ruffling his plumage. |
| IV. DEAD METAPHOR: | He strutted. |

## I. Simile

The simile is the most obvious form the metaphor can take and hence would seem elementary. But it has powers of its own, particularly where the writer seems to be trying urgently to express the inexpressible, comparing his subject to several different possibilities, no one wholly adequate. In *The Sound and the Fury*, Faulkner thus describes two jaybirds (my italics):

> [they] whirled up on the blast *like gaudy scraps of cloth or paper* and lodged in the mulberries, . . . screaming into the wind that *ripped* their harsh cries onward and away *like scraps of paper or of cloth* in turn.

The simile has a high poetic energy. D. H. Lawrence uses it frequently, as here in *The Plumed Serpent* (my italics):

> The lake was quite black, *like a great pit*. The wind suddenly blew with violence, with a strange ripping sound in the mango trees, *as if some membrane in the air were being ripped*.

Derek Walcott heightens his extended metaphor with a charge of simile (my italics):

> Prose is the squire of conduct, poetry the knight
> who leans into the flaming dragon with a pen's
>     lance,

is almost unhorsed *like a picador,* but tilts
straight
in the saddle.\*

## II. Plain Metaphor

The plain metaphor makes its comparison in one imaginative leap. It is shorthand for "as if he were a peacock"; it pretends, by exaggeration (*hyperbole*), that he *is* a peacock. We move instinctively to this kind of exaggerated comparison as we try to convey our impressions with all their emotional impact. "He was a maniac at Frisbee," we might say, or "a dynamo." The metaphor is probably our most common figure of speech: *the pigs, the swine, a plum, a gem, a phantom of delight, a shot in the arm.* It may be humorous or bitter; it may be simply and aptly visual: "The road was a ribbon of silver." Thoreau extends a metaphor through several sentences in one of his most famous passages:

> Time is but a stream I go a-fishing in. I drink at it; but while I drink I see the sandy bottom and detect how shallow it is. Its thin current slides away, but eternity remains. I would drink deeper; fish in the sky, whose bottom is pebbly with stars.

## III. Implied Metaphor

The implied metaphor is even more widely used. It operates most often among the verbs, as in *swelled, displayed,* and *ruffled,* the verbs suggesting "peacock." Most ideas can suggest analogues of physical processes or natural history. Give your television system *tentacles* reaching into every home, and you have compared TV to an octopus, with all its lethal and wiry suggestions. You can have your school spirit *fall below zero,* and you have implied that your school spirit is like temperature, registered on a thermometer in a sudden chill. Malcolm Cowley writes metaphorically about Hawthorne's style, first in a direct simile (*like a footprint*) and then in a metaphor implying that phrases are people walking at different speeds:

> He dreamed in words, while walking along the seashore or under the pines, till the words fitted themselves to his stride. The result was that his eighteenth-century English developed into a natural, a *walked,* style, with a phrase for every step and a comma after every phrase like a footprint in the sand. Sometimes the phrases hurry, sometimes they loiter, sometimes they march to drums.†

---

\*From "Italian Eclogues," *The New York Review of Books,* Aug. 8, 1996, p. 8.
†*The Portable Hawthorne* (New York: Viking, 1948).

### IV. Dead Metaphor

The art of resuscitation is the metaphorist's finest skill. It comes from liking words and paying attention to what they say. Simply add onto the dead
metaphor enough implied metaphors to get the circulation going again: *He
strutted, swelling and ruffling his plumage*. *He strutted* means by itself "walked
in a pompous manner." By bringing the metaphor back to life, we keep the
general meaning but also restore the physical picture of a peacock puffing
up and spreading his feathers. We recognize *strut* concretely and truly for
the first time. We know the word, and we know the man. We have an
image of him, a posture strongly suggestive of a peacock.

Perhaps the best dead metaphors to revive are those in proverbial
clichés. See what Thoreau does (in his *Journal*) with *spur of the moment*:

> **I feel the spur of the moment thrust deep into my side. The present
> is an inexorable rider.**

Or again, when in *Walden* he speaks of wanting "to improve *the nick of time*,
and notch it on my stick too," and of not being *thrown off the track* "by
every nutshell and mosquito's wing that falls on the rails." In each case, he
takes the proverbial phrase literally and physically, adding an attribute or
two to bring the old metaphor back alive.

You can go too far, of course. Your metaphors can be too thick and
vivid, and the obvious pun brings a howl of protest. I have myself advised
scholars against metaphors because they are so often overworked and so
often tangled in physical impossibilities, becoming "mixed" metaphors.
"The violent population explosion has paved the way for new intellectual
growth" looks pretty good—until you realize that explosions do not pave
and that new vegetation does not grow up through solid pavement.
Changing *paved* to *cleared* would clear the confusion. "He will have a hard
road to hoe" confuses two colloquial metaphors into physical absurdity.
The metaphor, then, is your most potent device. It makes your thought concrete and your writing vivid. It tells in an instant how your subject looks to
you. But it is dangerous. It should be quiet, almost unnoticed, with all
details agreeing, and all absolutely consistent with the natural universe.

## ALLUSION

## Illuminate the Dim with a Familiar Light

Allusions also illustrate your general idea by referring it to something else,
making it take your reader as Grant took Richmond, making you the

Mickey Mantle of the essay, or the Mickey Mouse. Allusions depend on common knowledge. Like the metaphor, they illustrate the remote with the familiar—a familiar place, or event, or personage. "He looked . . . like a Japanese Humphrey Bogart," writes William Bittner of French author Albert Camus, and we instantly see a face like the one we know so well (a glance at Camus's picture confirms this allusion as surprisingly accurate). Perhaps the most effective allusions depend on a knowledge of literature. When Thoreau writes that "the winter of man's discontent was thawing as well as the earth," we get a secret pleasure from recognizing this as an allusive borrowing from the opening lines of Shakespeare's *Richard III:* "Now is the winter of our discontent / Made glorious summer by this sun of York." Thoreau flatters us by assuming we are as well read as he. We need not catch the allusion to enjoy his point, but if we catch it, we feel a sudden fellowship of knowledge with him. We now see the full metaphorical force, Thoreau's and Shakespeare's both, heightened as it is by our remembrance of Richard Crookback's twisted discontent, an allusive illustration of all our pitiful resentments now thawing with the spring.

Allusions can also be humorous. The hero of Peter De Vries's "The Vale of Laughter," alluding to Lot's wife looking back on Sodom (Gen. 19:26) as he contemplates adultery for a moment, decides on the path toward home and honor:

> If you look back, you turn into a pillar of salt. If you look ahead, you turn into a pillar of society.

# DICTION

## Reach for Both the High and the Low

"What we need is a mixed diction," said Aristotle, and his point remains true 24 centuries and several languages later. The aim of style, he says, is to be clear but distinguished. For clarity, we need common, current words; but, used alone, these are commonplace, and as ephemeral as everyday talk. For distinction, we need words not heard every minute, unusual words, large words, foreign words, metaphors; but used alone, these become bogs, vapors, or at worst, gibberish. What we need is a diction that weds the popular with the dignified, the clear current with the sedgy margins of language and thought.

Not too low, not too high; not too simple, not too hard—an easy breadth of idea and vocabulary. English is peculiarly well endowed for this Aristotelian mixture. The long abstract Latin words and the short concrete

Anglo-Saxon ones give you all the range you need. For most of your ideas, you can find Latin and Anglo-Saxon partners. In fact, for many ideas, you can find a whole spectrum of synonyms from Latin through French to Anglo-Saxon, from general to specific—from *intrepidity* to *fortitude* to *valor* to *courage* to *bravery* to *pluck* to *guts*. Each of these *denotes* or specifies the same thing: being brave. But each has a different *connotation*, or aura of meaning (see 128). You can choose the high word for high effect, or you can get tough with Anglo-Saxon specifics. But you do not want all Anglo-Saxon, and you must especially guard against sobriety's luring you into all Latin. Tune your diction agreeably between the two extremes.

Indeed, the two extremes generate incomparable zip when tumbled side by side, as in *incomparable zip, inconsequential snip, megalomaniacal creep*, and the like. Rhythm and surprise conspire to set up the huge adjective first and then to add the small noun, like a monumental kick. Here is a passage from Edward Dahlberg's *Can These Bones Live*, which I opened completely at random to see how the large fell with the small (my italics):

> Christ walks on a *visionary sea*; Myshkin . . . has his ecstatic premonition of infinity when he has an *epileptic fit*. We know the inward size of an artist by his *dimensional thirsts*. . . .

This mixing of large Latin and small Anglo-Saxon, as John Crowe Ransom has noted, is what gives Shakespeare much of his power:

> This my hand will rather
> The multitudinous seas incarnadine,
> Making the green one red.

The short Anglo-Saxon *seas* works sharply between the two magnificent Latin words, as do the three short Anglo-Saxons that bring the big passage to rest, contrasting the Anglo-Saxon *red* with its big Latin kin, *incarnadine*. William Faulkner, who soaked himself in Shakespeare, gets much the same power from the same mixture. He is describing a very old black woman in *The Sound and the Fury* (the title itself comes from Shakespeare's *Macbeth*, the source of the *multitudinous seas* passage). She has been fat, but now she is wrinkled and completely shrunken except for her stomach:

> . . . a paunch almost dropsical, as though muscle and tissue had been courage or fortitude which the days or the years had consumed

until only the indomitable skeleton was left rising like a ruin or a landmark above the somnolent and impervious guts . . . .

The impact of that short, ugly Anglo-Saxon *guts*, with its slang metaphorical pun, is almost unbearably moving. And the impact would be nothing, the effect slurring, without the grand Latin preparation.

A good diction takes work. It exploits the natural but does not come naturally. It demands a wary eye for the way meanings sprout, and it demands the courage to prune. It has the warmth of human concern. It is a cut above the commonplace, a cut above the inaccuracies and circumlocutions of speech, yet within easy reach. Clarity is the first aim; economy, the second; grace, the third; dignity, the fourth. Our writing should be a little strange, a little out of the ordinary, a little beautiful, with words and phrases not met every day but seeming as right and natural as grass. A good diction takes care and cultivation.

It can be overcultivated. It may seem to call attention to itself rather than to its subject. Suddenly we are aware of the writer at work, and a little too pleased with himself or herself, reaching for the elegant cliché and the showy phrase. Some readers find this very fault with my own writing, though I do really try to saddle my maverick love of metaphor. If I strike you in this way, you can use me profitably as a bad example along with the following passage. I have italicized elements that individually may have a certain effectiveness, but that cumulatively become mannerism, as if the writer were watching himself gesture in a mirror. Some of his phrases are redundant; some are trite. Everything is somehow cozy and grandiose, and a little too nautical:

> *There's* little excitement *ashore* when merchant ships from *far-away* India, Nationalist China, or Egypt *knife through* the *gentle swells* of Virginia's Hampton Roads. This *unconcern* may simply reflect the *nonchalance* of people who live by *one of the world's great seaports.* Or perhaps *it's just* that *folk* who *dwell* in the *home towns* of atomic submarines and Mercury astronauts are not likely to be impressed by a visiting freighter, *from however distant a realm.* . . . *Upstream a bit* and also *to port*, the mouth of the Elizabeth River leads to Portsmouth and a major naval shipyard. *To starboard lies* Hampton, where at Langley Air Force Base the National Aeronautics and Space Administration prepares to send a man *into the heavens.*

| **SUGGESTIONS FOR EXERCISE** |

**1.** *As a warm-up, clear the preceding example of its overdone phrases.*

**2.** *Revise the following sentences to make them more vivid and distinct by replacing as many of the abstract terms as possible with concrete terms.*

1. For the better part of a year, she was without gainful employment.
2. Of the students who go to college outside their own state, 70 percent do not go back after completing their studies.
3. A sizable proportion of those people who use long-distance movers are large-corporation employees whose moving expenses are entirely underwritten by their companies.
4. His great-grandfather once ran successfully for high public office, but he never served because his opponent mortally wounded him in a duel with pistols.
5. There was a severe disturbance in Jackson prison one day in the spring—convicts, armed with makeshift weapons, took some of the prison personnel hostage.
6. Her husband had one extramarital relationship after another and finally disappeared with a hotel dining room employee in one of our larger midwestern cities.
7. Rejected by the military because of an impairment of his vision, Ernest became a journalist with a midwestern newspaper.
8. Disadvantaged people are often maltreated by the very social-service agencies ostensibly designed to help them.
9. The newspaper reported that a small foreign car had overturned on the expressway just north of town.
10. The new contract offers almost no change in the fringe-benefit package.

**3.** *Look up in your dictionary six of the Latin and Greek constituents listed below. Illustrate each with several English derivatives closely translated, as in these two examples:* con *(with)—convince (conquer with), conclude (shut with), concur (run with);* chron- *(time)—chronic (lasting a long time), chronicle (a record of the time), chronometer (time measurer).*

> LATIN: *a- (ab-), ad-, ante-, bene-, bi-, circum-, con-, contra-, di-(dis-), e- (ex-), in- (two meanings), inter-, intra-, mal-, multi-, ob-, per-, post-, pre-, pro-, retro-, semi-, sub- (sur-), super-, trans-, ultra-.*

> GREEK: *a- (an-), -agogue, allo-, anthropo-, anti-, apo-, arch-, auto-, batho-, bio-, cata-, cephalo-, chron-, -cracy, demo-, dia-, dyna-, dys-, ecto-, epi-, eu-, -gen, geo-, -gon, -gony, graph-,*

*gyn-, hemi-, hepta-, hetero-, hexa-, homo-, hydr-, hyper-, hypo-,
log-, mega-, -meter, micro-, mono-, morph-, -nomy, -nym,
-pathy, penta-, -phagy, phil-, -phobe (ia), -phone, poly-, pseudo-,
psyche-, -scope, soph-, stereo-, sym- (syn-), tele-, tetra-, theo-,
thermo-, tri-, zoo-.*

**4.** *Revise the following sentences so as to clear up the illogical or unnat-
ural connections in their metaphors and similes.*

1. The violent population explosion has paved the way for new
   intellectual growth.
2. The book causes a shock, like a bucket of icy water suddenly
   thrown on a fire.
3. The whole social fabric will become unstuck.
4. The tangled web of Jane's business crumbled under its own weight.
5. His last week had mirrored his future, like a hand writing on the
   wall.
6. The recent economic picture, which seemed to spell prosperity,
   has wilted beyond repair.
7. They were tickled to death by the thunderous applause.
8. Stream-of-consciousness fiction has gone out of phase with the
   new castles in the air of fantasy.
9. The murmured protests drifted from the convention floor to the
   podium, cracking the façade of her imperturbability.
10. Richard was ecstatic with his success. He had scaled the mountain
    of difficulties and from here on out he could sail with the breeze.
11. She pitches a high profile that sometimes backfires.

**5.** *Write a sentence for each of the following dead metaphors, bringing it
to life by adding implied metaphorical detail, as in "She bridled, snort-
ing and tossing her mane," or by adding a simile, as in "He was dead
wrong, laid out like a corpse on a slab."*

> dead center, pinned down, sharp as a tack, stick to, whined,
> purred, reflected, ran for office, yawned, take a course.

**6.** *Write a sentence for each of the following, in which you allude either
humorously or seriously to:*

1. A famous—or infamous—person (Caesar, Cleopatra, Napoleon,
   Barnum, Lincoln, Stalin, Picasso, Bogart)
2. A famous event (the Declaration of Independence, the Battle of
   Waterloo, the landing on Plymouth Rock, the Battle of the Bulge, the
   signing of the Magna Carta, Custer's Last Stand, the Watergate affair)
3. A notable place (Athens, Rome, Paris, London Bridge, Jerusalem,
   the Vatican)

4. This famous passage from Shakespeare, by quietly borrowing some of its phrases:

> To be, or not to be—that is the question:
> Whether 'tis nobler in the mind to suffer
> The slings and arrows of outrageous fortune,
> Or to take arms against a sea of troubles,
> And by opposing end them.

7. *Write a paragraph in which you mix your diction as effectively as you can, with the big Latin word and the little Anglo-Saxon word, the formal word and just the right touch of slang, working in at least two combinations of the extremes, on the pattern of* multitudinous seas, diversionary thrust, incomparable zip, *underlining these for your instructor's convenience.*

8. *Write a* TERRIBLE ESSAY. *Have some fun with this perennial favorite, in which you reinforce your sense for clear, figurative, and meaningful words by writing the muddiest and wordiest essay you can invent, gloriously working out all your bad habits. Organize in the usual way with a thesis, a good beginning, middle, and end, but parody the worst kind of sociological and bureaucratic prose. Here are the rules:*

   1. Put EVERYTHING in the passive voice.
   2. Modify nouns *only* with nouns, preferably in strings of three or four, never with adjectives: *governmental spending* becomes *government level spending;* an *excellent idea* becomes *quality program concept.*
   3. Use only big abstract nouns—as many *-tion*s as possible.
   4. Use no participles: not *dripping faucets* but *faucets which drip;* and use as many *which*s as possible.
   5. Use as many words as possible to say the least.
   6. Work in as many trite and wordy expressions as possible: *needless to say, all things being equal, due to the fact that, in terms of, as far as that is concerned.*
   7. Sprinkle heavily with *-wise*-type and *type-* type expressions, and say *hopefully* every three or four sentences, along with *near-perfect, near-hysterical,* and the other woolly *near*s.
   8. Compile and use a basic terrible vocabulary: *situation, aspect, function, factor, phase, process, procedure, utilize, the use of,* and so on. The class may well cooperate in this.

9. *Refine your sense of diction and meanings still further by writing an* IRONIC ESSAY, *saying the opposite of what you mean, as in "The party was a dazzling success," "The Rockheads are the solidest group in town," "Our team is the best in the West."*

# HANDBOOK

PART I: GRAMMAR

PART II:
PUNCTUATION, SPELLING,
CAPITALIZATION

PART III: GLOSSARY

# I The Trouble with Grammar

### AGREEMENT: SUBJECTS AND VERBS

Disagreement is our trouble—especially between subjects and verbs. The English *s* troubles dialect speakers and learners from other countries. In the present tense, right now, *s* makes singular verbs—*gets*, *goes*, *operates*—but, always, plural nouns—*grades*, *places*, *businesses*. The puzzled learner avoids the *s*, even in the basic verb *is*:

> When Joe *get* good *grade,* he *say* he happy.

When he means:

> When Joe *gets* good *grades,* he *says* he *is* [he's] happy.

Or he levels everything to *s*:

> They [I, you, he, she, it] knows horses goes faster than mules.

When he means

> They [I, you] know horses go faster than mules.

The trouble is that, with verbs, *s* signals only the third person singular (he, she, it), and only in the present tense:

**140**

| | SINGULAR | PLURAL |
|---|---|---|
| FIRST PERSON | I get | we get |
| SECOND PERSON | you get | you get |
| THIRD PERSON | he, she, it getS | they get |

The varied forms in our most frequent verb, *to be*, also cause trouble:

| | SINGULAR | PLURAL |
|---|---|---|
| FIRST PERSON | I am | we are |
| SECOND PERSON | you are | you are |
| THIRD PERSON | he, she, it is | they are |

Dialect speakers level this to *is* throughout—I *is*, you *is*, we *is*, they *is*—or to *be*, especially in the progressive forms: I *be* going, you *be* going, they *be* going.

So this is the most basic problem of agreement—matching singular subjects with singular verbs, plurals with plurals. First, find the verb because that names the action—*sways* in the following sentence: "The poplar tree *sways* in the wind, dropping yellow leaves on the lawn." Then ask *who* or *what* sways, and you have your simple subject: *tree*, a singular noun. Then make sure that your singular subject matches its singular verb. (Again, contrary to most nouns, singular verbs end in *s*—in the third person—"The actor performs; actors perform.") You will have little trouble except when subject and verb are far apart or when the number of the subject itself is doubtful. (Is *family* singular or plural? What about *none*? What about *neither he nor she?*)

> FAULTY: **Revision of their views about markets and averages *are* mandatory.**
>
> REVISED: **Revision of their views about markets and averages *is* mandatory.**

Subject and Verb Widely Separated

Sidestep the plural constructions that fall between your singular subject and its verb:

> FAULTY: **The *attention* of the students *wander* out the window.**
>
> REVISED: **The *attention* of the students *wanders* out the window.**
>
> FAULTY: **The *plaster*, as well as the floors, *need* repair.**
>
> REVISED: **The *plaster*, as well as the floors, *needs* repair.**

Mistaken Plurals

Collective nouns (*committee, jury, herd, group, family, kind, quartet*) are single units (plural in British usage); give them singular verbs or plural members:

<table>
<tr><td>Collective<br>Nouns</td><td>FAULTY: Her family were ready.<br>REVISED: Her family was ready.<br>FAULTY: The jury have disagreed among themselves.<br>REVISED: The jurors have disagreed among themselves.<br>FAULTY: These kind of muffins are delicious.<br>REVISED: These muffins are delicious.<br>REVISED: This kind of muffin is delicious.</td></tr>
</table>

Watch out for the indefinite pronouns—*each, neither, anyone, everyone, no one, none, everybody, nobody.* Each of these is (not *are*) singular in idea; yet each one flirts with the crowd from which it singles out its idea: each of *these*, either of *them*, none of *them*. Give all of them singular verbs.

Indefinite    *None* of these men *is* a failure.
Pronouns      *None* of the class, even the best prepared, *wants* the test.
              *Everybody,* including the high-school kids, *goes* to Andy's
                   Drive-In.
              *Neither* the right nor the left *supports* the issue.

*None of them are* is very common. From Shakespeare's time to ours, it has persisted alongside the more precise *none of them is*, which seems to have the edge in careful prose.

When one side of the *either-or* contrast is plural, you have a problem, conventionally solved by matching the verb to the nearer noun:

"Either–Or"    **Either the players or the coach *is* bad.**

Because *players is* disturbs some feelings for plurality, the best solution is probably to switch your nouns:

**Either the coach or the players *are* bad.**

When both sides of the contrast are plural, the verb is naturally also plural:

**Neither the rights of man nor the needs of the commonwealth *are* relevant to the question.**

Don't let a plural noun in the predicate lure you into a plural verb:

> FAULTY: His most faithful rooting *section are* his family and his girlfriend.
> REVISED: His most faithful rooting *section is* his family and his girlfriend.
> REVISED: His family and his girlfriend *are* his best rooting section.

## ALIGNING THE VERBS

Verbs have *tense* (past, present, future), *mood* (indicative, imperative, subjunctive), and *voice* (active, passive). These can sometimes slip out of line, as your thought slips, so a review should be useful here.

### Use the Tense That Best Expresses Your Idea

Each tense (from Latin *tempus*, meaning time) has its own virtues for expressing what you want your sentences to say. Use the *present tense*, of course, to express present action: "Now she *knows*. She *is leaving*." Use the present also for habitual action: "He *sees* her every day," and for describing literary events: "Hamlet *finds* the king praying, but he *is* unable to act; he *lets* the opportunity slip." And use the present tense to express timeless facts: "The Greeks knew that the world *is* round." The present can also serve for the future: "Classes begin next Monday." Apply the *past tense* to all action before the present:

> One day I *was watching* television when the phone *rang*. It *was* the police.
> In the center of the cracked façade, the door *sagged*. Rubble *lay* all around the foundations.

Use the *future tense* for action expected after the present:

> He *will finish* it next year.
> When he *finishes* next year, . . . [The present functioning as future]
> He *is going to finish* it next year. [The "present progressive" *is going* plus an infinitive, such as *to finish*, commonly expresses the future.]

Use the *present perfect tense* for action completed ("perfected") but relevant to the present moment:

> I *have gone* there before.
> He *has sung* 40 concerts.
> She *has driven* there every day.

Use the *past perfect tense* to express "the past of the past":

> "When we *arrived* [past], they *had finished* [past perfect]."

Similarly, use the *future perfect tense* to express "the past of the future":

> When we *arrive* [future], they *will have finished.* [future perfect]
> You *will have worked* 30 hours by Christmas. [future perfect]
> The flare *will signal* [future] that he *has started.* [perfect]

Set your tense and then move your readers clearly forward or back from it as your thought requires:

Shifting Tenses    **Hamlet *finds* the king praying. He *had sworn* instant revenge the night before, but he *will achieve* it only by accident and about a week later. Here he *is* unable to act; he *loses* his best opportunity.**

But avoid mixtures like this: "Hamlet *finds* the king praying, but he was unable to act; he *let* the opportunity slip." Here, all the verbs should be in the present, corresponding to *finds*.

Confusing the past tense of *lie* with the verb *lay* is a frequent error. *Lie* is intransitive, taking no object: *Lie* down; I *lie* down; I *lay* down yesterday; I have *lain* down often. *Lay* is transitive, taking an object: I *lay* carpets; I *laid* one yesterday; I have *laid* them often. When someone says incorrectly "He is *laying* down," ask yourself the impudent questions "Who is Down?" or "Is he laying goosefeathers?"—and you might remember to say, and write: "He is *lying* down."

## Irregular Verbs

The irregular verbs, such as *lie*, frequently slip into disagreement, not because of the third-person s, but because their past tense and past participle do not always match in the regular way: "She *played*; she has *played*. She *won*; she has *won*." Some of the irregulars also match: "He *bid*; he has *bid*." But most do not:

He *arose*.

He has *arisen*.

She *swam*.

She has *swum*.

Here are some to watch. Alternate forms are in parentheses. (Also see Glossary for *hanged, hung; lay, lie; rise, raise; set, sit*.)

arise, arose, arisen
awake, awoke, awaked (*but* was awakened)
bear, bore, borne
beat, beat, beaten
begin, began, begun
bid ("order"), bade, bidden
bid ("offer"), bid, bid
burst, burst, burst
drag, dragged (not drug), dragged
fit, fitted (fit, *especially intransitively*), fitted (*but* a fit person)
fling, flung, flung
get, got, got (gotten)
hang, hanged, hanged
hang, hung, hung
lay, laid, laid
lie, lay, lain

light, lit (lighted), lit (lighted)
prove, proved, proven (proved)
ride, rode, ridden
rise, rose, risen
set, set, set
sew, sewed, sewn (sewed)
shine ("glow"), shone, shone
shine ("polish"), shined, shined
show, showed, shown (showed)
shrink, shrank (shrunk), shrunk (shrunken)
sit, sat, sat
sow, sowed, sown (sowed)
spring, sprang, sprung
swim, swam, swum
swing, swung, swung
wake, woke (waked) waked
waken, wakened, wakened

## Keep Your Moods in Mind

The *indicative mood*, which indicates matters of fact (our usual verb and way of writing), and the *imperative mood*, which commands ("Do this," "Keep your moods in mind"), will give you no trouble. The *subjunctive mood*, which expresses an action or condition not asserted as actual fact, occasionally will. The conditional, provisional, wishful, suppositional ideas expressed by the subjunctive are usually subjoined (*subjunctus*, "yoked under") in subordinate clauses. The form of the verb is often plural and often in past tense, even though the subject is singular and the condition present or future.

> She looked as if she *were* confident.
> If I *were* you, Miles, I would ask her myself.
> If this *be* error, and upon me [*be*] proved . . .
> *Had* she *been* sure, she would have said so.
> I demand that he *make* restitution.
> I move that the nominations *be closed* and that the secretary
>     *cast* a unanimous ballot.

Don't let *would have* (colloquial *would've*) seep into your conditional clause from your main clause:

> FAULTY: If he *would have known,* he never would have said that.
> REVISED: If he *had known,* he never would have said that.
> REVISED: *Had* he *known,* he never would have said that.

Be careful not to write *would of* or *should of* for *would have* (*would've*) or *should have* (*should've*).

## Beware of Faulty Predication

Your verbs can mismatch your subjects in unsuspected ways. An active verb, for instance, can say that your subject is doing what it cannot do:

> FAULTY: The joy of cooking constantly crammed her refrigerator.

The impersonal, abstract joy doesn't do the cramming; she does.

> REVISED: Her joy in cooking constantly made her cram her
>     refrigerator.
> FAULTY: Your computer screen corrects your errors in a wink.

The inert screen cannot correct anything; you with your computer do the correcting that appears on the screen.

> REVISED: With your computer, you can correct your errors in a
>     wink.

Linking verbs can throw you off. *Is* is the universal work horse, along with other intransitives like *seems.* But some active verbs also serve as inactive links: *feel, look, taste, smell.* The link makes A = B—makes the subject equal its complement on the other side of the sign: "A cat is a domestic feline." Something concrete equals something concrete; an abstract must equal an abstract. Again, you might erroneously link an abstract quality with a concrete complement:

FAULTY: **Enthusiasm is an action helpful in your work.**

Enthusiasm, an abstract quality, usually does show up in some activity, but it is not itself an action.

REVISED: **Enthusiasm is a gift helpful in your work.**

Or again, a general subject like *kinds* on the near side of the linking verb *were* does not equal the specifics on the other side.

FAULTY: **The kinds of things they most enjoyed were sailing, snorkeling, and lying on the beach.**
REVISED: **The things they enjoyed most were sailing, snorkeling, and lying on the beach.**

Transitive verbs can also make faulty predications, pairing a subject with an object that does not logically suit it:

FAULTY: **The anonymous author makes the question of libel difficult.**

The author isn't making the question.

REVISED: **The author's anonymity makes the question of libel difficult.**

## Don't Mix Active and Passive Voice

Let's take one parting shot at our friend the passive voice. Avoid mis-aligning active with passive in the same sentence:

As she *entered* the room, muttering *was heard* [she *heard*].          Mixed Voices
After they *laid out* the pattern, electric shears *were used* [they *used* electric shears].

You can also think of this as an awkward shift of subject, from *she* to *muttering*, from *they* to *shears*. Here is a slippery sample, where the subject stays the same:

Past Tense; Not<br>Passive Voice

FAULTY: This plan *reduces* taxes and *has been used* successfully in three other cities.

REVISED: This plan *reduces* taxes and *has been* successful in three other cities.

REVISED: This plan *reduces* taxes and *has proved* workable in three other cities.

## AGREEMENT: PRONOUNS

## Match Your Pronouns to What They Stand For

Pronouns stand for (*pro*) nouns. They *refer* to nouns already expressed (*antecedents*), or they stand for conceptions (people, things, ideas) already established or implied, as in "*None of them* is perfect." Pronouns must agree with the singular and plural ideas they represent and must stand clearly as subjects or objects.

When a relative pronoun (*who, which, that*) is the subject of a clause, it takes a singular verb if its antecedent is singular, a plural verb if its antecedent is plural:

Phil is the only *one* of our swimmers WHO *has* won three gold medals. [The antecedent is *one,* not *swimmers.*]
Phil is one of the best *swimmers* WHO *have* ever been on the team. [The antecedent is *swimmers,* not *one.*]

Pronouns may stand either as subjects or objects of the action, and their form changes accordingly.

## Use Nominative Pronouns for Nominative Functions

Those pronouns in the predicate that refer to, or complement, the subject are troublesome; keep them nominative:

Subjective<br>Complement

He discovered that it was *I.*
It was *they* who signed the treaty.

This is she.
It is I.

Another example is that of the pronoun in *apposition* with the subject (that is, *positioned near, applied to*, and meaning the same thing as the subject):

*We* students would rather talk than sleep.                                  Apposition with Subject

After *than* and *as*, the pronoun is usually the subject of an implied verb:

She is taller than *I* [am].
You are as bright as *he* [is].
She loves you as much as *I* [do].                                          Implied Verb

But note: "She loves you as much as [she loves] *me*." Match your pronouns to what they stand for, subjects for subjects, objects for objects. (But a caution: use an objective pronoun as the subject of an infinitive.) See 192.

Use a nominative pronoun as subject of a noun clause. This is the trickiest of pronominal problems because the subject of the clause also looks like the object of the main verb:

FAULTY: The sergeant asked *whomever* did it to step forward.
REVISED: The sergeant asked *whoever* did it to step forward.

Similarly, parenthetical remarks like *I think*, *he says*, and *we believe* often make pronouns seem objects when they are actually subjects:

FAULTY: Ellen is the girl *whom* I think *will succeed.*
REVISED: Ellen is the girl *who* I think *will succeed.*

## Use Objective Pronouns for Objective Functions

Compound objects give most of the trouble:

They want you and *I* and the working poor to provide them with everything.
                                        **Edward Koch, when Mayor of New York**

Want *I?* No! Want *me*. This is the test to keep you straight. Try the pronoun by itself to hear the disagreement: "invited *I*," "for *I*," "between *I*," "sent *he*." The following examples are all correct:

Compound
Objects

They want you and *me* and the working poor . . . .
The mayor invited my wife and *me* to dinner. [*not* my wife and I]
Can you play tennis with Charlie and *me?* [*not* with Charlie and I]
Between *her* and *me,* an understanding grew.
They sent it to Stuart and *him.*
. . . for you and *me.*

Again, *see if the pronoun would stand by itself* ("for I"? No, *for me*):

FAULTY: The credit goes to *he* who tries. ["to he"?]
REVISED: The credit goes to *him* who tries.

Pronouns in apposition with objects must themselves be objective:

Apposition with
Object

FAULTY: The mayor complimented us both—Bill and *I.*
REVISED: The mayor complimented us both—Bill and *me.*
FAULTY: She gave the advice specifically to us—Helen and *I.*
REVISED: She gave the advice specifically to us—Helen and *me.*
FAULTY: Between us—Elaine and *I*—an understanding grew.
REVISED: Between us—Elaine and *me*—an understanding grew.
FAULTY: He would not think of letting *we* women help him.
REVISED: He would not think of letting *us* women help him.

Notice this one:

FAULTY: Will you please help Leonard and *I* find the manager?
REVISED: Will you please help Leonard and *me* find the manager?

*Leonard and me* are objective both as objects of the verb *help* and as subjects
of the shortened infinitive to *find.* Subjects of infinitives are always in the
objective case, as in "She saw *him* go"; "She helped *him* find his keys."

## Use a Possessive Pronoun Before a Gerund

Because gerunds are *-ing* words used as nouns, the pronouns attached to
them must say what they mean:

FAULTY: She disliked *him* hunting.
REVISED: She disliked *his* hunting.

The object of her dislike is not *him* but *hunting.*

## Keep Your Antecedents Clear

If an antecedent is missing, ambiguous, vague, or remote, the pronoun will suffer from "faulty reference" and disagreement.

> MISSING: In Texas *they* produce a lot of oil.
> REVISED: Texas produces a lot of oil.
> AMBIGUOUS: Paul smashed into a woman's *car who* was visiting his sister.
> REVISED: Paul smashed into the car of a *woman* visiting his sister.
> VAGUE: Because Ann had never spoken before an audience, she was afraid of *it*.
> REVISED: Because Ann had never spoken before an audience, she was afraid.
> REMOTE: The castle was built in 1537. The rooms and furnishings are carefully kept up, but the entrance is now guarded by a coin-fed turnstile. *It* still belongs to the Earl.
> REVISED: The castle, which still belongs to the Earl, was built in 1537. The rooms and furnishings are carefully kept up, but the entrance is now guarded by a coin-fed turnstile.

*This* poses a special problem, especially when heading a sentence ("This is a special problem"). Many good stylists insist that every *this* refer back to a specific noun—*report* in the following example:

> The commission submitted its *report. This* proved windy, evasive, and ineffectual.                    "This"

Others occasionally allow (as I do) a more colloquial *this*, referring back more broadly:

> The commission submitted its report. This ended the matter.

## Give an Indefinite or General Antecedent a Singular Pronoun

> FAULTY: Each of the students hoped to follow in *their* teacher's footsteps.
> REVISED: Each of the students hoped to follow in *his or her* teacher's footsteps.
> REVISED: *All* of the students hoped to follow in *their* teacher's footsteps. [Here, we have a single class.]

FAULTY: If the *government* dares to face the new philosophy, *they* should declare *themselves*.

REVISED: If the *government* dares to face the new philosophy, *it* should declare *itself*.

## Keep Person and Number in Agreement

Don't slip from person to person (*I* to *they*); don't fall among singulars and plurals—or you will have bad references:

FAULTY: *They* have reached an age when *you* should know better.

REVISED: *They* have reached an age when *they* should know better.

FAULT: A motion *picture* can improve upon a book, but *they* usually do not.

REVISED: A motion *picture* can improve upon a book, but *it* usually does not.

## MODIFIERS MISUSED AND MISPLACED

## Keep Your Adjectives and Adverbs Straight

The adjective sometimes wrongly crowds out the adverb: "He played a *real conservative game*." And the adverb sometimes steals the adjective's place, especially when the linking verb looks transitive but isn't (*feels, looks, tastes, smells*), making the sense wrong: "He feels *badly*" (adverb) means incompetence, not misery. The cure is to modify your nouns with adjectives and everything else with adverbs:

He played a *really* conservative game. [adverb]
He feels *bad*. [adjective]
This tastes *good*. [adjective]
I feel *good*. [adjective—spirit]
I feel *well*. [adjective—health]
This works *well*. [adverb]

Some words serve both as adjectives and adverbs: *early, late, near, far, hard, only, little, right, wrong, straight, well, better, best, fast,* for example, to be squeezed for their juice.

Think *little* of *little* things.

*Near* is a hard case, serving as an adjective (*the near future*) and as an adverb of place (*near the barn*), and then also trying to serve for *nearly*, the adverb of degree:

> FAULTY: We are nowhere *near* knowledgeable enough.
> REVISED: We are not *nearly* knowledgeable enough.
> FAULTY: It was a *near* treasonous statement.
> REVISED: It was a *nearly* treasonous statement.
> FAULTY: With Dodge, he has a tie of *near*-filial rapport.
> REVISED: With Dodge, he has an *almost* filial rapport.

*Slow* has a long history as an adverb, but *slowly* keeps the upper hand in print. Notice that adverbs usually go after, and adjectives before:

> The *slow* freight went *slowly*.

## Make Your Comparisons Complete

Ask yourself "Than what?"—when you find your sentences ending with a *greener* (adjective) or a *more smoothly* (adverb):

> FAULTY: The western plains are *flatter*.
> REVISED: The western plains are *flatter than* those east
>     of the Mississippi.
> FAULTY: He plays more *skillfully*.
> REVISED: He plays more *skillfully than* most boys his age.
> FAULTY: Jane told her more than Ellen.
> REVISED: Jane told her more than she told Ellen.
> FAULTY: His income is lower than a *busboy*.
> REVISED: His income is lower than a *busboy's*.

## Don't Let Your Modifiers Squint

Some modifiers squint in two directions at once. Place them to modify one thing only.

> FAULTY: They agreed *when both sides ceased fire* to open
>     negotiations.
> REVISED: They agreed to open negotiations *when both sides
>     ceased fire.*
> FAULTY: Several delegations *we know* have failed.
> REVISED: *We know* that several delegations have failed.
> FAULTY: They hoped to try *thoroughly* to understand.
> REVISED: They hoped to try to understand *thoroughly.*

The split infinitive (see 81, 263–264) can also make a modifier squint:

> FAULTY: He resolved to *dependably* develop plans.
> REVISED: He resolved to develop *dependable* plans.

## Don't Let Your Modifiers or References Dangle

The *-ing* words (the gerunds and participles) tend to slip loose from the sentence and dangle, referring to nothing or to the wrong thing.

> FAULTY: Going home, the walk was slippery. [participle]
> REVISED: Going home, I found the walk slippery.
> FAULTY: When getting out of bed, her toe hit the dresser. [gerund]
> REVISED: When getting out of bed, she hit her toe on the dresser.

Infinitive phrases also can dangle badly:

> FAULTY: To think clearly, some logic is important.
> REVISED: To think clearly, you should learn some logic.

Any phrase or clause may dangle:

> FAULTY: When only a freshman [phrase], Jim's history teacher
>     inspired him.
> REVISED: When Jim was only a freshman, his history teacher
>     inspired him.
> FAULTY: After he had taught for 30 years [clause], the average student still seemed average.
> REVISED: After he had taught for 30 years, he found the average student still average.

## SUGGESTIONS FOR EXERCISE

*Here is an assortment of the usual disagreements. Making them agreeable is probably best done in class orally—to hear the disagreements first.*

**1.**   *Straighten out these disagreements and misalignments:*

1. These kinds of questions are sheer absurdities.
2. Her clothes feel too flashy.
3. Conservatism, as well as liberalism, are summonses for change in American life, as we know it.
4. Neither the make of his car nor the price of his stereo impress us.
5. Her family were bitter about it.
6. The thought of the expense cooled her parents' picture of a happy vacation.
7. The grazing ground of both the antelope and the wild horses are west of this range.
8. The campus, as well as the town, need to wake up.
9. The extinction of several species of whales are threatened.
10. None of the group, even Smith and Jones, want to play.
11. If I would have studied harder, I would have passed.
12. First she investigated the practical implications, and then the moral implications that were involved were examined.

**2.**   *Revise these faulty pronouns and their sentences where necessary:*

1. None of us are perfect.
2. Doug is the only one of the boys who always stand straight.
3. He took my wife and I to dinner.
4. She disliked him whistling the same old tune.
5. He will give the ticket to whomever wants it: he did it for you and I.
6. My mother insists on me buying my own clothes: everyone likes their independence.

**3.**   *Straighten out these adjectives and adverbs:*

1. The demonstration reached near riot proportions.
2. It smells awfully.
3. The dress fitted her perfect.
4. He has a reasonable good chance.
5. Her car had a special built engine.

**4.** *Complete and adjust these partial thoughts:*

1. She swims more smoothly.
2. The pack of a paratrooper is lighter than a soldier.
3. The work of students is more intense than their parents.

**5.** *Unsquint these modifiers:*

1. She planned on the next day to call him.
2. They asked after ten days to be notified.
3. The party promised to completely attempt reform.
4. Several expeditions we know have failed.

**6.** *Mend these danglers:*

1. What we need is a file of engineers broken down by their specialties.
2. Following the games on television, the batting average of every player was at her fingertips.
3. When entering the room, the lamp fell over.
4. After he arrived at the dorm, his father phoned.

**7.** *Correct the following:*

1. No one likes dancing backward all their lives.
2. His pass hit the wide receiver real good.
3. The ball was laying under the bench.
4. If they would of come earlier, they would of seen everything.
5. I feel badly about it.

**8.** *Clear up the following:*

1. The professor as well as the students were glad the course was over.
2. We study hard at State, but you do not have to work all the time.
3. As he looked up, a light could be seen in the window.
4. A citizen should support the government, but they should also be free to criticize it.
5. She hated me leaving so early.
6. This is one of the best essays that has been submitted.
7. The responsibility falls upon you and I.

# II
# Punctuation, Spelling, Capitalization

Punctuation gives the silent page some of the breath of life. It marks the pauses and emphases with which speakers point their meanings. Loose punctuators forget what every good writer knows: that even silent reading produces an articulate murmur in our heads, that language springs from the breathing human voice, that the beauty and meaning of language depend on what the written word makes us *hear*, that is, on the sentence's tuning of emphasis and pause. Commas, semicolons, colons, periods, and other punctuation transcribe our meaningful pauses to the printed page.

## THE PERIOD: MARKING THE SENTENCE

A period marks a sentence, a subject completed in its verb:

**She walked.**

A phrase—which lacks a verb, though it may contain a verb *form* (*seeing, going*)—subordinates this idea, making it *depend* on the sentence's main clause:

**While *walking*, she thought.**

A subordinate clause does the same, making the whole original sentence subordinate:

*While she walked,* she thought.

Like a period and a question mark, an exclamation mark marks a sentence but much more emphatically: *Plan to revise!* Use it sparingly if you want it to count rhetorically.

Take special care not to break off a phrase or clause with a period, making a fragment that looks like a sentence but isn't (unless you intend a rhetorical fragment—see 106-107), and don't use the comma as a period (see 209).

> FAULTY: She dropped the cup. Which had cost twenty dollars.
> REVISED: She dropped the cup, which had cost twenty dollars.
> FAULTY: He swung furiously, the ball sailed into the lake.
> REVISED: He swung furiously. The ball sailed into the lake.

## THE COMMA

Here are the four basic commas:

> I. THE INTRODUCER—after introductory phrases and clauses.
> II. THE COORDINATOR—between "sentences" joined by *and, but, or, nor, yet, so, still, for.*
> III. THE INSERTER—a PAIR around any inserted word or remark.
> IV. THE LINKER—when adding words, phrases, or clauses.

## I. The Introducer

A comma after every introductory word or phrase makes your writing clearer, more alive with the breath and pause of meaning:

> Indeed, the idea failed.
> After the first letter, she wrote again.
> In the autumn of the same year, he went to Paris.

Without the introductory comma, your reader frequently expects something else:

> After the first letter she wrote, she ...
> In the autumn of the same year he went to Paris, he ...

Notice how the introducer changes the meaning of *However* in these two sentences:

> **However she goes, she goes in style.**
> **However, she goes when she feels like it.**

You can usually avoid the danger of forgetting the comma and spoiling the sense by substituting *But* for your introductory *Howevers*: "But she goes . . . ." Put your *howevers* within the sentence between commas:

> **She goes, however, when she feels like it.**

But beware! What looks like an introductory phrase or clause may actually be the subject of the sentence *and should take no comma*. A comma can break up a good marriage of subject and verb. The comma in each of these is an interloper and should be removed:

> **That handsome man in the ascot tie, is the groom.**
> **The idea that you should report every observation, is wrong.**
> **The realization that we must be slightly dishonest to be truly kind,**
>     **comes to all of us sooner or later.**

If your clause-as-subject is unusually long or confusing, you may relieve the pressure by inserting some qualifying remark after it between two commas:

> **The idea that you should report every observation, *however insignif-***
>     ***icant,* is wrong.**
> **The realization that we must be slightly dishonest to be truly kind,**
>     ***obviously the higher motive,* comes to all of us sooner or later.**

## II. The Coordinator

This comma goes between "sentences" joined by coordinate conjunctions. You will often see the comma omitted when your two clauses are short: "He hunted and she fished." But nothing is wrong with "He hunted, and she fished." The comma, in fact, shows the slight pause you make when you say it.

Think of the "comma-and" (**, and**) as a unit equivalent to the period. The period, the semicolon, and the "comma-and" (**, and**) all designate independent clauses—independent "sentences"—but give different emphases:

> He was tired. He went home.
> He was tired; he went home.
> He was tired, and he went home.

A comma tells your reader that another subject and predicate are coming:

> He hunted the hills and dales.
> He hunted the hills, and she fished in the streams.
> She was naughty but nice.
> She was naughty, but that is not our business.
> Wear your jacket or coat.
> Wear your jacket, or you will catch cold.
> It was strong yet sweet.
> It was strong, yet it was not unpleasant.

Of course, you may use a comma in *all* the examples above if your sense demands it. The contrasts set by *but, or,* and *yet* often urge a comma, and the even stronger contrasts with *not* and *either-or* demand a comma, whether or not full predication follows:

> It was strong, yet sweet.
> It was a battle, not a game.
> . . . either a bird in the hand, or two in the bush.

Commas signal where you would pause in speaking.

The meaningful pause also urges an occasional comma in compound predicates, usually not separated by commas:

> He granted the usual permission and walked away.
> He granted the usual permission, and walked away.

Both are correct. In the first sentence, however, the granting and walking are perfectly routine, and the temper is unruffled. In the second, some kind of emotion has forced a pause and a comma, after *permission*. Similarly, meaning itself may demand a comma between the two verbs:

> He turned and dropped the vase.
> He turned, and dropped the vase.

In the first sentence, he turned the vase; in the second, himself. Your **, and** in compound predicates suggests some touch of drama, some meaningful distinction, or afterthought.

You need a comma before *for* and *still* even more urgently. Without the comma, their conjunctive meaning changes; they assume their ordinary roles, *for* as a preposition, and *still* as an adjective or adverb:

> She liked him still. . . . [That is, either *yet* or *quiet!*]
> She liked him, still she could not marry him.
> She liked him for his money.
> She liked him, for a good man is hard to find.

An observation: *for* is the weakest of all the coordinators. Almost a subordinator, it is perilously close to *because*. *For* can seem moronic if cause and effect are fairly obvious: "She liked him, for he was kind." Either make a point of the cause by full subordination—"She liked him *because* he was kind"—or flatter the reader with a semicolon: "She liked him; he was kind." *For* is effective only when the cause is somewhat hard to find: "Blessed are the meek, for they shall inherit the earth."

To summarize the basic point about the comma as coordinator: put a comma before the coordinator ( ,*and* ,*but* ,*or* ,*nor* ,*yet* ,*so* ,*still* ,*for*) when joining independent clauses, and add others necessary for emphasis or clarity.

## III. The Inserter

Put a **pair** of commas around every inserted word, phrase, or clause—those expressions that seem parenthetical and are called "nonrestrictive." When you cut a sentence in two to insert something necessary, you need to tie off *both* ends, or your sentence will die on the table:

> Abilene, Kansas looks promising. [, Kansas,]
> When he packs his bag, however he goes. [, however,]
> The car, an ancient Packard is still running. [, an ancient Packard,]
> April 10, 1999 is agreeable as a date for final payment. [, 1999,]
> John Jones, Jr. is wrong. [, Jr.,]
> I wish, Sandra you would do it. [, Sandra,]

You do not mean that 1999 is agreeable, nor are you telling John Jones that Junior is wrong. Such parenthetical insertions need a **pair** of commas:

The case, *nevertheless*, was closed.
She will see, *if she has any sense at all*, that he is right.
Sam, *on the other hand*, may be wrong.
Note, *for example*, the excellent brushwork.
John Jones, *M.D.*, and Bill Jones, *Ph.D.*, doctored the punch to
    perfection.
He stopped at Kansas City, *Missouri*, for two hours.

The same rule applies to all *nonrestrictive* remarks, phrases, and clauses—all elements simply additive, explanatory, and hence parenthetical:

John, *my friend*, will do what he can.
Andy, *his project sunk, his hopes shattered*, was speechless.
The taxes, *which are reasonable*, will be paid.
That man, *who knows*, is not talking.

Think of *nonrestrictive* as "nonessential" to your meaning, hence set off by
commas. Think of *restrictive* as essential and "restricting" your meaning,
hence not set off at all (use *which* for nonrestrictives, and *that* for restrictives; see 116–117).

RESTRICTIVES
The taxes that are reasonable will be paid.
Southpaws who are superstitious will not pitch on Friday nights.
The man who knows is not talking.

NONRESTRICTIVES
The taxes, which are reasonable, will be paid.
Southpaws, who are superstitious, will not pitch on Friday nights.
The man, who knows, is not talking.

The difference between restrictives and nonrestrictives is one of meaning,
and the comma pair signals that meaning. Our first "Southpaw" sentence
says that only the superstitious ones lie low on Fridays; our second one, that
*all* of them do. Now, how many grandmothers do I have in the first sentence below (restrictive)? How many in the second (nonrestrictive)?

My grandmother who smokes pot is 90.
My grandmother, who smokes pot, is 90.

In the first sentence, I still have two grandmothers, because I am distinguishing one from the other by my restrictive phrase (no commas) as the

one with the unconventional habit. In the second sentence, I have but one grandmother, about whom I am adding an interesting though nonessential, nonrestrictive detail within a pair of commas. Read the two aloud, and you will hear the difference in meaning and how the pauses at the commas signal that difference. Commas are often optional, of course. The difference between a restrictive and a nonrestrictive meaning may sometimes be very slight. For example, you may take our recent bridegroom either way (but not halfway):

> That handsome man, in the ascot tie, is the groom. [nonrestrictive]
> That handsome man in the ascot tie is the groom. [restrictive]

Your meaning will dictate your choice. But use **pairs** of commas or none at all. Never separate subject and verb, or verb and object, with just one comma.

Some finer points. One comma of a pair enclosing an inserted remark may coincide with, and, in a sense, overlay, a comma "already there":

> In each box, a bottle was broken.
> In each box, however, a bottle was broken.
> The team lost, and the school was sick.
> The team lost, in spite of all, and the school was sick.
> The program will work, but the cost is high.
> The program will work, of course, but the cost is high.

Between the coordinate clauses, however, a semicolon might have been clearer:

> The team lost, in spite of all; and the school was sick.
> The program will work, of course; but the cost is high.

Beware: *however*, between commas, cannot substitute for *but*, as in the perfectly good sentence: "He wore a hat, *but* it looked terrible." You would be using a comma where a full stop (period or semicolon) should be:

> WRONG
> He wore a hat, however, it looked terrible.

> RIGHT (*notice the two meanings*):
> He wore a hat; however, it looked terrible.
> He wore a hat, however; it looked terrible.

But a simple **,but** avoids both the ambiguity of the floating *however* and the ponderosity of anchoring it with a semicolon, fore or aft: "He wore a hat, but it looked terrible."

Another point. *But* may absorb the first comma of a pair enclosing an introductory remark (although it need not do so):

> At any rate, he went.
> But, at any rate, he went.
> But at any rate, he went.
> But [,] if we want another party, we had better clean up.
> The party was a success, but [,] if we want another one, we had better clean up.

But avoid a comma *after* "but" in sentences like this:

> I understand your argument, but [,] I feel your opponent has a stronger case.

Treat the "he said" and "she said" of dialogue as a regular parenthetical insertion, within commas, and without capitalizing, unless a new sentence begins:

> "I'm going," he said, "whenever I get up enough nerve."
> "I'm going," he said. "Whenever I get up enough nerve, I'm really going."

And American usage puts the comma *inside* ALL quotation marks:

> "He is a nut," she said.
> She called him a "nut," and walked away.

Finally, the comma goes after a parenthesis, never before:

> On the day of her graduation (June 4, 1989), the weather turned broiling hot.

## IV. The Linker

This is the usual one, linking on additional phrases and afterthoughts:

> They went home, having overstayed their welcome.
> The book is too long, overloaded with examples.

It also links items in series. Again, the meaningful pause demands a comma:

> words, phrases, or clauses in a series
> to hunt, to fish, and to hike
> He went home, he went upstairs, and he could remember nothing.
> She liked oysters, soup, roast beef, and song.

Put a linker before the concluding *and*. By carefully separating all elements in a series, you keep alive a final distinction long ago lost in the daily press, the distinction Virginia Woolf makes (see 107): "urbane, polished, brilliant, imploring and commanding him . . . ." *Imploring and commanding* is syntactically equal to each one of the other modifiers in the series. If Woolf customarily omitted the last comma, as she does not, she could not have reached for that double apposition. The muscle would have been dead. These other examples of double apposition will give you an idea of its effectiveness:

> They cut out his idea, root and branch.
> She lost all her holdings, houses and lands.
> He loved to tramp the woods, to fish and hunt.

A comma makes a great deal of difference, of sense and distinction.

But adjectives in series, as distinct from nouns in series, change the game a bit. Notice the difference between the following two strings of adjectives:

> a good, unexpected, natural rhyme
> a good old battered hat

With adjectives in series, only your sense can guide you. If each seems to modify the noun directly, as in the first example above, use commas. If each seems to modify the total accumulation of adjectives and noun, as with *good* and *old* in the second phrase, do not use commas. Say your phrases aloud, and put your commas in the pauses that distinguish your meaning.

Finally, a special case. Dramatic intensity sometimes allows you to join clauses with commas instead of conjunctions:

> She sighed, she cried, she almost died.
> I couldn't do it, I tried, I let them all get away.
> It passed, it triumphed, it was a good bill.
> I came, I saw, I conquered.

The rhetorical intensity of this construction—the Greeks called it *asyndeton*—is obvious. The language is breathless, or grandly emphatic. As Aristotle once said, it is a person trying to say many things at once. The subjects repeat themselves, the verbs overlap, the idea accumulates a climax. By some psychological magic, the clauses of this construction usually come in threes. The comma is its sign. But unless you have a stylistic reason for such a flurry of clauses, go back to the normal comma and conjunction, the semicolon, or the period.

## FRAGMENTS, COMMA SPLICES, AND RUN-ONS

These are the most persistent problems in using the comma—either missing it or misusing it. The rhetorical fragment, as we have seen (106–107), may have great force: "So what." But the grammatical one needs repairing with a comma:

> FAULTY: She dropped the cup. Which had cost twenty dollars.
> REVISED: She dropped the cup, which had cost twenty dollars.
> FAULTY: He does not spell everything out. But rather hints
>    that something is wrong, and leaves the rest up to the
>    reader.
> REVISED: He does not spell everything out, but rather hints . . . ,
>    and leaves . . . .
> FAULTY: . . . and finally, the book is obscure. Going into lengthy
>    discussions and failing to remind the reader of the point.
> REVISED: . . . and finally, the book is obscure, going into lengthy
>    discussion . . . .
> FAULTY: Yet here is her husband treating their son to all that
>    she considers evil. Plus the fact that the boy is offered
>    beer.
> REVISED: Yet here is her husband treating their son to all that
>    she considers evil, especially beer.
> FAULTY: She points out that one never knows what the future will
>    bring. Because it is actually a matter of luck.
> REVISED: She points out that one never knows what the future
>    will bring because it is actually a matter of luck.
> FAULTY: They are off. Not out of their minds exactly but driven,
>    obsessed.
> REVISED: They are off, not out of their minds exactly, but driven,
>    obsessed.

# Beware the Comma Splice, and the Run-On

The comma splice is the beginner's most common error, the opposite of the fragment—putting a comma where we need a period rather than putting a period where we need a comma—splicing two sentences together with a comma:

> **The comma splice is a common error, it is the opposite of a fragment.**    Comma Splice

Of course, you will frequently see comma splices, particularly in fiction and dialogue, where writers are conveying colloquial speed and the thoughts come tumbling fast. Some nonfiction writers borrow this same speed here and there in their prose. But you should learn to recognize these as comma splices and generally avoid them because they may strike your readers as the errors of innocence. Like the rhetorical fragment, a comma splice between short clauses can be most effective (see *asyndeton*, 208): "If speech and cinema are akin to music, writing is like architecture; *it endures, it has weight.*"*

The run-on sentence (fortunately less common) omits even the splicing comma, running one sentence right on to another without noticing:

> **The comma splice is a common error it is the opposite of a fragment.**    Run-On

Here the writer is in deeper trouble, having somehow never gotten the feel of a sentence as based on subject and verb and thus needing special help. But most of us can see both the comma splice and run-on as really being two sentences, to be restored as such:

> **The comma splice is a common error. It is the opposite of a fragment.**

Or to be coordinated by adding a conjunction after the comma:

> **The comma splice is a common error, and it is . . . .**

Or to be subordinated by making the second sentence a phrase:

> **The comma splice is a common error, the opposite . . . .**

---

*Italics added. Richard Lloyd-Jones, "What We May Become," *College Composition and Communication* 33 (1952): 205.

Here are some typical comma splices:

> She cut class, it was boring.
> The class was not merely dull, it was useless.
> Figures do not lie, they mislead.
> He was more than satisfied, he was delighted.

Each of these pulls together a pair of closely sequential sentences. But a comma without its *and* or *but* will not hold the coordination. Either make them the sentences they are:

> She cut class. It was boring.
> Figures do not lie. They mislead.

Or coordinate them with a colon or dash (with a semicolon *only* if they contrast sharply):

> The class was not merely dull: it was useless.
> He was more than satisfied—he was delighted.

Or subordinate in some way:

> She cut class because it was boring.
> The class was not merely dull but useless.
> More than satisfied, he was delighted.

Here are some more typical splices, all from one set of papers in advanced freshman composition dealing with Shakespeare's *The Tempest*. I have circled the comma where the period should be:

> She knows nothing of the evil man is capable of⊙ to her every man is beautiful.
> The question of his sensibility hovers⊙ we wonder if he is just.
> Without a doubt, men discourage oppression⊙ they strive to be free.
> Ariel is civilized society⊙ besides being articulate, he has direction and order.
> Stephano and Trinculo are the comics of the play⊙ never presented as complete characters, they are not taken seriously.

You will accidentally splice with a comma most frequently when adding a thought (a complete short sentence) to a longer sentence:

> The book describes human evolution in wholly believable terms, comparing the social habits of gorillas and chimpanzees to human behavior, it is very convincing.

But you have confused your readers. Which way is that *comparing* phrase supposed to go? You must help them by repairing your splice with a period, either like this:

> The book describes human evolution in wholly believable terms, comparing the social habits of gorillas and chimpanzees to human behavior. It is very convincing.

Or like this:

> The book describes human behavior in wholly believable terms. Comparing the social habits of gorillas and chimpanzees to human behavior, it is very convincing.

In short, be sure to attach all accidental fragments—that *comparing* phrase, by itself, would be a fragment—to your main sentence. But be sure each complete sentence—*It is very convincing*—stands clear and alone with its own capital and period.

Conjunctive adverbs (*however, therefore, nevertheless, moreover, furthermore,* and others) may also cause comma splices and trouble:

> She continued teaching, however her heart was not in it.

Here are three mendings:

> She continued teaching, but her heart was not in it.
> She continued teaching; however, her heart was not in it.
> She continued teaching; her heart, however, was not in it.

Similarly, transitional phrases (*in fact, that is, for example*) may splice your sentences together:

> He disliked discipline, that is, he really was lazy.

You can strengthen the weak joints like this:

> He disliked discipline; that is, he really was lazy.
> He disliked discipline, that is, anything demanding.

# SEMICOLON AND COLON

*Use the semicolon only where you could also use a period, unless desperate.* This dogmatic formula, which I shall loosen up in a moment, has saved many a punctuator from both despair and a reckless fling of semicolons. Confusion comes from the belief that the semicolon is either a weak colon or a strong comma. It is most effective as neither. It is best, as we have seen (94–95), in pulling together and contrasting two independent clauses that could stand alone as sentences:

> **The novel concentrates on character. The film intensifies the violence.**
> **The novel concentrates on character; the film intensifies the violence.**

Semicolon

This compression and contrast by semicolon can go even farther, allowing us to drop a repeated verb in the second element (note also how the comma marks the omission):

> **Golf demands the best of time and space; tennis demands the best**
> **of personal energy.**
> **Golf demands the best of time and space; tennis, the best of personal**
> **energy.**
> **Tragedy begins with the apple; comedy, with the banana peel.\***

Thomas Jefferson drops the verb completely as he sums up his Epicurean philosophy:

> **Happiness, the Aim of Life; Virtue, the Foundation of Happiness;**
> **Utility, the Test of Virtue.**

Use a semicolon with a transitional word (*moreover, therefore, then, however, nevertheless*) to signal close contrast and connection:

> **He was lonely, blue, and solitary; moreover, his jaw ached.**

Used sparingly, the semicolon emphasizes your crucial contrasts; used recklessly, it merely clutters your page. *Never* use it as a colon: its effect is exactly

---

*Adapted from Guy Davenport, *Life*, 27 Mar. 1970: 12.

opposite. A colon, as in the preceding sentence, signals the meaning to go ahead; a semicolon, as in this sentence, stops it. The colon is a green light; the semicolon is a stop sign.

Consequently, a wrong semicolon frequently makes a fragment. *Use a semicolon only where you could also use a period*—forget the exceptions—or you will make semicolon fragments like the italicized phrases following the erroneous semicolons circled below:

> The play opens on a dark street in New York City ⟨;⟩ *one streetlight giving the only illumination.*
> The geese begin their migration in late August or early September ⟨;⟩ *some groups having started, in small stages, a week or so earlier.*

Each of those semicolons should have been a comma.

Of course, you may occasionally need a semicolon to unscramble a long line of phrases and clauses, especially those in series and containing internal commas:

> Composition is hard because we often must discover our ideas by writing them out, clarifying them on paper; because we must also find a clear and reasonable order for ideas the mind presents simultaneously; and because we must find, by trial and error, exactly the right words to convey our ideas and our feelings about them.

The colon waves the traffic on through the intersection: "Go right ahead," it says, "and you will find what you are looking for." The colon emphatically and precisely introduces a series, the clarifying detail, the illustrative example, and the formal quotation:

> The following players will start: Corelli, Smith, Jones, Baughman, and Stein.     Colon
> Pierpont lived for only one thing: money.
> In the end, it was useless: Adams really was too green.
> We remember Sherman's words: "War is hell."

Both the semicolon and the colon, unlike the comma and the period, go *outside* quotation marks:

> He called it a "generation gap"; she called it a "gaping generation."
> This was no "stitch in time": it was complete reconstruction.

## PARENTHESES AND DASH

The dash says aloud what the parentheses whisper. Both enclose interruptions too extravagant for a pair of commas to hold. The dash is the more useful—because whispering tends to annoy—and will remain useful only if not overused. It can serve as a conversational colon. It can set off a concluding phrase—for emphasis. It can bring long introductory matters to focus, concluding a series of parallel phrases: "—all these are crucial." It can insert a full sentence—a clause is really an incorporated sentence—directly next to a key word. The dash allows you to insert—with a kind of shout!—an occasional exclamation. You may even insert—and who would blame you?—an occasional question. The dash affords a structural complexity with all the tone and alacrity of talk.

    With care, you can get much the same power from parentheses:

> Many philosophers have despaired (somewhat unphilosophically) of discovering any certainties whatsoever.
> Thus did Innocent III (we shall return to him shortly) inaugurate an age of horrors.
> But in such circumstances (see 34), be cautious.
> Delay had doubled the costs (a stitch in time!), so the plans were shelved.

But dashes seem more generally useful, and here are some special points. When one of a pair of dashes falls where a comma would be, it absorbs the comma.

> If one wanted to go, he certainly could.
> If one wanted to go—whether invited or not—he certainly could.

Not so with the semicolon:

> He wanted to go—whether he was invited or not; she had more sense.

To indicate the dash, type two hyphens (--) flush against the words they separate—not one hyphen between two spaces, nor a hyphen spaced to look exactly like a hyphen.

    Put commas and periods *outside* a parenthetical group of words (like this one), even if the parenthetical group could stand alone as a sentence (see the preceding "Innocent III" example). (But if you make an actual full sentence parenthetical, put the period inside.)

Change has had its way with the parentheses around numbers. Formal print and most guides to writing, including this one, still hold to the full parentheses:

> **The sentence really has only two general varieties: (1) the "loose" or strung-along, in Aristotle's phrase, and (2) the periodic. She decided (1) that she did not like it, (2) that he would not like it, and (3) that they would be better off without it.**

Numbered Items

Popular print now omits the first half of the parentheses:

> **. . . decided 1) that she did not like it, 2) that he . . .**

But for your papers—keep the full parentheses.

## BRACKETS

Brackets indicate your own words inserted or substituted within a quotation from someone else: "Byron had already suggested that [they] had killed John Keats." You have substituted "they" for "the gentlemen of the *Quarterly Review*" to suit your own context. You do the same when you interpolate a word of explanation: "Byron had already suggested that the gentlemen of the *Quarterly Review* [especially Croker] had killed John Keats." *Do not use parentheses:* they mark the enclosed words as part of the original quotation. Don't claim innocence because your typewriter lacks brackets. Just leave spaces and draw them in later, or type slant lines and tip them with pencil or with the underscore key:

$$[\ldots]$$

In the example below, you are pointing out with a *sic* (Latin for "so" or "thus"), which you should not italicize, that you are reproducing an error exactly as it appears in the text you are quoting:

> **"On no occassion [sic] could we trust them."**

Similarly, you may give a correction after reproducing the error:

> **"On the twenty-fourth [twenty-third], we broke camp."**
> **"In not one instance [actually, Baldwin reports several instances] did our men run under fire."**

Use brackets when you need parentheses within parentheses:

> (see Donald Allenberg, *The Future of Television* [New York, 1991]:15–16)

Your instructor will probably put brackets around the wordy parts of your sentences, indicating what you should cut:

> In fact, [the reason] he liked it [was] because it was different.

## QUOTATION MARKS AND ITALICS

Put quotation marks around quotations that "run directly into your text" (like this), but *not* around quotations set off from the text and indented. You normally inset poetry, as it stands, without quotation marks:

> An aged man is but a paltry thing,
> A tattered coat upon a stick, unless
> Soul clap its hands and sing . . . .

But if you run it into your text, use quotation marks, with virgules (slants) showing the line-ends: "An aged man is but a paltry thing, / A tattered coat . . . ." Put periods and commas *inside* quotation marks; put semicolons and colons *outside:*

| | |
|---|---|
| Period | Now we understand the full meaning of "give me liberty, or give me death." |
| Comma | "This strange disease of modern life," in Arnold's words, remains uncured. |
| Semicolon | In Greece, it was "know thyself"; in America, it is "know thy neighbor." |
| Colon | He left after "Hail to the Chief": he could do nothing more. |

Although logic often seems to demand the period or comma outside the quotation marks, convention has put them inside for the sake of appearance, even when the sentence ends in a single quoted word or letter:

> Clara Bow was said to have "It."
> Mark it with "T."

If you have seen the periods and commas outside, you were reading a British book or some of America's little magazines.

When you have dialogue, signal each change of speaker with a paragraph's indentation:

> "What magazines in the natural sciences should I read regularly?" inquired the student.
>
> "Though moderately difficult, *Scientific American* and *Science* are always worth your time, but you'll want to explore afield from these," responded her advisor.

If in a dialogue a single speaker carries on for several paragraphs, place quotation marks before *each* paragraph, but after only the *last* paragraph.

Omit quotation marks entirely in *indirect* quotations:

> She asked me if I would help her.
>
> The insurance agent told Mr. Jones that his company would pay all valid claims within 30 days.
>
> In his review of the play, J. K. Beaumont praised the plot as strong and incisive but faulted the dialogue as listless and contrived in a few scenes. [Here, you are summarizing the reviewer's comments.]

If you are quoting a phrase that already contains quotation marks, reduce the original double marks (") to single ones ('):

| ORIGINAL | YOUR QUOTATION | |
|---|---|---|
| Hamlet's "are you honest?" is easily explained. | He writes that "Hamlet's 'are you honest?' is easily explained." | Single Quotation Marks (on the Right) |

Notice what happens when the quotation within your quotation falls at the end:

| ORIGINAL | YOUR QUOTATION |
|---|---|
| A majority of the informants thought *infer* meant "imply." | Kirk reports that "a majority of the informants thought *infer* meant 'imply.'" |

And notice that a question mark or exclamation point falls between the single and the double quotation marks at the end of a quotation containing a quotation:

> "Why do they call it 'The Hippocratic oath'?" she asked.
> "Everything can't be 'cool'!" he said.

But heed the following exception:

> "I heard someone say, 'Is anyone home?'" she declared.

Do not use *single* quotation marks for your own stylistic flourishes; use *double* quotation marks or, preferably, none:

> It was indeed an "affair," but the passion was hardly "grand."
> It was indeed an affair, but the passion was hardly grand.
> Some "cool" pianists use the twelve-tone scale.

Once you have thus established this slang meaning of *cool,* you may repeat the word without quotation marks. In general, of course, you should favor that slang which your style can absorb without quotation marks.

Do not use quotation marks for calling attention to words as words. Use italics (an underscore when typing) for the words, quotation marks for their meanings.

Italics       **This is taking *tergiversation* too literally.**
              **The word *struthious* means "like an ostrich."**

Similarly, use italics for numbers as numbers and letters as letters:

> He writes a **5** like an *s.*
> Dot your *i*'s and cross your *t*'s.

But common sayings like "Watch your p's and q's" and "from A to Z" require no italics.

Use quotation marks for titles *within* books and magazines: titles of chapters, articles, short stories, songs, and poems, and for unpublished works, lectures, courses, TV episodes within a series. But use italics for titles or names of books, newspapers, magazines, plays, films, TV series, long poems, sculptures, paintings, ships, trains, and airplanes.

Poe's description of how he wrote "The Raven" was attacked in the
    *Atlantic Monthly* [or: the *Atlantic.*]
We saw Michelangelo's *Pietà,* a remarkable statue in white
    marble.
We took the Sante Fe *Chief* from Chicago to Los Angeles.
She read all of Frazer's *The Golden Bough.*
His great-grandfather went down with the *Titanic.*
She read it in *The New York Times.*
They loved *Dirty Dancing* [film].

Handle titles within titles as follows:

"*Tintern Abbey*" *and Nature in Wordsworth* [book]
"'Tintern Abbey' and Natural Imagery" [article]
"The Art of *Tom Jones*" [article]
*The Art of* Tom Jones [book]

In the last example, notice that what is ordinarily italicized, like the title of a book (*Tom Jones*), is set in roman when the larger setting is in italics.

Italicize foreign words and phrases, unless they have been assimilated into English through usage (your dictionary should have a method for noting the distinction; if not, consult one that has):

The statement contained two clichés and one *non sequitur.*
The author of this naïve exposé suffers from an *idée fixe.*

Other foreign expressions not italicized are: etc., e.g., et al., genre, hubris, laissez-faire, leitmotif, roman á clef, raison d'être, tête-à-tête.

Use neither quotation marks nor italics for the Bible, for its books or parts (Genesis, Old Testament), for other sacred books (Koran, Talmud, Upanishad), for famous documents such as the Magna Carta, the Declaration of Independence, the Communist Manifesto, and the Gettysburg Address, or for instrumental music known by its form, number, and key:

Beethoven's C-minor Quartet
Brahms's Symphony No. 4, Opus 98

When a reference in parentheses falls at the end of a quotation, the quotation marks *precede* the parentheses:

As Ecclesiastes tells us, "there is no new thing under the sun" (1.9).

## ELLIPSIS

1. Use three spaced periods . . . (the ellipis mark) when you omit something from a quotation. Do *not* use them in your own text in place of a dash or in mere insouciance.
2. If you omit the end of a sentence, put in a period (no space) and add the three spaced dots. . . .
3. If your omission falls after a completed sentence, just add the three spaced dots to the period already there. . . . It looks the same as case 2.

Here is an uncut passage, followed by a shortened version illustrating the three kinds of ellipsis:

> To learn a language, learn as thoroughly as possible a few everyday sentences. This will educate your ear for all future pronunciations. It will give you a fundamental grasp of structure. And start soon.

> (1)
> To learn a language, learn . . . a few everyday sentences.
> (2)
> This will educate your ear. . . . It will give you a fundamental
> (3)
> grasp of structure. . . .

The ellipsis mark may fall on either side of any punctuation:

> as many . . . , and several others are
> as many; . . . others are

DO NOT break an ellipsis at the end of your line:

> "Every accident may claim lives. .
> . . Insurance is mandatory."

Either stretch it two dots more, which is best, or start it on the next line:

> "Every accident may claim lives
> . . . . Insurance is mandatory."

You can omit beginning and ending ellipses when you use a quotation within a sentence:

Lincoln was determined that the Union, "cemented with the blood of . . . the purest patriots," would not fail.

Use a full line of spaced dots when omitting a line or more of poetry:

A cloud comes over the sunlit arch,
. . . . . . . . . . . . . . . . .
And you're two months back in the middle of March.

# APOSTROPHE

*It's* may be overwhelmingly our most frequent misspelling, as in "The dog scratched *it's* ear." No, no! *It's* means *it is*. *Who's* means *who is*. *They're* means *they are*. NO pronoun spells *its* possessive with an apostrophe: *hers, its, ours, theirs, yours, whose, oneself*.

For nouns, add apostrophes to form the singular possessive: *dog's life, hour's work, Marx's ideas*. Add apostrophes even to singular words already ending in s: *Yeats's poems, Charles's crown. Sis' plans* and *the boss' daughter* are not what we say. We say *Sissuz* and *bossuz* and *Keatsuz* and should say the same in our writing: *sis's, boss's, Keats's*. Plurals not ending in s also form the possessive by adding *'s: children's hour, women's rights*. But most plurals take the apostrophe after the s already there: *witches' sabbath, ten cents' worth, three days' time, the Joneses' possessions*.

I repeat: the rule for making singulars possessive is to add *'s* regardless of length and previous ending. French names ending in silent *s*-sounds also add s: *Camus's works, Marivaux's life, Berlioz's Requiem*. If your page grows too thick with double s's, substitute a few pronouns for the proper names, or rephrase: *the death of Themistocles, the Dickens character Pip*.

The apostrophe can help to clarify clusters of nouns. These I have actually seen: *Alistair Jones Renown Combo, the church barbecue chicken sale, the uniform policeman training program, the members charter plane*. And, of course, *teachers meeting* and *veterans insurance* are so common as to seem almost normal. But an apostrophe chips one more noun out of the block. It makes your meaning one word clearer, marking *teachers'* as a modifier and distinguishing *teacher* from *teachers*. Inflections are helpful, and the written word needs all the help it can get: *Jones's Renowned, church's barbecued, uniformed policeman's, members' chartered*. Distinguish your modifiers, and keep your possessions.

Compound words take the *'s* on the last word only: *mother-in-law's hat, the brothers-in-law's attitude* (all the brothers-in-law have the same attitude), *somebody else's problem.* Joint ownership may similarly take the 's only on the last word (*Bill and Mary's house*), but *Bill's and Mary's* house is more precise, and preferable.

Again, possessive pronouns have no apostrophe: *hers, its, theirs, yours, whose, oneself.* Remember that *it's* means *it is*, and that *who's* means *who is*; for possession, use *its* and *whose*.

The double possessive uses both an *of* and an 's: *a friend of my mother's, a book of the teacher's, a son of the Joneses', an old hat of Mary's.* Note that the double possessive indicates one possession among several of the same kind: mother has several friends; the teacher, several books.

Use the apostrophe to indicate omissions: *the Spirit of '76, the Class of '02, can't, won't, don't.* Finally, use the apostrophe when adding a grammatical ending to a number, letter, sign, or abbreviation: *1920's; his 3's look like 8's; p's and q's; she got four A's; too many of's and and's; she X'd each box; K.O.'d* in the first round. (Some of these are also italics, or underlined when typed. See 218.) Contemporary usage omits the apostrophe in some of these: *1920s, 8s, two ts.*


## HYPHEN

For clarity, hyphenate groups of words acting as one adjective or one adverb: *eighteenth-century attitude, early-blooming southern crocus, of-and-which disease.* Distinguish between a *high school*, and a *high-school teacher.* Similarly, hyphenate compound nouns when you need to distinguish, for example, *five sentence-exercises* from *five-sentence exercises.*

Hyphenate prefixes to proper names: *ex-Catholic, pro-Napoleon,* and all relatively new combinations like *anti-marriage.* Consult your dictionary.

Hyphenate after prefixes that demand emphasis or clarity: *ex-husband, re-collect* ("to collect again," as against *recollect,* "to remember"), *re-create, re-emphasize, pre-existent.*

When you must break a word at the end of a line, hyphenate where your dictionary marks the syllables with a dot; *syl•lables, syl-lables.* If you must break a hyphenated word, break it after the hyphen: *self-/sufficient.* Don't hyphenate an already hyphenated word: *self-suf-/ficient.* It's hard on the eyes and the printer. When you write for print, underline those line-end hyphens you mean to keep as hyphens, making a little equals sign: self=/sufficient.

Hyphenate suffixes to single capital letters (*T-shirt, I-beam, X-ray*). Hyphenate *ex-champions* and *self-reliances.* Hyphenate to avoid double *i's* and triple consonants: *anti-intellectual, bell-like.*

Hyphenate two-word numbers: *twenty-one, three-fourths*. Use the "suspensive" hyphen for hyphenated words in series: "We have ten-, twenty-five-, and fifty-pound sizes."

## VIRGULE (SLANT, SLASH)

Spare this "little rod" (/), and don't spoil your work with the legalistic *and/or*. Don't write "bacon and/or eggs"; write "bacon or eggs, or both." Likewise, don't use it for a hyphen: not "male/female conflict" but "male-female conflict." Use the virgule when quoting poetry in your running text: "That time of year thou mayst in me behold / When yellow leaves, . . ."

## SPELLING

The dictionary is your best friend as you face the inevitable anxieties of spelling, but three underlying principles and some tricks of the trade can help immeasurably.

## Principle I

Letters represent sounds: proNUNciation can help you spell. No one proNOUNcing his words correctly would make the familiar errors of "similiar" and "enviorment." Simply sound out the letters: *envIRONment* and *goverNment* and *FebRUary* and *intRAmural*. Of course, you will need to be wary of some words not pronounced as spelled: *Wednesday* pronounced "*Wenzday*," for instance. But sounding the letters can help your spellings. You can even say "convertible" and "indelible" and "plausible" without sounding like a fool, and you can silently stress the *able* in words like "prob*able*" and "immov*able*" to remember the difficult distinction between words ending in *-ible*, and *-able*.

Consonants reliably represent their sounds. Remember that *c* and often *g* go soft before *i* and *e*. Consequently, you must add a *k* when extending words like *picnic* and *mimic—picnicKing, mimicKing*—to keep them from rhyming with *slicing* or *dicing*. Conversely, you just keep the *e* (where you would normally drop it) when making *peace* into *peacEable* and *change* into *changEable*, to keep the *c* and *g* soft.

Single *s* is pronounced *zh* in words like *vision, occasion, pleasure*. Knowing that *ss* hushes ("sh-h-h") will keep you from errors like *occassion*, which would sound like *passion*.

Vowels sound short and light before single consonants: *hat, pet, kit, hop, cup*. When you add any vowel (including *y*), the first vowel will say its name: *hate, Pete, kite, hoping, cupid*. Notice how the *a* in *-able* keeps the main vowel saying its name in words like *unmistakable, likable,* and *notable*. Therefore, to keep a vowel short, protect it with double consonants: *petting, hopping*. This explains the troublesome *rr* in *occuRRence*: a single *r* would make it say *cure* in the middle. *Putting* a golf ball and *putting* something on paper must both use *tt* to keep from being pronounced *pewting*. Compare *stony* with *sonny* and *bony* with *bonny*. The *y* is replacing the *e* in *stone* and *bone*, and the rule is working perfectly. It works in any accented syllable: compare *forgeTTable* as against *markeTing*, *begiNNing* as against *buttoNing*, and *compeLLing* as against *traveLing*. Likewise, when *full* combines and loses its stress, it also loses an *l*. Note the single and double *l* in *fulFILLment*. Similarly, SOUL*ful*, GRATE*ful*, AW*ful*—even SPOON*ful*.

## Principle II

Here is the old rule of *i* before *e*, and its famous exceptions:

> **I** before *e*
> **Except after** *c*,
> **Or when sounded like** *a*
> **As in** *neighbor* **and** *weigh*.

It works like a charm: *achieve, believe, receive, conceive*. Note that *c* needs an *e* to make it sound like *s*. Remember also that *foreign* was once pronounced "forayn," *heifer*, "hayfer," and *leisure*, "laysure." *Their* still sounds "thayr," and *vein* "vayn." Memorize these important exceptions:

> **counterfeit, either, forfeit, neither, protein, seize, sheik, weird**

Note that all are pronounced "ee" (with a little crowding) and that the *e* comes first. Another small group pronounces both the *i* and the *e* (again with a little crowding):

> **ancient, conscience, efficient, science**

Finally, another little group goes the other way, with the long *i* sound of the German "Heil":

height, sleight, seismograph, kaleidoscope

*Financier,* another exception, follows its French origin and its original sound. *Deity* sounds both vowels.

### Other "ees" That Drive You Nuts

These words are thorny—especially *proceed* and *precede*—but their numbers are few:

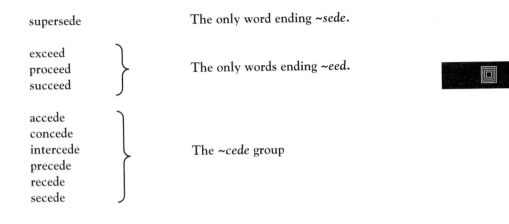

| | |
|---|---|
| supersede | The only word ending *~sede.* |
| exceed<br>proceed<br>succeed | The only words ending *~eed.* |
| accede<br>concede<br>intercede<br>precede<br>recede<br>secede | The *~cede* group |

## Principle III

Most big words, following the Latin or French from which they came, spell their sounds letter for letter. Look up the derivations of the words you misspell (note that double *s,* and explain it). You will never again have trouble with *desperate* and *separate* once you discover that the first comes from *de-spero,* "without hope," and that SePARate divides equals, the PAR values in stocks or golf. Nor with *definite* or *definitive,* once you see the kinship of both with *finite* and *finish.* Derivations can also help you a little with the devilment of *-able* and *-ible,* since, except for a few ringers, the *i* remains from Latin, and the *-ables* are either French (*ami-able*) or Anglo-Saxon copies (*workable*). Knowing origins can help at crucial points: *resemblAnce* comes from Latin *simulAre,* "to copy"; *existEnce* comes from Latin *existEre;* "to stand forth."

The biggest help comes from learning the common Latin prefixes, which, by a process of assimilation (*ad-similis,* "like to like"), account for the double consonants at the first syLLabic joint of so many of our words:

AD- (toward, to): *abbreviate* (shorten down), *accept* (grasp to).
CON- (with): *collapse* (fall with), *commit* (send with).
DIS- (apart): *dissect* (cut apart), *dissolve* (loosen apart).
IN- (into): *illuminate* (shine into), *illusion* (playing into).
IN- (not): *illegal* (not lawful), *immature* (not ripe).
INTER- (between): *interrupt* (break between), *interrogate* (task
    between).
OB- (toward, to): *occupy* (take in), *oppose* (put to), *offer* (carry to).
SUB- (under): *suffer* (bear under), *suppose* (put down).
SYN- ("together"—this one is Greek): *symmetry* (measuring
    together), *syllogism* (logic together).

Spelling takes a will, an eye, and an ear—and a dictionary. Keep a list
of your favorite enemies. Memorize one or two a day. Write them in the air
in longhand. Visualize them. Imagine a blinking neon sign, with the
wicked letters red and tall—definIte—definIte. Then print them once,
write them twice, and blink them a few times more as you go to sleep. But
best of all, make up whatever devices you can—the crazier the better—to
remember their tricky parts:

DANCE attenDANCE.

EXISTENCE is TENSE.

There's IRON in this envIRON-
    ment.

The resisTANCE took its STANCE.

There's an ANT on the defen-
    dANT.

LOOSE as a goose.

LOSE loses an o.

ALLOT isn't A LOT.

Already isn't ALL RIGHT.

I for gaIety.

The LL in paraLLel gives me
*el.*

PURr in PURsuit.

When an unaccented syllable leads to misspelling, you can also get
some help by trying to remember a version of the word that accents the
troublesome syllable: academy—acaDEMic; definitely—defiNItion; irritable—irriTATE; mandatory—manDATE; preparation—prePARE.

Many foreign words, though established in English, retain their native
diacritical marks, which aid in pronunciation; *naiveté, résumé, séance, tête-
à-tête, façade, Fräulein, mañana, vicuña.* Many names are similarly treated:
*Müller, Gödel, Göttingen, Poincaré, Brontë, Noël Coward, García Lorca,
Havlíček.* As always, your dictionary is your best guide, as it is, indeed, to
all words transliterated to English from different alphabets and systems of
writing (Russian, Arabic, Chinese, Japanese, and so on).

Here are more of the perpetual headaches:

accept—except
accommodate
acknowledgment—judgment
advice—advise
affect—effect*
all right*—a lot*
allusion—illusion—disillusion*
analysis—analyzing
argue—argument
arrangement
businessman
capital (city)—capitol (building)*
censor—censure*
committee
complement—compliment*
continual—continuous*
controversy
council—counsel—consul*
criticize—criticism
curriculum*—career—occurrence
obstacle
possession
primitive
principal—principle*
proceed—precede—procedure
rhythm
questionnaire
stationary—stationery

decide—divide—devices
desert—dessert
dilemma—condemn
disastrous
discreet—discrete*
embarrassment—harassment
eminent—imminent—immanent*
exaggerate
explain—explanation
familiar—similar
forward—foreword
genius—ingenious*—ingenuous*
height—eighth
hypocrisy—democracy
irritable
its—it's*
lonely—loneliness
marriage—marital—martial
misspell—misspelling
potatoes—heroes—tomatoes
succeed—successful
suppressed
their—they're
truly
until—till
unnoticed
weather—whether
who's—whose*

# CAPITALIZATION

You know about sentences and names, certainly; but the following points are troublesome. Capitalize:

1. Names of races, languages, and religions—Asian, Caucasian, Mongolian, Protestant, Jewish, Christian, Roman Catholic, Indian, French, English, Black (as in Black English). But "blacks and whites in this neighborhood," "black entrepreneurs," "white storekeepers,"—especially in phrases that contrast blacks and whites, since *white* is never capitalized.

*In the Glossary of Usage.

2. North, South, East, and West *only when they are regions*—the mysterious East, the new Southwest—or parts of proper nouns: the West Side, East Lansing.

3. The *complete* names of churches, rivers, hotels, and the like—the First Baptist Church, the Mark Hopkins Hotel, the Suwannee River (not First Baptist church, Mark Hopkins hotel, Suwannee river).

4. All words in titles, except prepositions, articles, conjunctions, and the "to" of infinitives. But capitalize even these if they come first or last, or if they are longer than four letters—"I'm Through with Love," *Gone with the Wind*, "I'll Stand By," *How to Gain Friends and Influence People, Out of Africa, To Kill a Mockingbird*. Capitalize nouns, adjectives, and prefixes in hyphenated compounds—*The Eighteenth-Century Background, The Anti-Idealist* (but *The Antislavery Movement*). But hyphenated single words, the names of numbered streets, and the written-out numbers on your checks are *not* capitalized after the hyphen: *Self-fulfillment, Re-examination, Forty-second Street, Fifty-four . . . Dollars.*

When referring to magazines, newspapers, and reference works in sentences, footnotes, and bibliographies, you may drop the *The* as part of the title; the *Atlantic Monthly*, the *Kansas City Star*, the *Encyclopaedia Britannica.* (Euphony and sense preserve *The* for a few: *The New Yorker, The Spectator.*)

5. References to a specific section of a work—the Index, his Preface, Chapter 1, Volume IV, Act II, but "scene iii" is usually not capitalized because its numerals are also in lower case.

6. Abstract nouns, when you want emphasis, serious or humorous— ". . . the truths contradict, so what is Truth?"; Very Important Person; the Ideal.

*Do not* capitalize the seasons—spring, winter, midsummer.

*Do not* capitalize after a colon, unless what follows is normally capitalized:

> **Again we may say with Churchill: "Never have so many owed so
>     much to so few."**
> ***Culture, People, Nature: An Introduction to General Anthropology***
>     **[title of book]**
> **Many lost everything in the earthquake: their homes had vanished
>     along with their supplies, their crops, their livestock.**

*Do not* capitalize proper nouns serving as common nouns: *china, cognac, napoleon* (a pastry), *chauvinist, watt* (electricity). Usage divides on some proper adjectives: *French [french] pastry, Cheddar [cheddar] cheese, German [german] measles, Venetian [venetian] blinds.* Also somewhat uncertain are names with lowercase articles or prepositions like [Charles] de Gaulle, [John] von Neumann; in such cases, follow the lowercase form within sentences—*de Gaulle, von Neumann*—but always capitalize in full at the beginning of a sentence: *De Gaulle, Von Neumann.* (Many names, however, drop the article or preposition when the surname appears alone: [Ludwig van] *Beethoven,* [Guy de] *Maupassant.*) Breeds of animals, as in *Welsh terrier,* and products of a definite origin, as in *Scotch whiskey,* are less uncertain. When in doubt, your best guides are your dictionary and, for proper names, a biographical dictionary or an encyclopedia.

## SUGGESTIONS FOR EXERCISE

**1.** *Correct these omissions of the comma, and, in your margin, label the ones you insert as* INTRODUCER, COORDINATOR, INSERTER, *or* LINKER:

1. We find however that the greatest expense in renovation will be for labor not for materials.
2. They took chemistry fine arts history and English.
3. We met June 1 1989 to discuss the problem which continued to plague us.
4. A faithful sincere friend he remained loyal to his roommate even after the unexpected turn of events.
5. Though she was a junior-college instructor teaching advanced calculus given at night during the winter did not intimidate her.
6. C. Wright Mills's *The Power Elite* which even after almost three decades is still one of the finest examples of sociological analysis available ought to be required reading in any elementary sociology course.
7. My father, who is a good gardener keeps things well trimmed.

**2.** *Correct these fragments, comma splices, and run-ons, adding commas and other marks as necessary:*

1. His lectures are not only hard to follow they are boring.
2. Stephano and Trinculo are the comics of the play never presented as complete characters they are not taken seriously.
3. The book deals with the folly of war its stupidity, its cruelty however in doing this the author brings in too many characters repeats episodes over and over and spoils his comedy by pressing too hard.

4. He left his second novel unfinished. Perhaps because of his basic uncertainty, which he never overcame.

5. She seems to play a careless game. But actually knows exactly what she is doing, and intends to put her opponent off guard.

6. His idea of democracy was incomplete, he himself had slaves.

7. She knows her cards that is she never overbids.

8. The problem facing modern architects is tremendous, it involves saving energy on a grand scale with untested devices and still achieving beautiful buildings.

9. The solution was elegant, besides being inexpensive, it was a wholly new approach.

10. Don't underestimate the future, it is always there.

**3.** *Add or subtract commas and semicolons as necessary in these sentences:*

1. Their travels are tireless, their budget however needs a rest.

2. They abhor economizing, that is, they are really spendthrifts.

3. Muller wants efficiency, Smithers beauty.

4. Abramson won the first set with a consistent backhand; some beautiful forehand volleys also helping at crucial moments.

5. The downtown parking problem remains unsolved; the new structures, the new meters, and the new traffic patterns having come into play about three years too late.

**4.** *Adjust the following sentences concerning the colon:*

1. Many things seem unimportant, even distasteful, money, clothes, popularity, even security and friends.

2. People faced with inflation, of which we have growing reminders daily, seem to take one of two courses; either economizing severely in hopes of receding prices, or buying far beyond their immediate needs in fear of still higher prices.

3. Depressed, refusing to face the reality of his situation, he killed himself, it was as simple as that.

4. To let him go was unthinkable: to punish him was unbearable.

**5.** *Add quotation marks and italics to these:*

1. Like the farmer in Frost's Mending Wall, some people believe that Good fences make good neighbors.

2. Here see means understand, and audience stands for all current readers.

3. For him, the most important letter between A and Z is I.

4. Why does the raven keep crying Nevermore? he asked.

5. In America, said the Chinese lecturer, people sing Home, Sweet Home; in China, they stay there.

6. The boys' favorite books were Huckleberry Finn, the Bible, especially Ecclesiastes, and Walden.
7. Germaine Greer's The Female Eunuch is memorable for phrases like I'm sick of peering at the world through false eyelashes and I'm a woman, not a castrate.

**6.**  *Make a list of your ten most frequent misspellings. Then keep it handy and active, removing your conquests and adding your new troubles.*

**7.**  *Capitalize the following, where necessary:*

go west, young man.
the south left the union.
the east side of town
the introduction to *reestablishing toryism*
east side, west side
the tall black spoke french.
she loved the spring.
*health within seconds* [book]
*clear through life in time* [book]
a doberman pinscher
the methodist episcopal church

the missouri river
my christian name begins with c.
the new york public library
the *neo-positivistic approach* [book]
the st. louis post-dispatch [add italics]
twenty-five dollars [on a check]
33 thirty-third street
the tundra occupies a large portion of northern canada.

# III
# A Glossary of Usage*

Speech keeps a daily pressure on writing, and writing returns the compliment, exacting sense from new twists in the spoken language and keeping old senses straight. Usage, generally, is "the way they say it." Usage is the current in the living stream of language; it keeps us afloat, it keeps us fresh—as it sweeps us along. But to distinguish yourself as a writer, you must always swim upstream. You may say, *hoojaeatwith?*; but you will write: *With whom did they compare themselves? With the best, with whoever seemed admirable.* Usage is, primarily, talk; and talk year by year gives words differing social approval and differing meanings. Words move from the gutter to the penthouse and back down the elevator shaft. *Bull*, a four-letter Anglo-Saxon word, was unmentionable in Victorian circles. One had to say *he-cow*, if at all. Phrases and syntactical patterns also have their fashions, mostly bad. *Like unto me* changes to *like me* to *like I do*; *this type of thing* becomes *this type thing; wise*, after centuries of dormancy in only a few words (*likewise, clockwise, otherwise*), suddenly sprouts out the end of everything: *budgetwise, personalitywise, beautywise, prestigewise. Persuade them to vote* becomes *convince them to vote.* Suddenly, everyone is saying *hopefully*, and *near-perfect* shoves old *nearly* off the page. As usual, the marketplace changes more than your money.

But the written language has always refined the language of the marketplace. The Attic Greek of Plato and Aristotle (as Aristotle's remarks about local usages show) was distilled from commercial exchange. Cicero and Catullus and Horace polished their currency against the archaic and the Greek. Mallarmé claimed that Poe had given *un sens plus pur aux mots de la*

---

*\*The American Heritage Dictionary* includes comments on various usages, summarizing the practices and judgments of its Usage Panel, a spectrum of 150 scholars, editors, and writers, of which I am one.

*tribu*—which Eliot rephrases for himself: "to purify the dialect of the tribe." Writing has done just that, and writers have dreamed they have done so:

> **I have laboured to refine our language to grammatical purity, and to clear it from colloquial barbarisms, licentious idioms, and irregular combinations. Something, perhaps, I have added to the elegance of its construction, and something to the harmony of its cadence.**

—wrote Samuel Johnson in 1752 as he closed his *Rambler* papers. And he had almost done what he hoped. He was to shape English writing and speech for the next 150 years, until it was ready for another dip in the stream and another purification. His work, moreover, lasts. We would not imitate it now, but we can read it with pleasure and imitate its enduring drive for excellence and meaning—making words mean what they say.

Johnson goes on to say that he has "rarely admitted any word not authorized by former writers." Writers provide the second level of usage, the paper money. But even this usage requires principle. If we accept "what the best writers use," we still cannot tell whether it is valid: we may be aping their bad habits. Usage is only a court of first appeal, where we can say little more than "He said it." Beyond that helpless litigation, we can test our writing by asking what the words mean and by simple principles: clarity is good, economy is good, ease is good, gracefulness is good, fullness is good, forcefulness is good. As with all predicaments on earth, we judge by appeal to meanings and principles, and we often find both in conflict. Do *near* and *nearly* mean the same thing? Do *convince* and *persuade*? *Lie* and *lay*? Is our writing economical but unclear? Is it full but cumbersome? Is it clear but too colloquial for grace? Careful judgment will give the ruling.

**A, an.**  A goes before consonants and *an* before vowels. But use *a* before *h* sounded in a first syllable: *a hospital, a hamburger.* Use *an* before a silent *h*: *an honor, an heir, an hour.* With *h*-words accented on the second syllable, most ears prefer *an*: *an hypothesis, an historical feat.* But *a hypothesis* is fully acceptable. Use *a* before vowels pronounced as consonants: *a usage, a euphemism.*

**Abbreviations.**  Use only those conventional abbreviations your reader can easily recognize: *Dr., Mr., Mrs., Ms., Messrs.* (for two or more men, pronounced "messers," as in *Messrs. Adams, Pruitt, and Williams*),

*Jr., St., Esq.* (Esquire, following a British gentleman's name, or, occasionally, a U.S. attorney's, between commas and with *Mr.* omitted), *S.J.* (Society of Jesus, also following a name). All take periods. College degrees are usually recognizable: *A.B., M.A., Ph.D., D.Litt., M.D., LL.D.* Similarly, dates and times: B.C., A.D., A.M., P.M. Though these are conventionally printed as small capitals, regular capitals in your classroom papers are perfectly acceptable, as are "lowercase" letters for a.m. and p.m. A.D. precedes its year (A.D. *1066*); B.C. follows its year. Write them without commas: *2000* B.C. *was Smith's estimate.* A number of familiar abbreviations go without periods: *TV, FBI, USSR, USA, YMCA,* though periods are perfectly *OK* or *O.K.* Certain scientific phrases also go without periods, especially when combined with figures: *55 mph, 300 rpm, 4000 kwh.* But *U.N.* and *U.S. delegation* are customary. Note that in formal usage *U.S.* serves only as an adjective; write out the *United States* serving as a noun.

Abbreviations conventional in running prose, unitalicized, are "e.g." (*exempli gratia,* "for example"), "i.e." (*id est,* "that is"), "etc." (*et cetera,* better written out "and so forth"), and "viz." (*videlicet,* pronounced "vi-DEL-uh-sit," meaning "that is," "namely"). These are followed by either commas or colons after the period:

**The commission discovered three frequent errors in management, i.e., failure to take appropriate inventories, erroneous accounting, and inattention to costs.**

**The semester included some outstanding extracurricular programs, e.g.: a series of lectures on civil rights, three concerts, and a superb performance of Oedipus Rex.**

The abbreviation *vs.,* usually italicized, is best spelled out, unitalicized, in your text: "The antagonism of Capulet versus Montague runs throughout the play." The abbreviation c. or ca., standing for *circa* ("around") and used with approximate dates in parentheses, is not italicized: "Higden wrote *Polychronicon* (c. 1350)." See also 160–163.

**Above.** For naturalness and effectiveness, avoid such references as "The above statistics are . . . ," and "The above speaks for itself." Simply use "These" or "This."

**Accidently.** A misspelling for *accidentally;* that is, the adjective *accidental* plus the adverbial *-ly.*

**Action.** A horribly overused catchall. Be specific: *invasion, rape, murder, intransigence, boycott.*

**A.D., B.C., a.m., p.m.**  A.D. (*anno Domini*, "the year of the Lord") goes *before* its year: A.D. 1990. B.C. ("before Christ") goes after: 320 B.C. Some scholars prefer B.C.E. ("Before Common Era"). The times, a.m., p.m., go after their numbers, and usually in small letters, though capitals are all right. Do not use either as a noun: "At seven in the p.m."; "Late in the a.m." Do not use with "o'clock" to distinguish seven in the morning from seven at night ("seven o'clock p.m."). Just write "seven p.m."

**Ad.**  In your papers, use *advertisement*.

**Adapt, adopt.**  To *adapt* is to adjust something to a new purpose. To *adopt* is to take it over as it is.

**Adverse, averse.**  Both turn away. But adverse means bad luck, and *averse* means opposed: "They ran into *adverse* winds, but were *averse* to changing course."

**Advice, advise.**  Frequently confused. *Advice* is what you get when advisers *advise* you.

**Aesthetic.**  An adjective: an *aesthetic* judgment, his *aesthetic* viewpoint. *Aesthetics* is a singular noun for the science of beauty: "Santayana's *aesthetics* agrees with his metaphysics."

**Affect, effect.**  *Affect* means "to influence, to produce an *effect*." Avoid *affect* as a noun; just say *feeling* or *emotion*. *Affective* is a technical term for *emotional* or *emotive*, which are clearer.

**Aggravate.**  Means to add gravity to something already bad enough. Avoid using it to mean "irritate."

| WRONG | RIGHT |
|---|---|
| He aggravated his mother. | The rum aggravated his mother's fever. |

**All, all of.**  Use *all* without the *of* wherever you can to economize: *all this, all that, all those, all the people, all her lunch.* But some constructions need *of: all of them, all of Faulkner.*

**All ready, already.**  Two different meanings. *All ready* means that everything is ready; *already* means "by this time."

**All right, alright.**  *Alright* is not *all right*; you are confusing it with the spelling of *already*. Never use *alright*.

**Allude, elude.**  *Allude* makes an indirect reference: "He is the Mickey Mouse of the essay." *Elude*, from Latin *ludere*, "to play," means to evade by wit or skill: "Mickey *eluded* the cat." Less specifically, a synonym for *escape*: "His meaning *eludes* me."

**Allude, refer.** You might confuse the indirect reference of *allusion*, with the direct *refer*, "to mention.":

> She *alluded* to past victories and *referred to* Coach Carr's inspirational work.

**Allusion, illusion, disillusion.** The first two are frequently confused, and *disillusion* is frequently misspelled *disallusion*. An *allusion* is a reference to something; an *illusion* is a mistaken conception. You disillusion someone by bringing him back to hard reality from his illusions.

**Alot.** You mean *a lot*, not *allot*.

**Also.** Do not use for *and*, especially to start a sentence: not "*Also*, it failed" but simply "And it failed." Not "They had three cats, *also* a dog" but "They had three cats and a dog."

**Among.** See *Between*.

**Amount of, number of.** Use *amount* with general heaps of things; use *number* with amounts that might be counted: *a small amount of interest, a large number of votes*. Use *number* with living creatures: *a number of applicants, a number of squirrels*.

**And/or.** An ungainly thought-stopper. See Virgule, 223.

**Angry, mad.** *Mad* is usually too colloquial for your papers. See *Mad*.

**Ante-, anti-.** *Ante-* means "before": an *antebellum* house (one built before the [Civil] War); *antedate* (to date before). *Anti-* means "against": *antifeminist, antiseptic*. Hyphenate before capitals, and before i and other vowels that confuse the reading: *anti-American, anti-intellectual, anti-acid, anti-ego*.

**Anxious.** Use to indicate *Angst*, agony, and anxiety. Does not mean cheerful expectation: "He was *anxious* to get started." Use *eager* instead.

**Any.** Do not overuse as a modifier.

| POOR | GOOD |
|---|---|
| She was the best of any senior in the class. | She was the best senior in the class. |
| If any people know the answer, they aren't talking. | If anyone knows the answer, that person is not talking. |

Add *other* when comparing likes: "She was better than *any other* senior in the class." But "This junior was better than any senior."

**Anybody, nobody, somebody.** Don't write as two words—*any body, no body, some body*—unless you mean it: "You have some body!"; "No body of water daunted him."

**Any more.** Written as two words, except when an adverb in negatives and questions:

> She never wins *anymore.*
> Does she play *anymore?*

**Anyone.** Don't write as two words—*any one*—unless you mean "any one thing."

**Anyplace, someplace.** Use *anywhere* and *somewhere* (adverbs), unless you mean "any *place*" and "some *place*."

**Anyways.** Nonstandard. "Even if you don't want to, write *anyway.*"

**Appear.** Badly overworked for *seem.*

**Appearing.** Don't write "an expensive-appearing house." "An expensive-looking house" is not much better. Write "an expensive house" or "the house looked expensive."

**Appreciate.** Means "recognize the worth of." Do not use to mean simply "understand."

| LOOSE | CAREFUL |
|---|---|
| I *appreciate* your position. | I *understand* your position. |
| I *appreciate* that your position is grotesque. | I *realize* your position is grotesque. |

**Apt to, likely to, liable to.** *Apt* is the more colloquial choice but fully acceptable for known physical tendencies: *He is apt to overshoot his volleys. Likely to* is for general probabilities: *It is likely to rain; She is likely to succeed. Liable to* implies vulnerability: *He is liable to lose on powder snow; Overconfidence is liable to end in disappointment.* Don't use *liable* or *apt* for mere probability: *She is liable [apt] to come tomorrow* for *She may come tomorrow.*

**Area.** Drop it. *In the area of finance* means *in finance,* and *conclusive in all areas* means simply *conclusive,* or *conclusive in all departments (subjects, topics).* Be specific.

**Around.** Do not use for *about:* it will seem to mean "surrounding."

| POOR | GOOD |
|---|---|
| *Around* thirty people came. | *About* thirty people came. |
| He sang at *around* ten o'clock. | He sang at *about* ten o'clock. |

**As.** This is the right one: not "Nobody loves you *like* I do" but "Nobody loves you *as* I do." (See also *Like.*)

Do not use *as* for *such as:* "Many things, *as* nails, hats, tooth-picks . . . ." Write "Many things, *such as* nails . . . ."

Do not use *as* for *because* or *since;* it is ambiguous:

| AMBIGUOUS | PRECISE |
|---|---|
| As I was walking, I had time to think. | Because I was walking, I had time to think. |

Do not use *as* to mean "that" or "whether" (as in "I don't know *as* he would like her").

**As . . . as.** Use positively, not forgetting the second *as:*

| WRONG | RIGHT |
|---|---|
| *as* long if not longer than the other | *as* long *as* the other, if not longer. |

Negatively, use *not so . . . as.* It is clearer (but more formal) than *as . . . as:*

It is *not so* long as the other.
His argument is *not so* clear *as* hers.

**As being.** Redundant. Cut the *being.* "Even his friends see him *as* [*being*] a waffler."

**As far as.** A wordy windup.

| WORDY | IMPROVED |
|---|---|
| As far as winter clothes are concerned, we are well supplied. | We have a good supply of winter clothes. |

**As if.** Takes the subjunctive: ". . . as if he **were** cold."

**As of, as of now.** Avoid, except for humor. Use *at,* or *now,* or delete entirely.

| POOR | IMPROVED |
|---|---|
| He left, as of ten'o'clock. | He left at ten o'clock. |
| As of now, I've sworn off. | I've just sworn off. |

**As to.** Use only at the beginning of a sentence: "As to his first allegation, I can only say . . . ." Change it to *about*, or omit it, within a sentence: "He knows nothing *about* the details"; "He is not sure [whether] they are right."

**As well as.** You may mean only *and*. Check it out. Avoid such ambiguities as *The Commons voted as well as the Lords*.

**Aspect.** Overused. Try *side*, *part*, *portion*. See *Jargon*.

**At.** Do not use after *where*. "Where is it *at*?" means "Where is it?"

**Authored.** Terrible. Write "She has *written* three plays."

**Awful.** Write *awfully* in your colloquial moments, but *very* is better, and nothing at all may be better yet

> She is awfully good.
> She is very good.
> She is good.

**Awhile, a while.** You usually want the adverb: *linger awhile, the custom endured awhile longer*. If you want the noun, emphasizing a period of time, make it clear: *the custom lasted for a while*.

**Back of, in back of.** *Behind* says it more smoothly.

**Bad, badly.** *Bad* is an adjective: *a bad trip. Badly* is an adverb: *he wrote badly*. Linking verbs take *bad: he smells bad; I feel bad; it looks bad*.

**Balance, bulk.** Make them mean business, as in "He deposited the balance of his allowance" and "The bulk of the crop was ruined." Do not use them for people:

| POOR | IMPROVED |
|---|---|
| The *balance* of the class went home. | The *rest* of the class went home. |
| The *bulk* of the crowd was indifferent. | *Most* of the crowd was indifferent. |

**Basis.** Drop it: *on a daily basis* means *daily*.

**Be sure and.** Write *be sure to*.

**Because of, due to.** See *Due to*.

**Being as, being that.** Redundancies for *because* and *since*.

| POOR | IMPROVED |
|---|---|
| Being as the windward leg was choppy, his boat sailed poorly. | Because the windward leg . . . . |

**Besides.** Means "in addition to," not "other than."

| POOR | IMPROVED |
|------|----------|
| Something *besides* smog was the cause [unless smog was also a cause]. | Something *other than* smog was the cause. |

**Better than.** Unless you really mean *better than*, use *more than*.

| POOR | IMPROVED |
|------|----------|
| The lake was *better than* two miles across. | The lake was *more than* two miles across. |

**Between, among.** *Between* ("by twain") has *two* in mind; *among* has more than two. *Between*, a preposition, takes an object; *between us, between you and me*. ("Between you and I" is sheer embarrassment; see *Me*, subsequently.) *Between* also indicates geographical placing: "It is midway between Chicago, Detroit, and Toledo." "The grenade fell between Jones and me and the gatepost"; but "The grenade fell among the fruit stands." "Between every building was a plot of petunias" (or "In between each building . . . .") conveys the idea, however nonsensical "between a building" is. "Between all the buildings were plots of petunias" would be better, though still a compromise.

**Bias.** Our language is biased by ages of patriarchs, warriors, subservient woman, and racial antipathies, and we are all biased by where we are from and what we are. As you write, reach beyond these limits to engage all shades and both genders of readers. A limiting reference by a *he* or a *his* frequently slips into our sentences. Change to the neutral and inclusive plural if you can:

| POOR | IMPROVED |
|------|----------|
| Every student should buy *his* own copy. | Students should buy their own copies. |

Or change *he* to *he or she*:

| POOR | IMPROVED | BETTER |
|------|----------|--------|
| Everyone knows when *he* has painted *himself* into a corner. | Everyone knows when *he or she* has painted *himself or herself* . . . . | We all know when *we* have painted *ourselves* . . . . |

Although "he or she" takes in the facts of gender, it still gives the male first place. Nevertheless, "she or he" puts the female first with a mildly aggressive push and may seem too fussy and self-conscious. Stick with "he or she." Such compromises as *s/he* and *she/he* are hard on the eye and unspeakable.

Look out for inadvertent assumptions of gender:

| POOR | IMPROVED |
|------|----------|
| The preschool program appeals to working *mothers*. | The preschool program appeals to working *parents*. |
| Businesswomen spend many hours in household chores. | *People in business*. . . . |
| Style comes from a *craftsman* who has discovered the gnarls in *his* material. | Style comes from a *craftsman or craftswoman* who has discovered the gnarls in *the* material. |

Be careful about stereotypes, such as assuming that all women are talkative, all men aggressive, all gays promiscuous, all blonds dizzy.

**Bimonthly, biweekly.** Careless usage has damaged these almost beyond recognition, confusing them with *semimonthly* and *semiweekly*. For clarity, better say "every two months" and "every two weeks."

**But, cannot but.** "He can but fail" is old but usable. After a negative, however, the natural turn in *but* causes confusion:

| POOR | IMPROVED |
|------|----------|
| He cannot but fail. | He can only fail. |
| He could not doubt but that it . . . . | He could not doubt that it . . . . |
| He could not help but take . . . . | He could not help taking . . . . |

When *but* means "except," it is a preposition. "Everybody laughed but me."

Similarly, *but*s too frequent keep your readers off balance:

| POOR | IMPROVED |
|------|----------|
| The campaign was successful *but* costly. *But* the victory was sweet. | The campaign was costly, *but* victory was sweet. |

**But that, but what.** Colloquial redundancies.

| POOR | IMPROVED |
|------|----------|
| There is no doubt but that John's is the best steer. | There is no doubt that John's is the best steer. |
| | John's is clearly the best steer. |
| There is no one but what would enjoy it. | Anyone would enjoy it. |

**Can, may (could, might).** *Can* means ability; *may* asks permission, and expresses possibility. *Can I go?* means, strictly, "Have I the physical capability to go?" In speech, *can* usually serves for both ability and permission, though the clerk will probably say, properly, "May I help you?" In assertions, the distinction is clear: "He can do it." "He may do it." "If he can, he may." Keep these distinctions clear in your writing.

Could and *might* are the past tenses, but when used in the present time they are subjunctive, with shades of possibility, and hence politeness: "*Could* you come next Tuesday?" "*Might* I inquire about your plans?" *Could* may mean ability almost as strongly as *can:* "I'm sure he could do it." But *could* and *might* are usually subjunctives, expressing doubt:

Perhaps he could make it, if he tries.
I might be able to go, but I doubt it.

**Cannot, can not.** Use either, depending on the rhythm and emphasis you want. *Can not* emphasizes the *not* slightly.

**Can't hardly, couldn't hardly.** Use *can hardly, could hardly* because *hardly* carries the negative sense.

**Can't help but.** A marginal mixture in speech of two clearer and more formal ideas, *I can but regret* and *I can't help regretting*. Avoid it in writing.

**Capital, capitol.** Frequently confused. You mean *capital*, the head thing (from Latin *capitalis*, "of the head")—the head city of a government, the head letter of a sentence or name, the top ("head") of a Greek column, the money that heads investments, the offense that once got your head chopped off ("capital punishment"). The Capitol, capitalized, is the Temple of Jupiter on the Capitoline Hill in Rome or the building and hill in Washington, D.C., named after them. The legislature sits in the Capitol in our capital. State legislatures also sit in their *capitols* (buildings; small c).

**Case.** Chop out this deadwood:

| POOR | IMPROVED |
|---|---|
| In many cases, ants survive . . . . | Ants often . . . . |
| In such a case, surgery is recommended | Then surgery is recommended. |
| In case he goes . . . . | If he goes . . . . |

| POOR | IMPROVED |
|---|---|
| Everyone enjoyed himself, except in a few scattered cases. | Almost everyone enjoyed himself and herself. |

**Cause, result.** Because *all* events are both causes and results, suspect yourself of wordiness if you write either word.

| WORDY | ECONOMICAL |
|---|---|
| The invasions caused depopulation of the country. | The invasions depopulated the country. |
| She lost as a result of poor campaigning. | She lost because her campaign was poor. |

**Cause-and-effect relationship.** Verbal adhesive tape. Recast the sentence, with some verb other than the wordy *cause*:

| POOR | IMPROVED |
|---|---|
| Othello's jealousy rises in a cause-and-effect relationship when he sees the handkerchief. | Seeing the handkerchief arouses Othello's jealousy. |

**Censor, censure.** Frequently confused. A *censor* cuts out objectionable passages. To *censor* is to cut or prohibit. To *censure* is to condemn: "The *censor censored* some parts of the play, and *censured* the author as an irresponsible drunkard."

**Center around.** A physical impossibility. Make it *centers on*, or *revolves around*, or *concerns*, or *is about*.

**Circumstances.** *In these circumstances* makes more sense than *under these circumstances* because the stances are standing around (*circum*), not standing under. Often jargon: *The economy is in difficult circumstances* means, simply, *The economy is in trouble*.

**Clichés.** Don't use unwittingly. But they can be effective. There are two kinds: (1) the rhetorical—*tried and true, the not too distant future, sadder* *but wiser, in the style to which she had become accustomed;* (2) the prover-bial—*apple of his eye, skin of your teeth, sharp as a tack, quick as a flash, twinkling of an eye.* The rhetorical ones are clinched by sound alone; the proverbial are metaphors caught in the popular fancy. Proverbial clichés can lighten a dull passage. You may even revitalize them because they are frequently dead metaphors (see 130, 132). Avoid the rhetorical clichés unless you turn them to your advantage; *tried and untrue, glad-der and wiser, a future not too distant.*

**Come and, be sure and, go and, try and.** All colloquial ways of saying *come to, be sure to, go to, try to,* "Come and see us" means *Come to see us,* and so forth.

**Compare to, compare with.** To compare *to* is to show similarities (and dif-ferences) between different kinds; to compare *with* is to show differences (and similarities) between like kinds.

> Composition has been compared to architecture.
> He compares favorably *with* Mickey Spillane.
> Compare Shakespeare *with* Ben Jonson.

**Complement, compliment.** Frequently confused. *Complement* is a com-pletion; *compliment* is a flattery: "When the regiment reached its full *complement* of recruits, the general gave it a flowery *compliment.*"

**Concept.** Often jargonish and wordy.

| POOR | IMPROVED |
|------|----------|
| The concept of multiprogramming allows .... | Multiprogramming allows .... |

**Conscience, conscious.** Sometimes confused. Your *conscience* is your inner voice whispering what is right. You are *conscious* when you are aware of your surroundings.

**Consensus.** The opinion of a majority. Don't write the redundant *con-sensus of opinion.*

**Considerable.** Jargon. Say *terrible, grim, excessive, worrysome, big.*

**Contact.** Don't *contact* anyone: call, write, find, tell him.

**Continual, continuous.** You can improve your writing by *continual* prac-tice, but the effort cannot be *continuous.* The first means "frequently repeated"; the second, "without interruption."

> It requires *continual* practice.
> There was a *continuous* line of clouds.

**Contractions.** We use them constantly in conversation: *don't, won't, can't, shouldn't, isn't.* Avoid them in writing, or your prose will seem too chummy. But use one now and then when you want some colloquial emphasis: *You can't go home again.*

**Convince, persuade.** *Convince* ... THAT and *persuade* ... TO are the standard idioms. *Convince* ... OF is also standard. Nevertheless, *convince* is frequently creeping in before infinitives with *to.*

| POOR | RIGHT |
|------|-------|
| They *convinced* him to run. | They *persuaded* him to run. |
| | They *convinced* him *that* he should run. |
| | They *convinced* him of their support. |

**Could, might.** See *Can, may.*

**Could care less.** You mean *couldn't care less.* Speech has worn off the *n't,* making the words say the opposite of what you mean. A person who cares a great deal could care a great deal less; one who does not care "*couldn't* care less": he's already at rock bottom.

**Could of, would of.** Phonetic misspellings of *could've* ("could have") and *would've* ("would have"). In writing, spell them out completely: *could have* and *would have.*

**Couldn't hardly.** Use *could hardly.*

**Council, counsel, consul.** *Council* is probably the noun you mean: a group of deliberators. *Counsel* is usually the verb "to advise." But *counsel* is also a noun: an adviser, an attorney, and their advice. Check your dictionary to see that you are writing what you mean. A *counselor* gives you his *counsel* about your courses, which may be submitted to an academic *council.* A *consul* is an official representing your government in a foreign country.

**Credible, credulous.** *Credible* is believable; *credulous* is willing to believe. "His testimony was not *credible,* but the jury was still *credulous.*

**Criteria.** Plural: *These criteria are.* The singular is *criterion.*

**Curriculum.** The plural is *curricula,* though *curriculums* will get by in informal prose. The adjective is *curricular.*

**Data.** A plural like *criteria, strata, phenomena:* "The data are inconclusive."

**Definitely.** A high-school favorite, badly overused.

**Denotation, Connotation.** See 128.

**Different from, different than.** Avoid *different than*, which confuses the idea of differing. Things *differ from* each other. Only in comparing several differences does *than* make clear sense: "All three of his copies differ from the original, but his last one is *more* different *than* the others." But here *than* is controlled by *more*, not by *different*.

| WRONG | RIGHT |
|---|---|
| It is different *than* I expected. | It is different *from* what I expected. |
| | It is not what I expected. |
| He is different *than* the others. | He is different *from* the others. |

**Discreet, discrete.** Frequently confused. *Discreet* means someone tactful and judicious; *discrete* means something separate and distinct: "She was *discreet* in examining each *discrete* part of the evidence."

**Disinterested.** Does not mean "uninterested" nor "indifferent." *Disinterested* means impartial, without private interests in the issue.

| WRONG | RIGHT |
|---|---|
| You seem disinterested in the case. | You seem uninterested in the case. |
| | The judge was disinterested and perfectly fair. |
| She was disinterested in it. | She was indifferent to it. |

**Double negative.** A negation that cancels another negation, making it accidentally positive: "He couldn't hardly" indicates that "He could easily," the opposite of its intended meaning. "They can't win nothing" really says that they *must* win something.

But some doubled negations carry an indirect emphasis—a mild irony, really—in such tentative assertions as "One cannot be certain that she will not prove to be the century's greatest poet," or "a not unattractive offer."

**Drastic.** A catchall for *severe, harsh, murderous, bold*.

**Due to.** Never begin a sentence with "**Due** to circumstances beyond his control, he . . . ." *Due* is an adjective and must always relate to a noun or pronoun: "The catastrophe *due* to circumstances beyond his control was unavoidable," or "The catastrophe was *due* to circumstances beyond his control" (predicate adjective). But you are still better off with *because of, through, by*, or *owing to. Due to* is usually a symptom of wordiness, especially when it leads to *due to the fact that*, a venerable piece of plumbing meaning *because*.

| WRONG | RIGHT |
|-------|-------|
| He resigned *due to* sickness. | He resigned *because of* sickness. |
| She succeeded *due to* hard work. | She succeeded *through* hard work. |
| He lost his shirt *due to* leaving it in the locker room. | He lost his shirt *by* leaving it in the locker room. |
| The Far East will continue to worry the West, *due to* a general social upheaval. | The Far East will continue to worry the West, *owing to* a general social upheaval. |
| The program failed *due to the fact that* a recession had set in. | The program failed *because* a recession had set in. |

**Effect.** See *Affect.*

**Elicit, illicit.** *Elicit* means "to draw forth." *Illicit* means "illegal."

**Either, neither.** One of two, taking a singular verb: *Either is a good candidate, but neither speaks well. Either . . . or (neither . . . nor)* are paralleling conjunctions. See 102–103.

**Eminent, imminent, immanent.** Often confused. *Eminent* is something that stands out; *imminent* is something about to happen. *Immanent,* much less common, is a philosophical term for something spiritual "remaining within, indwelling." You usually mean *eminent.*

**Enormity.** Means "atrociousness"; does not mean "enormousness."

the *enormity* of the crime
the *enormousness* of the mountain

**Enthuse.** Don't use it; it coos and gushes.

| WRONG | RIGHT |
|-------|-------|
| She *enthused* over her new job. | She gushed on and on about her new job. |
| He was *enthused.* | He was *enthusiastic.* |

**Environment.** Frequently misspelled *enviorment* or *envirnment.* It is business jargon, unless you mean the world around us.

| WORDY | IMPROVED |
|-------|----------|
| in an MVT environment | in MVT; with MVT; under MVT |
| They work in an environment of cost analysis. | They analyze cost. |

**Equally as good.** A redundant mixture of two choices, *as good as* and *equally good.* Use only one of these at a time.

**Etc.** Substitute something specific for it, or drop it, or write "and so forth."

**Everyday, every day.** You wear your *everyday* clothes *every day.*
**Everyone, everybody.** Avoid the common mismatching *their:*

"Everyone does *his or her* [not *their*] own thing."

**Exists.** Another symptom of wordiness.

| POOR | IMPROVED |
|---|---|
| a system like that which exists at the university | a system like that at the university |

**Facet.** Usually jargon. It means "little face," one of the many small *surfaces* of a diamond. Use it metaphorically or not at all.

| POOR | IMPROVED |
|---|---|
| This problem has several *facets.* | This problem has five parts. Each *facet* of the problem sparkles with implications. |

**The fact that.** Deadly with *due to,* and usually wordy by itself.

| POOR | IMPROVED |
|---|---|
| *The fact that* Rome fell *due to* moral decay is clear. | *That* Rome fell *through* moral decay is clear. |
| This disparity is in part *a result of the fact that* some of the best indicators make their best show-ings in an expanding market. | This disparity arises in part *because* some of the best indicators . . . . |

| POOR | IMPROVED |
|---|---|
| *In view of the fact that* more core is used . . . . | Because more core . . . . |

**Factor.** Avoid it. We've used it to death. Try *element* when you mean "ele-ment." Look for an accurate verb when you mean "cause."

| POOR | IMPROVED |
|---|---|
| The increase in female employment is a factor in juvenile delinquency. | The increase in female employment has contributed to juvenile delinquency. |
| Puritan self-sufficiency was an important factor in the rise of capitalism. | Puritan self-sufficiency favored the rise of capitalism. |

**Faith, fate.** Often confused, along with *faithful* and *faithless* as against *fateful* and other versions of *fate*. *Faith* is trust, a religious belief. *Fate* is destiny.

**Farther, further.** The first means distance, actual or figurative; the second means more in time or degree. You look *farther* and consider *further* before you go *farther* into debt.

**Feasible.** See *Viable*.

**Fewer, less.** See *Less, few*.

**The field of.** Try to omit it—you usually can—or bring the metaphor to life. It is trite and wordy.

| POOR | IMPROVED |
|---|---|
| He is studying in the field of geology. | He is studying geology. |

**Firstly.** Archaic. Trim all such terms to *first, second*, and so on.

**Flaunt, flout.** *Flaunt* means to parade, to wave impudently; *flout* means to scoff at. The first is metaphorical; the second, not: "She *flaunted* her wickedness and *flouted* the police."

**Flounder, founder.** Frequently confused. *Flounder* means to wobble clumsily, to flop around; *founder*, to sink (The *ship foundered*), or, figuratively, to collapse, or go lame (said of horses).

**For.** See 203.

**Former, latter.** Passable, but they often make the readers look back. Repeating the antecedents is clearer:

| POOR | IMPROVED |
|---|---|
| The Athenians and Spartans were always in conflict. *The former* had a better civilization; *the latter* had a better army. | The Athenians and Spartans were always in conflict. Athens had the better culture; Sparta, the better army. |

**Fun.** A noun. Avoid it as an adjective: *a fun party* ("The party was fun").

**Further.** See *Farther*.

**Good, well.** *Good* is the adjective: *good time*. *Well* is the adverb: *well done*. In verbs of feeling, we are caught in the ambiguities of health. *I feel good* is more accurate than *I feel well* because *well* may mean that your feelers are in working order. But *I feel well* is also an honest statement: "I feel that I am well." Ask yourself what your readers might misunderstand from your statements, and you will use these two confused terms clearly.

**Got, gotten.** Both acceptable. Your rhythm and emphasis will decide. America prefers the older *gotten* in many phrases; Britain goes mainly for *got*.

**Hanged, hung.** *Hanged* is the past of *hang* only for the death penalty.

**They hung the rope and hanged the man.**

**Hardly.** Watch the negative here. "I can't *hardly*" means "*I can* easily." Write: "One can hardly conceive the vastness."

**He, she.** Elude the dilemma with *he or she*. Evasions like *he/she* and *s/he* are not what we say and jar the eye in print. See *Bias*.

**Healthy, healthful.** Swimming is *healthful*; swimmers are *healthy*.

**Heaven sakes.** Should be *heaven's sake*, "For the sake of heaven, don't," or ". . . No!" An exclamation of disapproval or frustration.

**His/her, his (her).** Shift to the neutral plural ("Students should sign their exams on the first page."), employ an *occasional* "his or her," or otherwise rephrase: *s/he* is unpronounceable; *she/he*, not much better. See *Bias*.

**Hisself.** You mean *himself*.

**Historically.** A favorite windy throat-clearer. Badly overused.

**History.** The *narrative*, written or oral, of events, not the events themselves. Therefore, avoid the redundancy "*recorded* history," likewise "*annals* of history," "*chronicles* of history." *History* alone can suffice or even itself disappear. "Archeologists have uncovered evidence of events previously unknown to history" would be better without the misleading *to history*.

**Hopefully.** An inaccurate dangler, a cliché. "Hopefully, they are at work" does not mean that they are working hopefully. Simply use "I hope" or "one hopes" (but *not* "it is hoped"); not "They are a symbol of idealism, and, hopefully, are representative," but "They are a symbol of idealism and are, one hopes, representative."

**However.** Initial *however* should be an adverb: "However long the task takes, it will be done." For the "floating" *however*, and *however* versus *but*, see 32, 205, 211.

**Hung.** See *Hanged*.

**The idea that.** Like *the fact that*—and the cure is the same. Cut it.

**If, whether.** *If* is for uncertainties; *whether*, for alternatives. Usually the distinction is unimportant: *I don't know if it will rain; I don't know whether it will rain [or not]*.

**If not.** Usually ambiguous for *and indeed*. "They made good, *if not* excellent, profits" usually intends to say that the profits were really a bit better than good, but it actually says negatively that they were OK but not outstanding. Say "They made good, *and indeed* excellent, profits.

**Imminent, immanent.** See *Eminent*.

**Imply, infer.** The author *implies*; you *infer* ("carry in") what you think he means.

> He *implied* that all women are hypocrites.
> From the ending, we *infer* that tragedy ennobles as it kills.

> Perfect Communication
>
> Confusion would
> More surely fly
> If you'd infer
> What I imply.
>
> G. Sterling Leiby

**Importantly.** Often an inaccurate (and popular) adverb, like *hopefully*.

| INACCURATE | IMPROVED |
|---|---|
| *More importantly,* he walked home. | *More important,* he walked home. |

**In connection with.** Always wordy. Say *about*.

| POOR | IMPROVED |
|---|---|
| They liked everything *in connection with* the university. | They liked everything *about* the university. |

**Includes.** Jargonish, as a general verb for specific actions.

| POOR | IMPROVED |
|---|---|
| The report *includes* rural and urban marketing. | The report *analyzes* rural and urban marketing. |

**Incredible, incredulous.** Sometimes confused. The first means *unbelievable*, frequently a synonym for *amazing, astonishing,* and the like. The second indicates disbelieving, doubting, skepticism: "She gave him an *incredulous* look." See *Credible, credulous*.

**Individual.** Write *person* unless you really mean someone separate and unique.

**Infer.** See *Imply, infer.*

**Ingenious, ingenuous.** Sometimes confused. *Ingenious* means clever; *ingenuous*, naïve. *Ingenius* is a common misspelling for both.

**Inside of, outside of.** "They painted the *outside* of the house" means what it says, but these idioms can be redundant and inaccurate.

| POOR | IMPROVED |
| --- | --- |
| *inside* of half an hour | *within* half an hour |
| He had nothing for dinner *outside* of a few potato chips. | He had nothing for dinner *but* a few potato chips. |

**Instances.** Redundant. *In many instances* means *often, frequently.*

**Interesting.** Make what you say interesting, but never tell the readers *it is interesting*: they may not believe you. *It is interesting* is merely a lazy preamble.

| POOR | IMPROVED |
| --- | --- |
| It is interesting to note that nicotine is named for Jean Nicot, who introduced tobacco into France in 1560. | Nicotine is named for Jean Nicot, who introduced tobacco into France in 1560. |

**Into.** An all too popular evasion of precise meaning:

| POOR | IMPROVED |
| --- | --- |
| He is *into* programs. They are *into* antiques. | He is *writing* programs. They are *collecting* antiques. |

**Irregardless.** A faulty word. The *ir-* (meaning *not*) is doing what the *less* already does. You are thinking of *irrespective* and trying to say *regardless.*

**Is when, is where.** Avoid these loose attempts:

| LOOSE | SPECIFIC |
| --- | --- |
| Combustion is when [where] oxidation bursts into flame. | Combustion is oxidation bursting into flame. |

**It.** Give it a specific reference, as a pronoun. See 115, 193.

**Its, it's.** Don't confuse *its*, the possessive pronoun, with *it's*, the contraction of *it is*.

**-ize.** A handy way to make verbs from nouns and adjectives (*patron-ize*, *civil-ize*). But handle with care. Manufacture new *-izes* only with a sense of humor and daring ("they Harvardized the party"). Business overdoes the trick: *finalize* has provoked strong disapproval from writers who are not commercially familiarized.

**Jargon.** A technical, wordy phraseology that becomes characteristic of any particular trade, or branch of learning, frequently with nouns modifying nouns and in the passive voice. Break out of it by making words mean what they say.

| JARGON | CLEAR MEANING |
|---|---|
| The *plot structure* of the play provides no *objective correlative*. | The play fails to act out and exhibit the hero's inner conflicts. |
| | The plot is incoherent. |
| | The structure is lopsided. |
| The *character development* of the heroine is excellent. | The author sketches and deepens the heroine's personality skillfully. |
| | The heroine matures convincingly. |
| Three *motivation profile studies* were developed *in the area of production management*. | The company studied its production managers and discovered three kinds of motivation. |
| He *structured* the meeting | He organized (planned, arranged) the meeting. |

**Judgment, judgement.** Americans write *judgment*; the British, *judgement*, keeping the original *e*.

**Kind of, sort of.** Colloquialisms for *somewhat*, *rather*, *something*, and the like. Usable, but don't overuse.

**Lay.** Don't use *lay* to mean *lie*. To *lay* means "to put" and needs an object; to *lie* means "to recline." Memorize both their present and past tenses, frequently confused:

I *lie* down when I can: I *lay* down yesterday; I have *lain* down often. [Intransitive, no object.]

The hen *lays* an egg; she *laid* one yesterday; she has *laid* four this week. [Transitive, *lays* an object.]

Now I *lay* the book on the table; I *laid* it there yesterday; I have *laid* it there many times.

**Lead, led.**  Because *lead* (being in front) is spelled like the *lead* in *lead pencil*, people frequently misspell the past tense, which is *led*.

**Lend, loan.**  Don't use *loan* for *lend*. *Lend* is the verb; *loan*, the noun: "Please *lend* me a five; I need a *loan* badly." Remember the line: "I'll *send* you to a *friend* who'll be willing to *lend*."

**Less, few.**  Don't use one for the other. *Less* answers "How much?" *Few* answers "How many?"

| WRONG | RIGHT |
|---|---|
| We had *less* people than last time. | We had *fewer* people this time than last. |

**Level.**  Usually redundant jargon. *High level management* is *top management* and *college level courses* are *college courses*. What is a *level management* or a *level course* anyway?

**Lie, lay.**  See *Lay*.

**Lighted, lit.**  Equally good past tenses for *light* (both "to ignite, illuminate" and "to descend upon"), with *lit* perhaps more frequent. Rhythm usually determines the choice. *Lighted* seems preferred for adverbs and combinations: *a clean well-lighted place; it could have been lighted better*.

**Like, as, as if.**  Usage blurs them, but the writer should distinguish them before deciding to go colloquial. Otherwise, the writer may throw readers off.

He looks *like* me.
He dresses *as* [the way] I do.
He acts *as if* he were high.

Note that *like* takes the objective case and that *as*, being a conjunction, is followed by the nominative:

She looks like *her*.
She is as tall as *I* [am].
She is tall, like *me*.

*Like* sometimes replaces *as* where no verb follows in phrases other than comparisons (*as . . . as*):

It works *like* a charm. ( . . . *as* a charm *works*.)
It went over *like* a lead balloon. ( . . . *as* a lead balloon *does*.)
They worked *like* beavers. ( . . . *as* beavers *do*.)

**Literally.** Often misused, and overused, as a general emphasizer: "We *literally* wiped them off the field." Say "We wiped them off the field."

**Loan.** See *Lend.*

**Loose, lose.** You will *lose* the game if your defense is *loose.*

**Lots, lots of, a lot of.** Conversational for *many, much, great, considerable.* Try something else. See *Alot.*

**Mad.** It means "insane," but it also became "angry" in ordinary speech as early as 1300. As *angry,* it is usually too colloquial for your papers.

**Majority.** Misused for *most:* "*The majority* of the play is comic" [wrong]. A *majority* is more than half in numbers of a class or group, at least 50.1 percent. A *plurality* is less than half but more than any other count made of two or more other competing groups.

**Man, Mankind.** Built into our thinking. Pope's "The proper study of Mankind is Man" lives in our consciousness. But to cut against the stereotype we must now think of alternatives: *men and women, people, humanity, humankind, the human race.*

**Many times.** Two wordy words for *often.*

**May.** See *Can, may.*

**Maybe.** Conversational for *perhaps.* Sometimes misused for *may be.* Unless you want an unmistakable colloquial touch, avoid it altogether.

**Manner.** A sign of amateur standing. Use *way,* or *like this,* not *in this manner.*

**Me.** Use *me* boldly. It is the proper object of verbs and prepositions. Nothing is sadder than faulty propriety: "between you and *I,*" or "They gave it to John and *I,*" or "They invited my wife and *I.*" Test yourself by dropping the first member "between *I*" (*no*), "gave it to *I*" (*no*), "invited *I*" (*no*). Do NOT substitute *myself.*

**Medium, media.** The singular and the plural. Avoid *medias,* and you will distinguish yourself from the masses.

**Midst, mist.** Sometimes you may write *mist,* dew in the air, when you mean *midst,* in the middle of, or *missed.*

**Might.** See *Can, may.*

**Might of.** You mean *might have.* "He *might have* killed her."

**Moral, morale.** The first is good behavior, or the point of a story illustrating it. The second is the inspiring spirit of a group.

**Most.** Does not mean *almost.*

| WRONG | RIGHT |
|---|---|
| **Most** everyone knows. | **Almost** everyone knows. |

**Must, a must.**  A *must* is popular jargon. Try something else:

| JARGON | IMPROVED |
|---|---|
| *Jurassic Park* is really *a must* for every viewer. | Everyone interested in film should see *Jurassic Park*. |
| This is *a must* course. | Everyone should take this course. |

**Must of.**  Like *might of*, a goof for *might have*.

**Myself.**  Use it only reflexively ("I hurt *myself*") or intensively ("I *myself* often have trouble"). Fear of *me* leads to the incorrect "They gave it to John and *myself*." Do not use *myself, himself, herself, themselves* for *me, him, her, them*.

**Nature.**  Avoid this padding. Do not write *moderate in nature, moderate by nature, of a moderate nature*; simply write *moderate*.

**Near.**  Avoid this wordy and popular atrocity: "*near* perfect"; "a *near* ecstatic applause"; "the *near* extermination of a species." Say *almost, nearly, virtually*, or nothing: "an ecstatic applause"; "almost exterminating the species."

**Neither.**  See *Either*.

**Nice.**  Overused for anything pleasing, proper, or skillful: "A nice day; a nice girl; a nice catch." Try for something more specific: "a balmy day; a friendly (pretty, well-mannered) girl; a skillful (remarkable, extraordinary) catch."

**No one.**  Two words in America, not *noone*, or *no-one* (British).

**None.**  This pronoun means "no one" and takes a singular verb, as do *each, every, everyone, nobody*, and other distributives. See 184.

**Nowhere near.**  Use *not nearly* or *far from*, unless you really mean *near*: "He was nowhere, near the end." See *Near*.

**Nowheres.**  You mean *nowhere*.

**Nohow.**  Colloquial talk for *not at all* or *in no way*. Don't write it.

**Number of.**  Usually correct. See *Amount of*.

**Numbers.**  Spell out those that take no more than two words (*twelve, twelfth, twenty-four, two hundred*); use numerals for the rest (*101, 203, 4,510*). This is MLA style. Informal styles write out only numbers from one to nine. Spell out *all* numbers beginning a sentence. But use numerals to make contrasts and statistics clearer: *20 as compared to 49; only 1 out of 40; 200 or 300 times as great*. Change a two-word number to numerals when it matches a numeral: *with 400* [not *four hundred*] *students and 527 parents*. Numbers are customary with streets: *42nd Street, 5th Avenue*, which may also be spelled out for aesthetic reasons: *Fifth Avenue*. Use numbers also with dates, times, measurements, and money:

*1 April 1996; 6:30* A.M. (but *half-past six*); *3 × 5 cards; 240 by 100 feet; 6'9"* (but *six feet tall*); *$4.99; $2 a ticket* (but *16 cents a bunch*). You may use Roman numerals (see your dictionary) with Arabic to designate parts of plays and books: "Romeo's mistake (II. iii. 69)"; "in *Tom Jones* (XII.iv.483)." But the new style is all Arabic: (2.3.69), (12.4.483). See 162–163. Also see *Per cent, percent, percentage.*

**Off of.** *Write from:* "He jumped *from* his horse."

**O.K., OK, okay.** The most popular expression around the globe. It originated in a Boston newspaper in the 1830s among a humorous series of abbreviations, this one standing for the dialectical "Orl (pronounced *awl* in Boston) Kerrect," for "all correct": "O.K." The preferred spelling is now "OK." Use it carefully as colloquial flavoring.

**On the part of.** Wordy.

POOR
There was a great deal of discontent *on the part of* those students who could not enroll.

IMPROVED
The students who could not enroll were deeply discontented.

**One.** As a pronoun—"*One* usually flunks the first time"—see 7–8. Avoid the redundant numeral:

POOR
One of the most effective ways of writing is rewriting.

IMPROVED
The best writing is rewriting.

POOR
*The Ambassadors* is one of the most interesting of James's books.
The meeting was obviously a poor one.

IMPROVED
*The Ambassadors* is James at his best.
The meeting was obviously poor.

In constructions such as "one of the best that . . ." and "one of the worst who . . . ," the relative pronouns often are mistakenly considered singular. The plural noun of the prepositional phrase (*the best, worst*), not the *one*, is the antecedent, and the verb must be plural too:

WRONG
one of the best [*players*] who *has* ever swung a bat

RIGHT
one of the best [*players*] who *have* ever swung a bat

**Only.** Don't put it in too soon; you will say what you do not mean.

WRONG                                RIGHT
He *only liked* mystery stories.     He liked *only* mystery stories.

**Overall.** Jargonish. Use *general,* or rephrase.

DULL                                 IMPROVED
The overall quality was good.        The lectures were generally good.

**Oversight.** An unintentional omission: "Leaving you off the list was an *oversight.*" Unfortunately, officialdom uses it for *overview* or *supervisory.* Congress now has more than one Oversight Committee—which sounds like a committee set up to catch omissions. Avoid this ambiguity. Keep your *oversights* meaning *oversights.*

**Passed, past.** The first is the verb; the second, the noun for time gone by. Because you *passed* your exam in that time and because they sound the same, you may confuse them. Keep them straight.

**Parent.** One of those nouns aping a verb: *to rear, bring up, supervise, raise, love.* As a verb, avoid it, and choose the more accurate verb for what you have in mind.

**Persecute, prosecute.** *To persecute,* coming from Latin *sequor,* "to follow," is to harass, harry, oppress, like a dog on a trail. *To prosecute,* from the same source, is to bring legal charges against presumed offenders.

**Per.** Use *a:* "He worked ten hours *a* day." *Per* is jargonish, except in conventional Latin phrases: *per diem, per capita* (not italicized in your running prose).

POOR                                 IMPROVED
This will cost us a manhour *per*    A year from now, this will cost us a
    machine *per* month a year from      manhour a machine a month.
    now.
As *per* your instructions.          According to your instructions.

**Per cent, percent, percentage.** *Percent* (one word) seems preferred, though *percentage,* without numbers, still carries polish: "A large *percentage* of nonvoters attended." Use both the % sign and numerals only when comparing percentages as in technical reports; elsewhere, use numerals with *percent* when your figures cannot be spelled out in one or two words (2 1/2 percent, 150 percent, 48.5 percent). Otherwise, spell out the numbers as well: *twenty-three percent, ten percent, a hundred percent.* See *Numbers.*

**Perfect.** Not "more perfect" but "more nearly perfect."

**Personal, personnel.** Something individual, private, pertaining to or directed at a particular person as distinguished from an entire staff of persons:

She made a *personal* appearance.
All the office *personnel* agreed that he was getting too *personal.*

**Personally.** Almost always superfluous.

| POOR | IMPROVED |
|---|---|
| I want to welcome them personally. | I want to welcome them [myself]. |
| *Personally,* I like it. | I like it. |

**Phase.** Do not use when *part* is wanted; "a *phase* of the organization" is better put as "a *part* of the organization." A phase is a stage in a cycle, as of the moon, of business, of the financial markets.

**Phenomena.** Frequently misused for the singular *phenomenon:* "This is a striking *phenomenon*" (not *phenomena*).

**Phenomenal.** Misused for a general intensive: "His popularity was *phenomenal.*" A phenomenon is a fact of nature, in the ordinary nature of things. Find another word for the extraordinary: "His success was *extraordinary*" (*unusual, astounding, stupendous*).

**Plan on.** Use *plan to.* "He planned on going" should be "He planned to go."

**Plus.** Say *and* unless you mean "two *plus* two": "The dinner was great, *and* it cost us nothing."

**Prejudice.** When you write "He was *prejudice,*" your readers may be *puzzle.* Give it a *d:* "He was *prejudiced*"; then they won't be *puzzled.*

**Presently.** Drop it, or use *now.* Many readers will take it to mean *soon:* "He will go *presently.*" It is characteristic of official jargon:

| POOR | IMPROVED |
|---|---|
| The committee is meeting *presently.* | The committee is meeting. |
| | The committee is meeting *soon.* |
| He is *presently* studying Greek. | He is studying Greek. |

**Principle, principal.** Often confused. *Principle* is a noun only, meaning an essential truth or rule: "It works on the *principle* that hot air rises." *Principal* is the adjective: The high-school *principal* acts as a noun because usage has dropped the *person* the adjective once modified. Likewise, *principal* is the principal amount of your money, which draws interest.

**Prioritize.** Business jargon. Another of those sprouting *-ize* words. Try *put first, rank, arrange,* or the like.

**Process.** Often verbal fat. For example, the following can reduce more often than not: *production process,* to *production; legislative* (or *legislation*) *process,* to *legislation; educational* (or *education*) *process,* to *education; societal process* to *social forces.*

**Proceed to.** Cut it:

| WORDY | IMPROVED |
|---|---|
| They *proceeded to* start the fireworks. | They *started* the fireworks. |

**Proof, evidence.** *Proof* results from enough *evidence* to establish a point beyond doubt. Be modest about claiming proof:

| POOR | IMPROVED |
|---|---|
| This *proves* that Fielding was in Bath at the time. | Evidently, Fielding was in Bath at the time. |

**Provide.** If you *absolutely* cannot use the meaningful verb directly, you may say *provide,* provided you absolutely cannot *give, furnish, allow, supply, enable, authorize, permit, facilitate, force, do, make, effect, help, be, direct, encourage* . . . .

**Providing that.** Use *provided,* and drop the *that. Providing,* with or without *that,* tends to make a misleading modification.

| POOR | IMPROVED |
|---|---|
| I will drop, *providing that* I get an incomplete. | I will drop, *provided* I get an incomplete. |

In "I will drop, *providing that* I get an incomplete," *you* seem to be providing, contrary to what you mean.

**Put across.** Try something else: *convinced, persuaded, explained, made clear. Put across* is badly overused.

**Quality.** Keep it as a noun. Too many *professional quality writers* are already producing *poor quality prose,* and *poor in quality* means *poor.*

**Quite.** An acceptable but overused emphatic: *quite good, quite expressive, quite a while, quite a person.* Try rephrasing it now and then: *good, very good, for some time, an able person.*

**Quote, quotation.** Quote your quotations, and put them in quotation marks. Distinguish the verb from the noun. The best solution is to use *quote* only as a verb and to find synonyms for the noun: *passage, remark, assertion.*

| WRONG | RIGHT |
|---|---|
| As the following *quote* from Milton shows: . . . | As the following *passage* [or quotation] from Milton shows: . . . |

**Raise.**  See *Rise, raise*.

**Rarely ever.**  Drop the ever: "Shakespeare *rarely* misses a chance for comedy."

**Real.**  Do not use for *very*. *Real* is an adjective meaning "actual":

| WRONG | RIGHT |
|---|---|
| It was *real* good. | It was *very* good. |
| | It was *really* good. |

But be careful with *really*. It can be too frequent and colloquial.

**Reason . . . is because.**  Knock out *the reason . . . is*, and *the reason why . . . is*, and you will have a good sentence.

> [The reason] they have difficulty with languages [is] because they have no interest in them.

**Refer, allude.**  See *Allude, refer*.

**Regarding, in regard to.**  Redundant or inaccurate.

| POOR | IMPROVED |
|---|---|
| *Regarding* the banknote, Jones was perplexed. [Was he *looking* at it?] | Jones was perplexed by the banknote. |
| He knew nothing *regarding* money. | He knew nothing about money. |
| She was careful *in regard to* the facts. | She respected the facts. |

**Regardless.**  This is correct. See *Irregardless* for the confusion.

**Relate.**  It can be stuffy and ambiguous. Write *tell* when you mean *tell*, rather than making a connection.

**Relate to.**  Colloquial and vague. Be specific.

| POOR | IMPROVED |
|---|---|
| He *related to* newspaper work. | He *liked* newspaper work. |

**Relevant.**  Something like *significant* will do, but *relevant* asks for specifics: relevant to abortion, the monetary crisis, working parents.

**Respective, respectively.**  Usually redundant.

| POOR | IMPROVED |
|---|---|
| The armies retreated to their *respective* trenches. | The armies retreated to their trenches. |
| Smith and Jones won the first and second prize *respectively*. | Smith won the first prize; Jones, the second. |

**Reverend, Honorable.** Titles of the clergy and congress. The fully proper forms, as in the heading of a letter (*the* would not be capitalized in your running prose), are *The Reverend Mr. Claude C. Smith; The Honorable Adam A. Jones.* In running prose, *Rev. Claude Smith* and *Hon. Adam Jones* will get by, but the best procedure is to give the title and name its full form for first mention and then continue with *Mr. Smith* and *Mr. Jones*. Do not use "Reverend" or "Honorable" with the last name alone.

**Rise, raise.** Frequently confused. *Rise, rose, risen* means to get up. *Raise, raised, raised* means to lift up. "He *rose* early and *raised* a commotion."

**Sanction.** Beautifully ambiguous, now meaning both "to approve" and "to penalize." Although it is firmly established as *penalize* and *a restriction*, you can distinguish yourself by sticking to the root and using it only "to bless," "to sanctify," "to approve," "to permit." Use *penalize* or *prohibit* when you mean just that. Instead of "They exacted *sanctions*," say "They exacted *penalties*" or "enacted *restrictions*."

**Sarcasm.** A cutting remark. Wrongly used for any irony.

**Seldom ever.** Redundant. Cut the *ever*. (But *seldom if ever* has its uses.)

**Set, sit.** Frequently confused. You *set* something down; you yourself *sit* down. Confine *sitting* mostly to people (*sit, sat, sat*), and keep it intransitive, taking no object. *Set* is the same in all tenses (*set, set, set*).

| CONFUSED | CLARIFIED |
|---|---|
| The house *sets* too near the street. | The house *stands* [*sits*] too near the street. |
| The package *set* where he left it. | The package *lay* [*sat*] where he left it. |
| She *has* set there all day. | She *has sat* there all day. |

**Sexism.** See *Bias*.

**Shall, will; should, would.** The older distinctions—*shall* and *should* reserved for I and we—have faded; *will* and *would* are usual: "I will go"; "I would if I could"; "he will try"; "they all would." But *shall* remains in first-person questions: *Shall I call you tomorrow? Shall* in the third person expresses determination: "They shall not pass." *Should*, in formal usage, is actually ambiguous: *We should be happy to comply*, intended to mean "would be happy," seems to say "ought to be happy."

**S/he.** Write "he or she," "he and she."

**Should of.** See *Could of, would of.*

**Similar to.** Use *like:*

POOR
This is *similar* to that.

IMPROVED
This is *like* that.

**Sit.** See *Set, sit.*

**Situate.** Usually wordy and inaccurate. Avoid it unless you mean, literally or figuratively, the act of determining a site or placing a building: "Do not *situate* heavy buildings on loose soil."

FAULTY
He is well *situated.*
Ann Arbor is a town *situated* on the Huron River.
The control panel is *situated* on the right.
The company is well *situated* to meet the competition.

IMPROVED
He is rich.
Ann Arbor is a town on the Huron River.
The control panel is on the right.
The company is well prepared to meet the competition.

**Situation.** Usually jargon. Avoid it. Say what you mean: *state, market, mess, quandary, conflict, predicament.*

**Size.** Often redundant. A *small-sized country* is a *small country. Large in size* is *large.*

**Slow.** Go SLOW is what the street signs and the people on the street all say, but write "Go Slowly."

**So.** Should be followed by *that* in describing extent: "It was *so* foggy *that* traffic almost stopped." Avoid its incomplete form, the gushy intensive—*so nice, so wonderful, so pretty*—though occasionally this is effective.

**Someplace, somewhere.** See *Anyplace.*

**Somewheres.** You mean *somewhere.*

**Sort of.** See *Kind of, sort of.*

**Split infinitives.** Improve them. You see them every day, of course. About 52 percent of magazine and newspaper editors now accept "to instantly trace," which 90 percent found unprintable eight years ago. Nevertheless, adolescents and beginners love them. They are cliché traps: *to really know, to really like, to better understand, to further improve*. They indicate a wordy writer and usually produce redundancies: *to really understand* is *to understand*. They are misleading: *to better . . . , to further, to well . . . , to even. . . .* All look like and sound like infinitives: *to further investigate* starts out like *to further our investigation*, throwing the readers off track. *To better know* is to make *know* better; *to even like* is to make *like* even—which is not what you mean.

The quickest cure is to drop the splitting adverb, giving *know* and *like* their full weight. Or you can spell out the adverbial thought: "To understand *completely for the first time*"; "to improve *even more*."

Or you can change the adverb to an adjective:

| POOR | IMPROVED |
|------|----------|
| *to adequately think* out solutions | *to think* out *adequate* solutions |
| to enable us *to effectively plan* our advertising | to enable us *to plan effective* advertising |

**Stationary, stationery.** *Stationary* is motionless. *Stationery* is the writing paper the stationer sells you.

**Suppose to.** You mean *supposeD to*, with the past-tense *d*.

**Than, then.** The misspelling *then* often slips in for a *than*. Then you don't mean *then*.

**That, which, who.** *That* defines and restricts; *which* is explanatory and nonrestrictive; *who* stands for people, and may be restrictive or nonrestrictive. See *Who*, and 97–98, 115–117, 204–205.

**Theirselves.** You mean *themselves*.

**There is, there are, it is.** However natural and convenient—it is WORDY. Notice that *it* here refers to something specific, differing distinctly from the *it* in "It is easy to write badly." (Better: "Writing badly is easy.") This indefinite subject, like *there is* and *there are*, gives the trouble. Of course, you will occasionally need an *it* or a *there* to assert existences:

| | |
|---|---|
| **There are ants in the cupboard.** | **There are craters on the moon.** |
| **There is only one Kenneth.** | **It is too bad.** |

**They.** Often a loose indefinite pronoun; tighten it. See 193–194.

**This.** Often a colloquially vague referent:

POOR

We ourselves could paint the apartment if we only had the time. But *this* is a problem.

IMPROVED

. . . . But we both work long hours.

Colloquially, *this* (and *these*) sometimes refers to nothing previously said:

He had *this* southern accent.

She wore *these* long red plastic fingernails.

He had *a* southern accent.

She wore long red plastic fingernails.

**Throne, thrown.** People frequently write *thrown* for *throne* but not the other way around. Check yourself.

**Thus, thusly.** *Thus* goes with a formal style—"Thus we ended the experiment"—but *in this way* or *like this* is more natural in spite of the nonreferential *this*. *Thusly* is cumbersome and incorrect.

**Till, until.** Both are respectable. Note the spelling. Do not use *'til*.

**Too.** Awful as a conjunctive adverb: "Too, it was unjust." Also poor as an intensive: "They did not do too well" (note the difference in Shakespeare's "not wisely but too well"—he really means it). Use *very* or (better) nothing: "They did not do well" (notice the nice understated irony).

**Tool.** Overused for "means." Try *instrument, means*.

**Toward, towards.** *Toward* is the better (*towards* in Britain), though both are acceptable.

**Trite.** From Latin *tritus*: "worn out." Many words become temporarily worn out and unusable—*emasculated, viable, situation*, to name a few—and many phrases are permanently frayed; see *Clichés*.

**Try and.** You mean *try to*.

**Type.** Banish it, abolish it. If you must use it, insert *of*: not *that type person* but *that type* OF *person*, though even this is really jargon for *that kind of person, a person like that*. See 119.

**Unique.**  Something unique has nothing in the world like it.

| WRONG | RIGHT |
|---|---|
| The more unique the organization | The *more nearly unique* ... |
| . . . . | |
| the *most unique* man I know | the *most unusual* man I know |
| a very *unique* personality | a *unique* personality |

**Upon.**  Stuffy. Make it *on.*
**Use, use of.**  A dangerously wordy word. See 117.
**Use to.**  A mistake for *used to.*
**Utilize, utilization.**  Like *use,* wordy. See 117.

| POOR | IMPROVED |
|---|---|
| He *utilizes* frequent dialogue to enliven his stories. | Frequent dialogue enlivens his stories. |
| The *utilization* of a scapegoat eases their guilt. | A scapegoat eases their guilt. |

**Very.**  Spare the *very* and the *quite, rather,* and *pretty.* I would hate to admit (and don't care to know) how many of these qualifiers I have cut from this text. You can do without them entirely, but they do ease a phrase now and then.
**Viable.**  With *feasible,* overworked. Try *practicable, workable, possible.*
**WASP.**  "White Anglo-Saxon Protestant." A pejorative loosely applied to any white. Avoid it.
**Ways.**  Avoid it for distance. Means *way:* "He went a short *way* into the woods."
**Well.**  See *Good.*
**Whether.**  See *If.*
**Which.**  See *Who, which, that.*
**While.**  Reserve for time only, as in "*While* I was talking, she smoked constantly." Do not use for *although.*

| WRONG | RIGHT |
|---|---|
| *While* I like her, I don't admire her. | *Although* I like her, I don't admire her. |

**Who, which, that.**  *Who* may be either restrictive or nonrestrictive: "The ones *who win* are lucky"; "The players, *who are all outstanding,* win often." *Who* refers only to persons. Use *that* for all other restrictives; *which* for all other nonrestrictives. Cut every *who*, *that*, and *which* not needed. See 115, "the *of-and-which* disease" 115–117, and, on restrictives, and nonrestrictives, 204–205.

Avoid *which* in loose references to the whole idea preceding, rather than to a specific word, because you may be unclear:

| FAULTY | IMPROVED |
|---|---|
| He never wore the hat, which his wife hated. | His wife hated his going bareheaded.<br>He never wore the hat his wife hated. |

**Whom, whomever.** The objective forms, after verbs and prepositions; but each is often wrongly put as the subject of a clause (191).

| WRONG | RIGHT |
|---|---|
| Give the ticket to *whomever* wants it. | Give the ticket to *whoever* wants it. [The whole clause is the object of *to*; whoever is the subject of *wants*.] |
| The president, *whom* he said would be late . . . . | The president, *who* he said would be late. . . .<br>[Commas around *he said* would clear the confusion.] |
| *Whom* shall I say called? | *Who* shall I say called? |

BUT:

They did not know *whom* to elect. [The infinitive takes the objective case.]

**Who's, whose.** Sometimes confused in writing. *Who's* means "who is?" in conversational questions: "*Who's* going?" Never use it in writing (except in dialogue), and you can't miss. *Whose* is the regular possessive of *who*: "The committee, *whose* work was finished, adjourned."

**Will.** See *Shall.*

**-wise.** Avoid all confections like *marketwise, customerwise, pricewise, gradewise, confectionwise*—except for humor.

**With regards to.** "Give My Regards to Broadway," the old song went, and, in a letter, you might also ask your correspondent to give your good wishes to someone. But drop the *s* when you mean "with reference to."

**Would.** For habitual acts, the simple past is more economical:

| POOR | IMPROVED |
|---|---|
| The parliament *would* meet only when called by the king. | The parliament *met* only when called by the king. |
| Every hour, the sentry *would make* his round. | Every hour, the sentry *made* his round. |

*Would* sometimes seeps into the premise of a supposition. Rule: Don't use *would* in an *if* clause.

| WRONG | RIGHT |
|---|---|
| If she *would have* gone, she would have succeeded. | If she *had* gone, she would have succeeded. |
| | *Had* she gone, she would have succeeded [more economical]. |

**Would of.** See *Could of, would of.*

**You (I, we, one).** See 7–9.

**Your, you're.** Because they sound alike, you may accidentally write one for the other. Your accident will show that you're not watching what you're saying.

# Index